ECHO

Wrapped in Memory

Louise Bourgeois

Simone Rocha

Anne Teresa De Keersmaeker

Lannoo

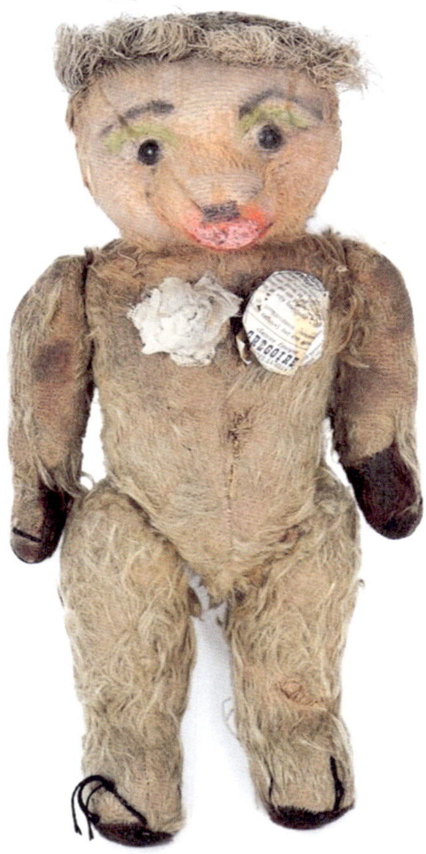

Jean Paul Gaultier's teddy bear Nana, 1957

TABLE OF CONTENTS

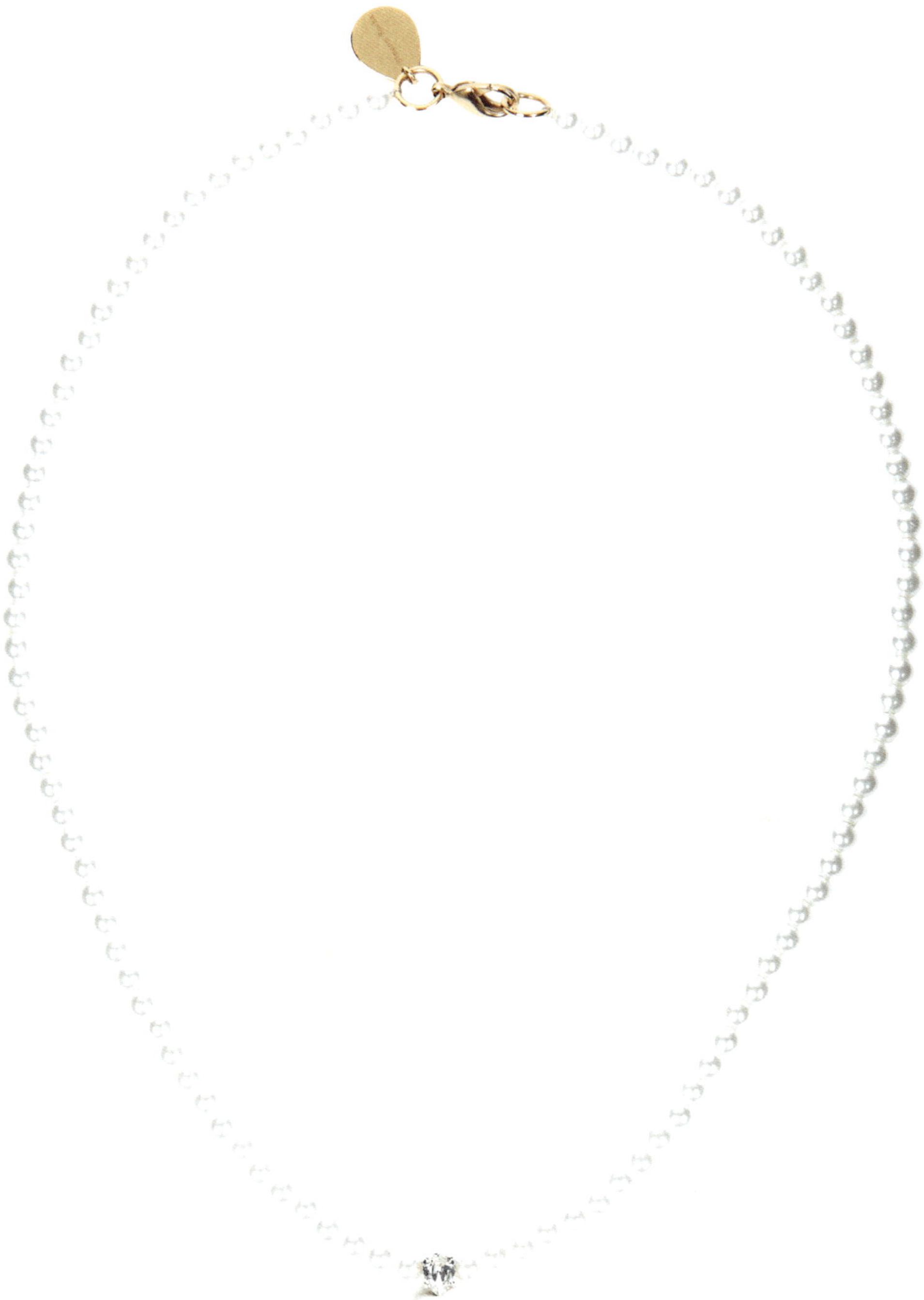

SIMONE ROCHA
Spring-Summer 2022

Foreword

KAAT DEBO
DIRECTOR MOMU —— FASHION MUSEUM ANTWERP

ECHO. Wrapped in Memory explores the relationship between clothing and memory, drawing on the work of Louise Bourgeois, Simone Rocha and Anne Teresa De Keersmaeker. Clothing is one of the most intimate things in our lives. It is what we wear closest to our bodies. We allow few other items to come into such direct contact with our skin. Our memories, too, are intimate, personal and subjective. They are tinted by positive or negative emotions, sometimes also by trauma, loss or fear, and can be evoked by smell, colour or tactility. All of this is why clothing is an ideal carrier of and portal to our memories.

Working every day with a collection of more than 38,000 objects gives MoMu's curators and researchers access to the echoes of a myriad of personal histories and events. Smells, stains and tears in clothing, or the way certain garments were altered or repaired in the past, are an inexhaustible source of stories and embody the passing of time. Contradictorily, museums typically prefer displaying objects considered to be of museum quality. In doing so, we frequently conceal the inescapable processes of ageing, and everyday wear and tear, as if these are things to be scrupulously hidden. *ECHO* features a unique selection of objects from the MoMu collection in different stages of degradation with their flaws, discolourations and traces of damage, and with just as many intriguing stories.

Since early childhood, all three protagonists in *ECHO* have had a personal connection with clothes, textiles or fashion. Anne Teresa De Keersmaeker recalls the bolts of fabric in the living room of her childhood home, and the annual visits to the dressmaker with her mother and siblings. But also, how clothes were passed on and reused between the sisters of the family. One of Simone Rocha's earliest memories plays out in the fabric archive of her father, the designer John Rocha. The aura of domesticity of crafts like embroidery and knitting, very present in her Irish childhood, still shines through in her work today. Louise Bourgeois also grew up in a textile family. Her parents had a carpet restoration workshop. She recalls hiding in the rolled-up carpets as a child, an echo of a past when, in old castles and mansions, enormous carpets and tapestries served as room dividers, creating what Bourgeois so beautifully describes as flexible architecture. This concept finds its translation in the beautiful scenography Janina Pedan designed for the exhibition *ECHO*. Integrating curtains and fabric walls, combined with lighting by Chris Pype and graphic design by Paul Boudens, her design immerses the visitor in an intimate and sensory journey.

We were able to realise this exhibition thanks to the loyal cooperation of the Easton Foundation, Xavier Hufkens and the archives of Rosas and Simone Rocha. My special thanks to their respective teams. Thanks to Elisa De Wyngaert, the curator of *ECHO. Wrapped in Memory*, for her unique research and passionate work on this exhibition and book. My sincere thanks also to the loaners, artists, designers, photographers, and authors whose work contributed significantly to this ambitious project. I am particularly grateful for the additional support of Naomi Milgrom of the Naomi Milgrom Foundation and Tanguy Van Quickenborne of the firm Van Den Weghe. Finally, I would like to thank the entire MoMu team who, as always, gave their best.

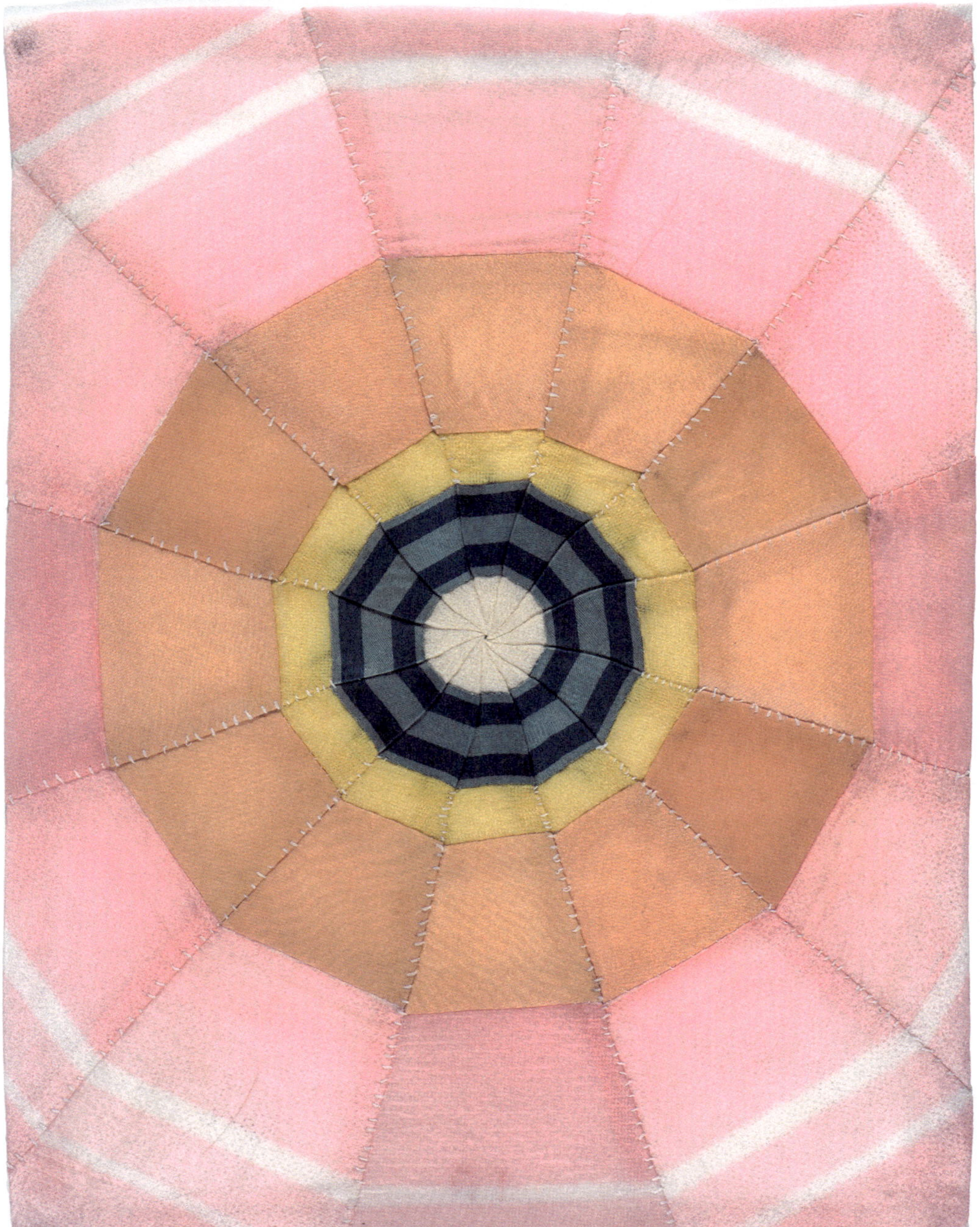

Louise Bourgeois
Dawn (detail), 2006

CHAPTER I

Wrapped in Memory

Louise Bourgeois
Simone Rocha
Anne Teresa De Keersmaeker

ELISA DE WYNGAERT

> "[...] you can retell your life and remember your life by the shape, the weight, the colour, the smell of the clothes in your closet. Fashion is like the weather, the ocean —— it changes all the time."[1]
>
> LOUISE BOURGEOIS

Jokingly, I have described this exhibition and accompanying publication as the closing chapter of a trilogy that started in 2021. The past few years have been an emotional turmoil for most of us, which is why psychology and emotions sat at the heart of these exhibitions. During the Covid-19 pandemic, I curated *E/MOTION. Fashion in Transition*, a show that explored how fashion has always been in dialogue with, and has even anticipated, different crises and transitions. Fashion, like no other medium, can magnify and reflect the raw emotions within a society.[2] In 2022, *E/MOTION* was followed by *MIRROR MIRROR. Fashion & the Psyche*, in which we traced the connections between fashion, psychology, self-image and identity.[3] *ECHO. Wrapped in Memory* closes the trilogy by reflecting on the intimate connection between clothing and memory. To me, *ECHO* is the sensitive, associative and tactile sister.

Artist Louise Bourgeois (1911–2010), fashion designer Simone Rocha (°1986) and choreographer and dancer Anne Teresa De Keersmaeker (°1960) will guide this story. Three women, working in different disciplines, who, to me, have always shared the astonishing quality of evoking and embracing echoes of the past in their work. In their own unique ways, they weave memories of clothing and textiles into their artistic language. What they create comes from a personal and emotional place, but the effects reach beyond the personal and touch many facets of the human experience.

Anne Teresa De Keersmaeker established the dance company Rosas in Brussels in 1983, while creating the work *Rosas danst Rosas*. It is well known that De Keersmaeker takes music as the blueprint for the choreography, but less well known is how essential clothing is to her, not only during the performance, but to the dancers and the choreography too. Some of her past choreographies even started from a garment. For example, her first solo in 1982, *Violin Phase*, was inspired by the movement of a rehearsal dress she had worn in the studio, which twirled pleasantly when she spun around. First there was the dance, then the choreography.

I am in no doubt that I (and probably many others) would be able to recognise a Rosas production only by looking at a lineup of dressed dancers. However subtle, there is an artistic consistency that is hard to pin down. Is it the flowing knee-length skirts and dresses? Is it the gender-nonconforming silhouettes? Is it the slightly ill-fitting jeans and colourful trainers? Does it lie in the vulnerable but seductive play of hiding and revealing? The sudden laying bare of just one shoulder? The cotton briefs, the act of dressing and undressing? To me, Rosas' stage clothes have come to embody a sense of purity, realism and subdued elegance. Recent productions are an ode to streetwear.

Clothing, accessories and shoes are treated with the utmost care in the Rosas archive, where pieces are repeatedly restored and reused until they are beyond repair. The archive holds memories of De Keersmaeker's circle of people: dancers and collaborators. Over the years, costumes have been created in tandem with trusted individuals like Martine André, Aouatif Boulaich, Inge Büscher, An D'Huys, Nathalie Douxfils, Elizabeth Jenyon, Lila John, Anne-Catherine Kunz, Carine Lauwers, Ester Manas, Fauve Ryckebusch, Rudy Sabounghi, Dries Van Noten, Tim Van Steenbergen and Ann Weckx.[4] But although she actively seeks out and values dialogue and co-creation, when it comes to the costumes, she wants to be in control. De Keersmaeker knows that she is directional when it comes to the costumes and values people who understand her vision without needing too many words: a shared sensitivity for the quality of fabrics, for the way clothes flow, the right balance between opaqueness and transparency, hiding and revealing. As such, many of her own garments end up being used or replicated in the performances. Her deep respect for craftsmanship and craftspeople is felt in the frequent use of both historic and vintage garments, which are often adapted to the dancers' bodies, or form the basis from which replicas are made.

> "Clothing is also an exercise of memory.
> It makes me explore the past: how did I feel when I wore that.
> They are like signposts in the search for the past."[5]
>
> LOUISE BOURGEOIS

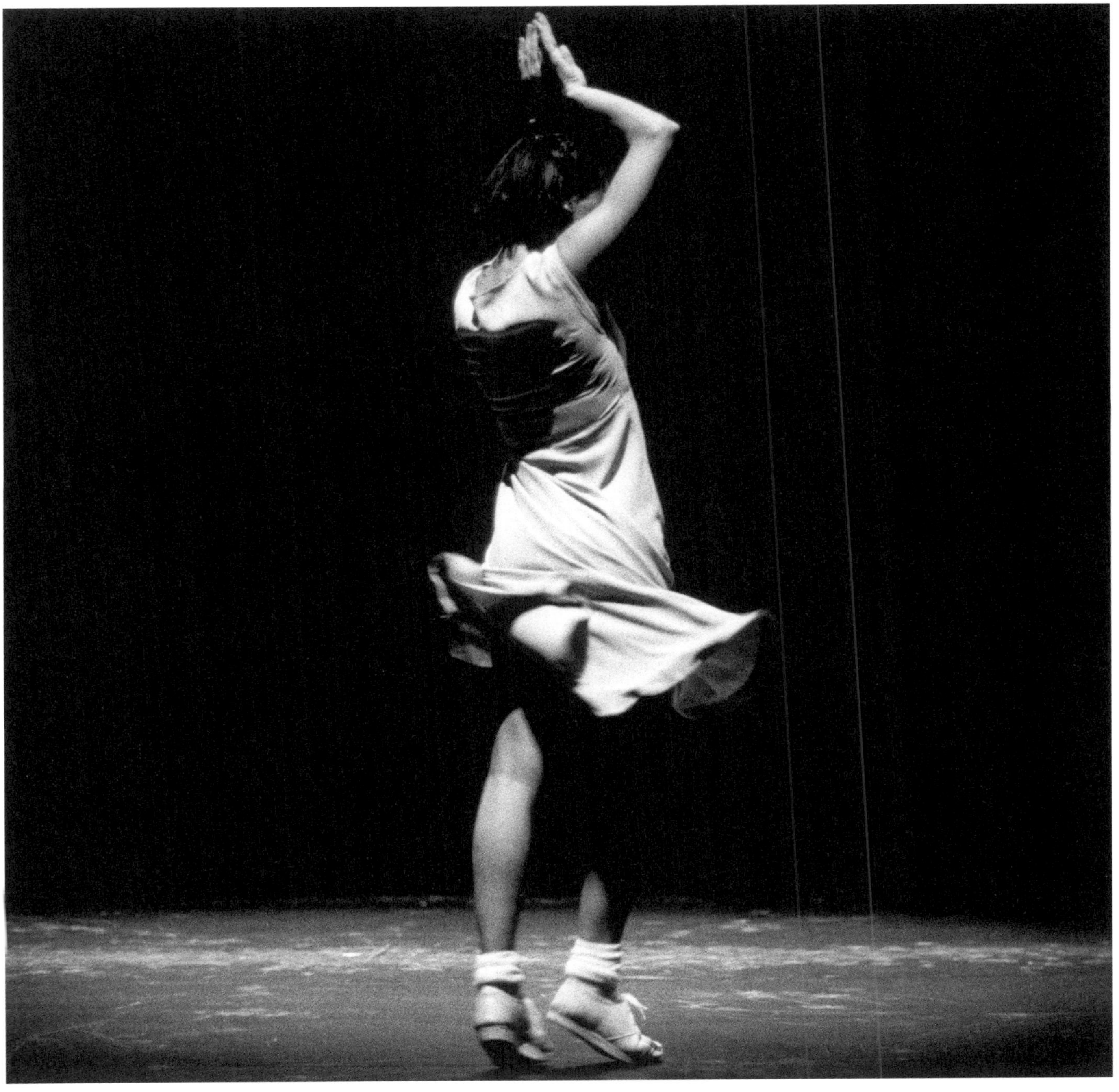

ANNE TERESA DE KEERSMAEKER/ROSAS
Fase, Four Movements to the Music of Steve Reich, 1982
Anne Teresa De Keersmaeker

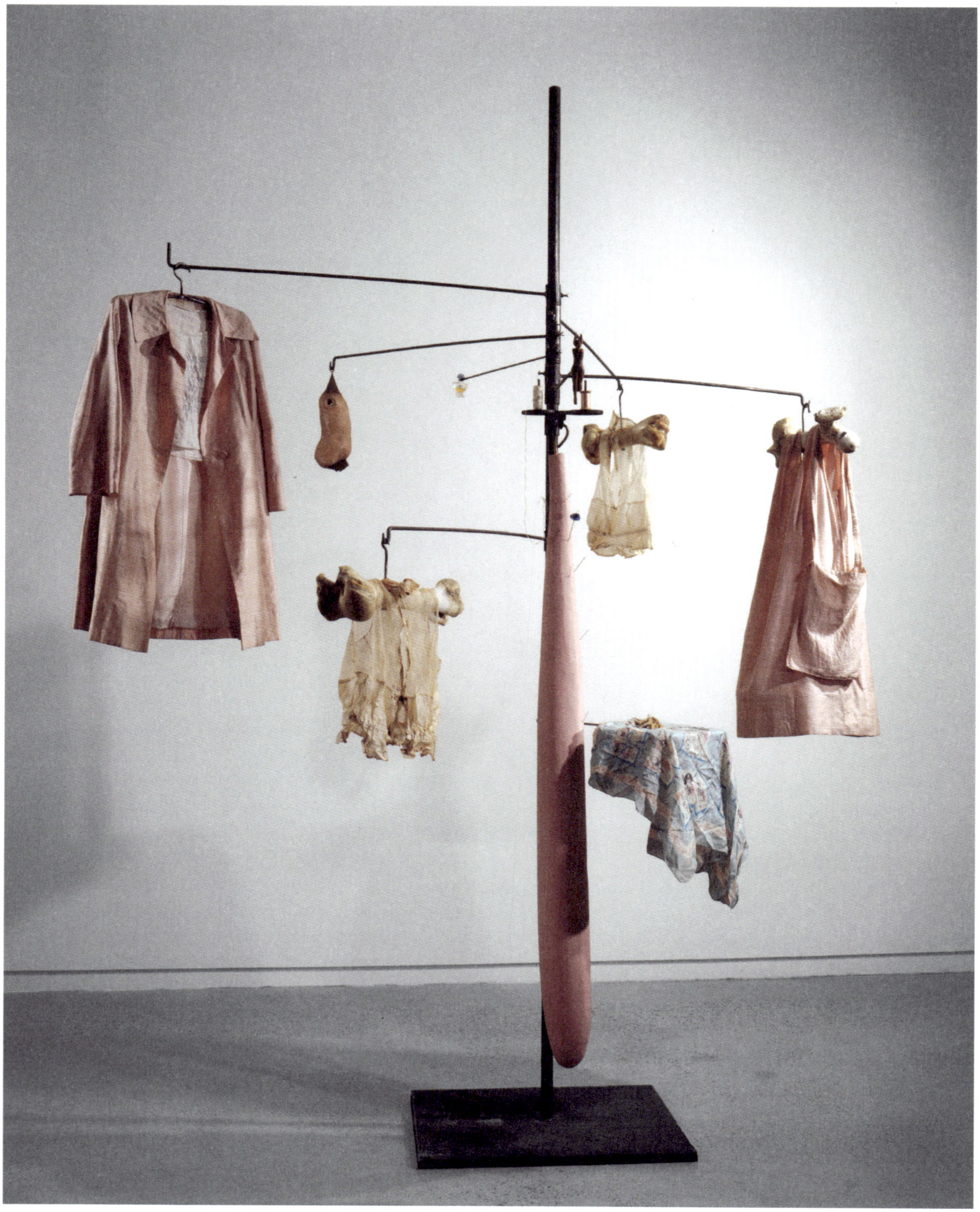

Louise Bourgeois
Pink Days and Blue Days, 1997

Over decades, fearful of throwing anything away, Louise Bourgeois accumulated not only a collection of her own garments, dating back to childhood, but also clothing that belonged to family members:

> "It gives me great pleasure to hold on to my clothes, my dresses, my stockings, I have never thrown away a pair of shoes of mine in 20 years [...] The pretext is that they are still good —— it's my past and as rotten as it was I would like to take it and hold it tight in my arms."[6]
>
> LOUISE BOURGEOIS

Then, one morning in the mid-1990s, when she was already well into her eighties, Bourgeois asked her long-time studio assistant Jerry Gorovoy to bring the contents of the upstairs wardrobes down to her basement studio. There, she suspended the clothes from hangers on the pipes on the ceiling and arranged them into colours. This exercise opened up a new, intimate dialogue with her memories. From these clothes and textiles, she developed an extensive new body of sculptures, installations, drawings, collages, books and prints. The garments that had a specific memory associated with them, or that were evocative of certain people or places, were kept intact and used in sculptural installations. Her more contemporary garments, as well as her household napkins, table linens, handkerchiefs, old towels and, later, tapestry fragments, were used less delicately. From these, Bourgeois made works that involved cutting up or altering, reconfiguring and stuffing the fabrics to create a range of expressive figurative forms, abject and distressed states of being. According to Gorovoy, Bourgeois's deep urge to embark on this new body of work came from her getting older and wondering what would happen to all the objects she had saved throughout her life. These fabric works were a way of processing her memories and experiences, thereby helping her to understand the sources of her anxieties and fear of abandonment. Like the pages of a diary, they allowed her to preserve significant people, places and events.

I can recognise a garment by Simone Rocha from across the street. Just like Bourgeois and De Keersmaeker, Rocha has a powerful, yet delicate, artistic language, with recurring motifs: references to children's clothing and historic dress, signature pearl and crystal embellishments, broderie anglaise, gilt brocades, ribboned lace, Alice bands, Aran knitting, chunky shoes and ballerinas. Her work speaks to the female gaze and there is a cheeky seduction in that. She designs for all genders and ages and, in doing so, embraces all things that would 'traditionally' be considered 'feminine'. Her world is filled with frills, tulle, lace, pastels and ruffles, but in this softness lies a twist, a darker edge; there is a more subversive side for those who care to see it. In these layers and juxtapositions, there is a kinship between Bourgeois, Rocha and De Keersmaeker.

Rocha clearly remembers seeing Bourgeois's work for the first time when she was 16 years old and visited the *Stitches in Time* exhibition at the Irish Museum of Modern Art in Dublin. Even as a teenager, Bourgeois's work resonated deeply with her. Bourgeois's motifs and use of textiles changed the way the young Rocha looked at art, fashion and her future. In her early twenties she moved from Dublin to London to complete her fashion design MA at Central Saint Martins where she graduated in 2010, the same year Bourgeois passed away. Not long after launching her own fashion house, Rocha saw her dream come true as she went from being an admirer to a collaborator with Louise Bourgeois's foundation, The Easton Foundation. Over the years, not only has Bourgeois's work been on display in Rocha's stores, but her spirit also continues to emanate from Rocha's designs. Her most direct references include the intricate spiderweb prints and embroideries of Bourgeois's late fabric works in the Autumn-Winter 2019-20 collection and a limited-edition series of *Spiral Woman* earrings in collaboration with Hauser & Wirth. But Bourgeois never leaves the collections. She is there in the subtleties too: in a specific pink hue, in the natural fibres against the man-made, in the tapestries from her childhood, the blood-red threads. If you know her work, you understand how Bourgeois's legacy is at home with Rocha.

These artists' echoes of personal memories do come with a freshness, an almost childlike perspective. What they each create, eventually takes us back to early life. As Siri Hustvedt writes so eloquently, 'Femininity and childhood have been continually linked in Western culture as conditions of shrunken intellect and dependence. And yet, the dependent child lives on in the adult, in every adult, in memory that is more feeling than autobiographical image.'[10]

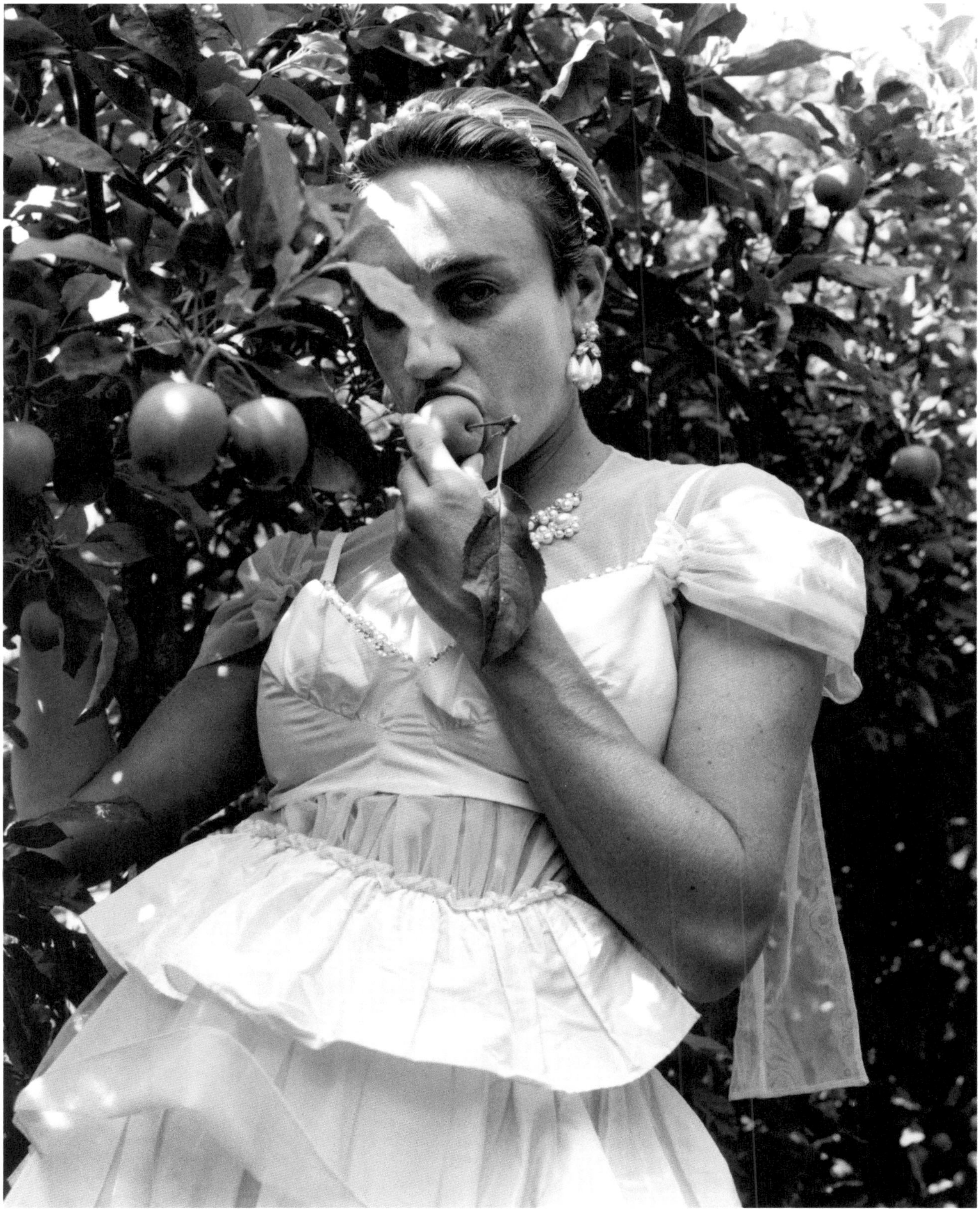

Simone Rocha
Autumn-Winter 2019-20

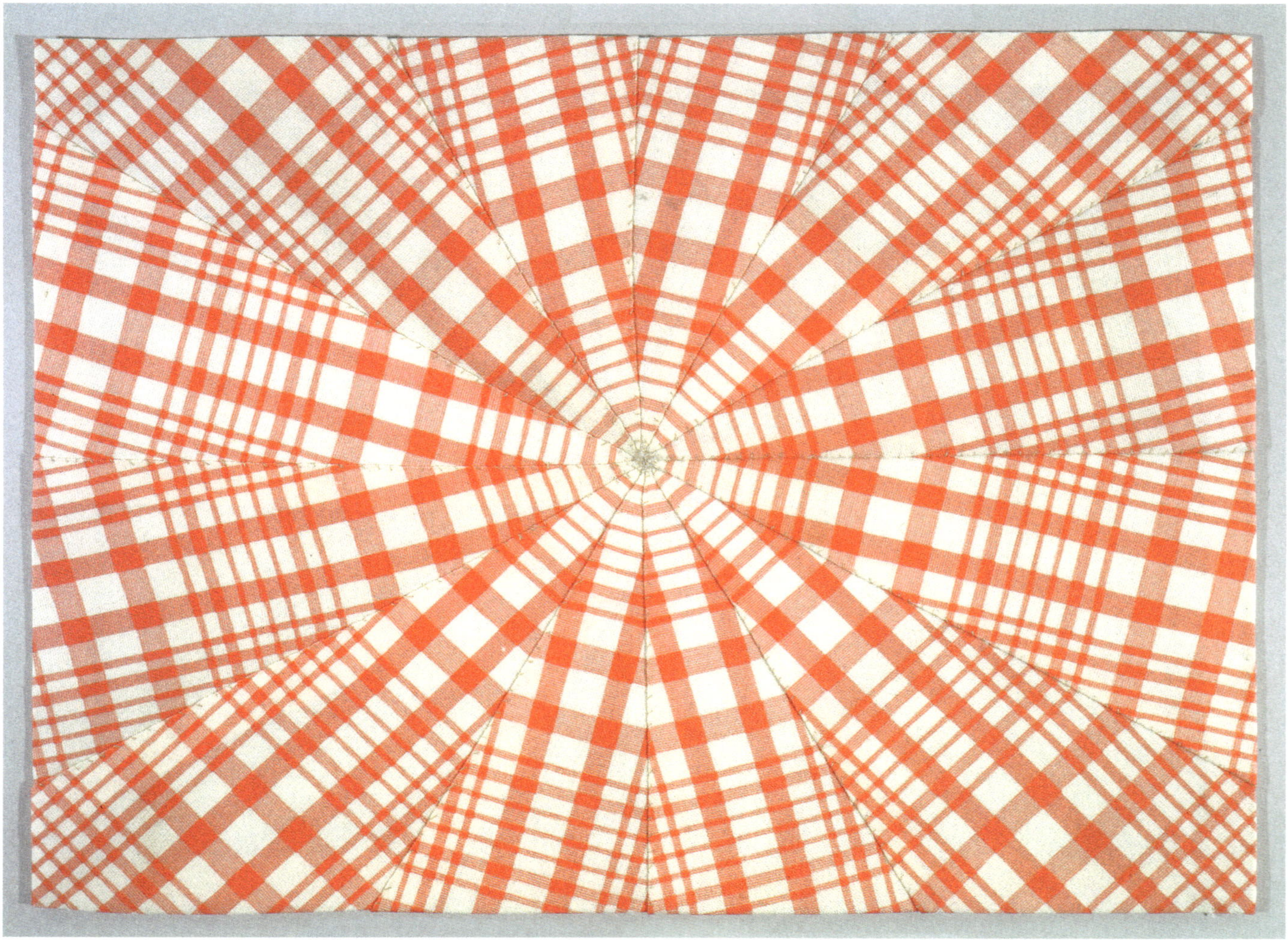

LOUISE BOURGEOIS
Untitled, 2003

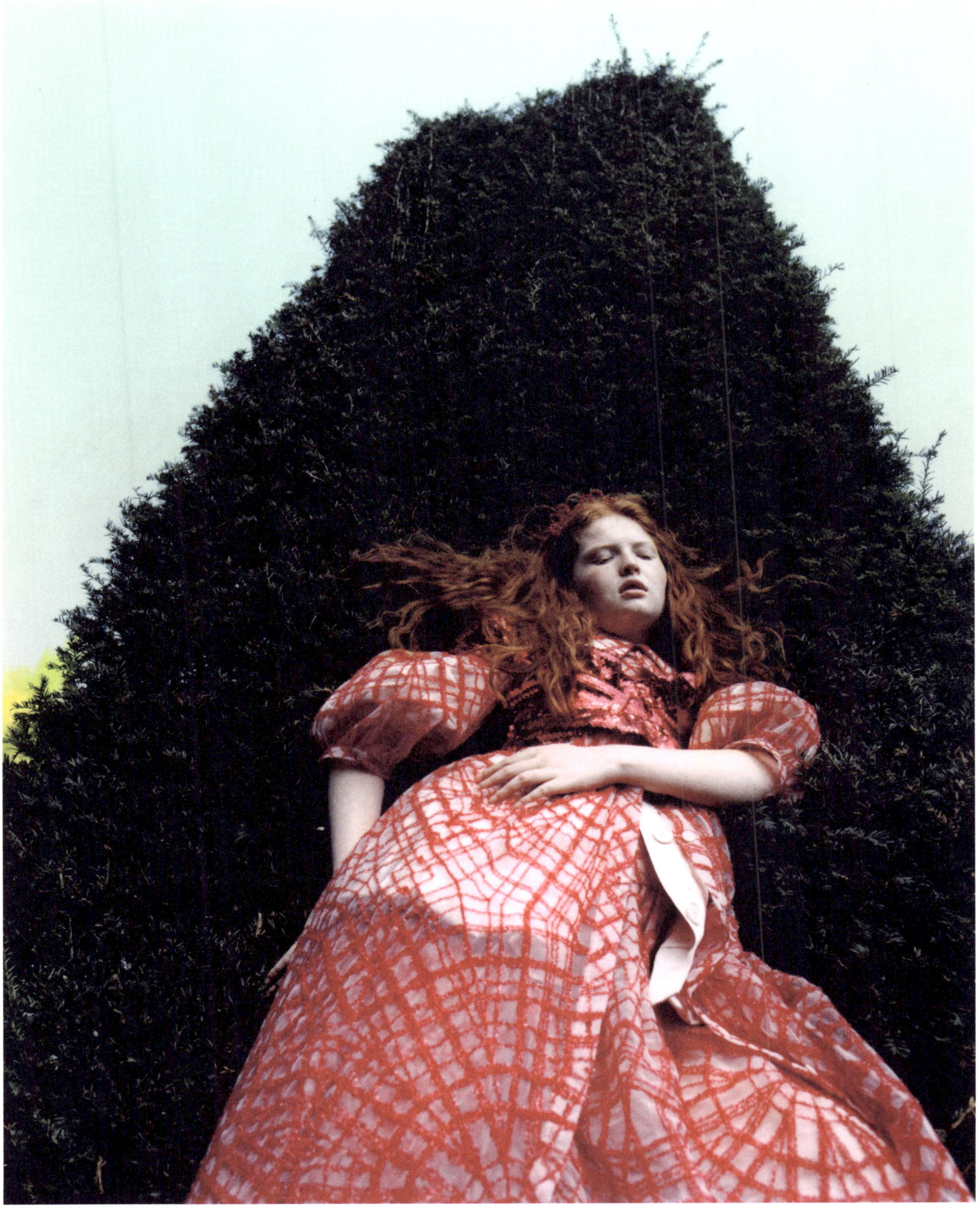

SIMONE ROCHA
Autumn-Winter 2019-20

One of five siblings, Anne Teresa De Keersmaeker was born in 1960 in Wemmel, not far from Brussels. Her parents had a farm where, in the 1960s-70s, she grew up surrounded by cows, horses, pigs, sheep, chickens, wheat, beets, potatoes, milk and butter: 'As a young girl, I was there all seasons. In winter to help cut beets and feed the cows in the barn. In summer to help bring in the harvest, plough with the tractor, and in the field illegally learning to drive a van when I was 12.'[11] When she was ten, she took her first class at her village's ballet school and, thanks to her inspirational teacher, she instantly fell in love. Today, De Keersmaeker still moves with the disarming energy, care and attention of that young girl. Thanks to her childhood, her work is authentically in tune with nature. Her dance vocabulary is minimalistic and unpretentious, intriguingly mundane. From her first choreographies, such as *Fase, Four Movements to the Music of Steve Reich* (1982), there is a childlike quality in the short and sharp movements, in the turning, jumping, swinging and waving of arms, in the twisting of skirts —— movements children would make if you asked them to dance:

> "It's a vocabulary which will make the audience members believe they'll be able to do, too —— movements people can see themselves doing as non-dancers. Very often you see people quietly trying the material of *Fase* at the bus stop after a performance. That potential for imitation is important, it is an important way for dancers to make a connection with their audience."[12]
>
> ANNE TERESA DE KEERSMAEKER

The clothes, too, evoke a sense of nostalgia for childhood, explains close collaborator An D'Huys: 'There are the school uniforms (*Rosas danst Rosas*, 1983), the pleated skirts *(Bartók/aantekeningen*, 1986), the laced boots with clean schoolgirl socks, but there are also the clothes from her own childhood and those of the adults around her, like the dresses from the 1950s and 1960s, men's suits in stiff wool with straight legs.'[13]

Sometimes, you swear you can sense some romanticism in the unexpected princess dress. One would never describe De Keersmaeker's work as sentimental, but like Bourgeois and Rocha, there is a tenderness to the way she cherishes the memories held in garments. 'Newness' is not an aspiration either; rather, she lives in tune with nature, believing that objects and clothing should live a long life. As D'Huys explains, 'this is beautifully symbolised by the rib-knitted vests from her youth (some with holes) that have been repeatedly darned and mended and that continue to be worn in her productions (like recently in *Forêt* at the Louvre)'.[14]

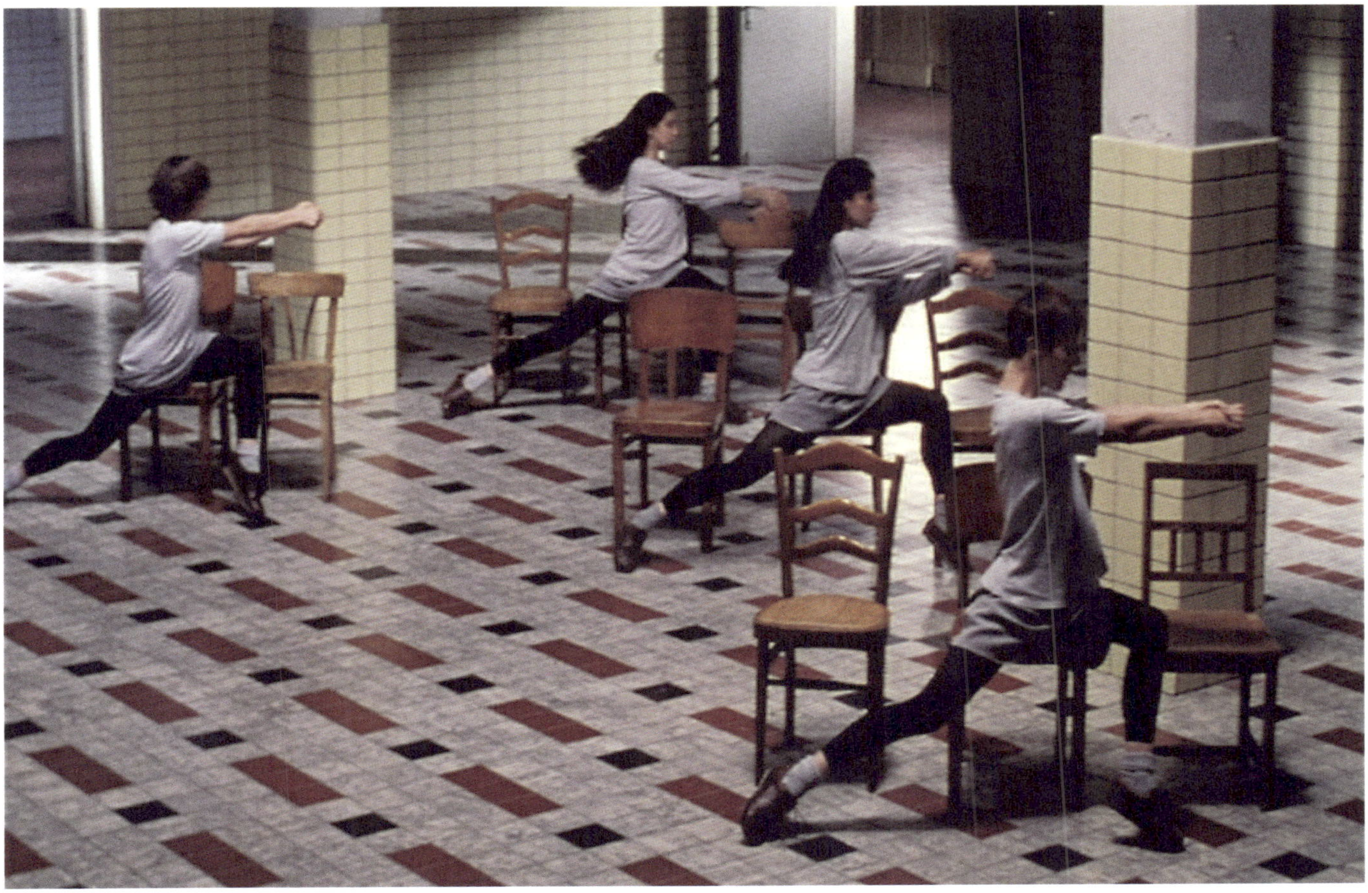

Thierry De Mey & Anne Teresa De Keersmaeker
Rosas danst Rosas, 1997, 35 mm, 57 min, colour
Samantha Van Wissen, Anne Mousselet, Cynthia Loemij, Sarah Ludi

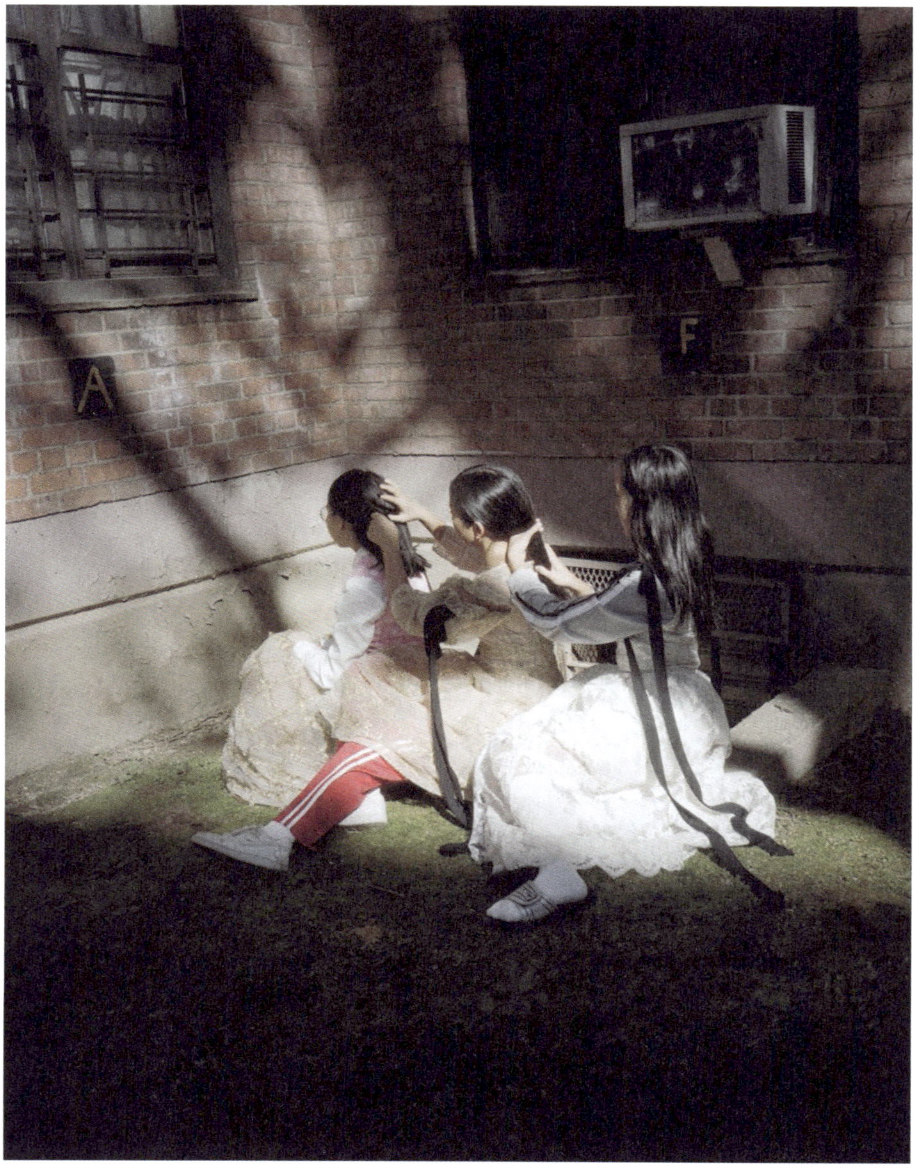

SIMONE ROCHA
Autumn-Winter 2018-19
Braiding hair series by Petra Collins

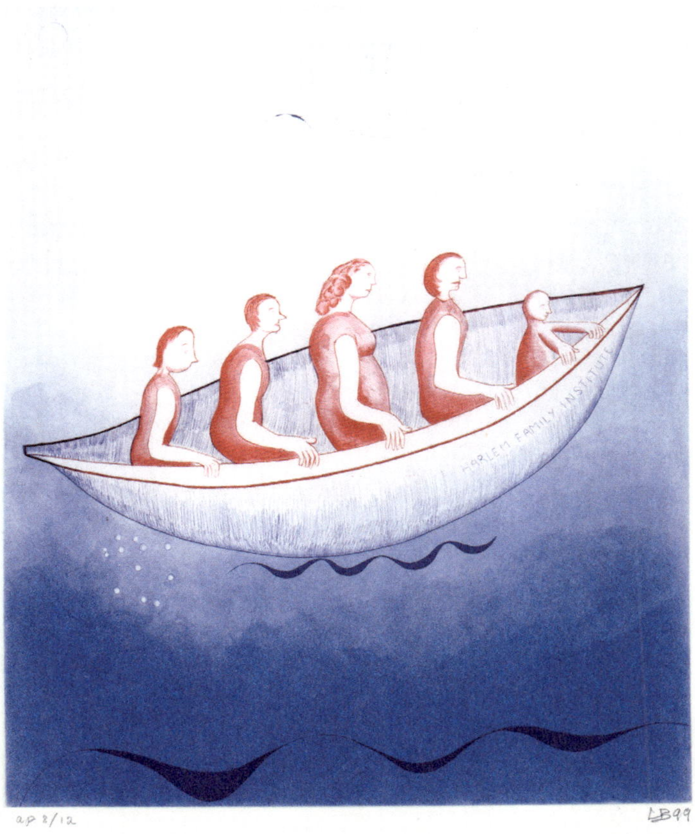

LOUISE BOURGEOIS
Follow the Child within You, 1999

> "My childhood has never lost its magic, it has never lost its mystery, and it has never lost its drama. All my work in the past 50 years, all my subjects, have found their inspiration in my childhood."[15]
>
> LOUISE BOURGEOIS

Bourgeois used her art to work through difficult childhood memories, which stemmed from the complex relationships and family dynamics at play. She was born in 1911 in Paris into a family of tapestry restorers. Her mother, Joséphine Bourgeois, ran the atelier in the suburbs of Paris, along the banks of the River Bièvre, while her father, Louis Bourgeois, sold the restored tapestries out of a gallery in Saint-Germain-des-Près. As a girl, she assisted her mother by drawing in the missing feet of figures in damaged tapestries. Her late-career fabric works, the techniques and the textiles, are her most direct return to childhood.

Rocha also grew up surrounded by textiles; her father is the designer John Rocha, who was born in Hong Kong. One of her first vivid memories is being in her father's Dublin studio, walking through his fabric room: 'A big, long room with doors at both ends —— almost like a corridor —— with rows and rows of material... I remember everything being extremely physical and tangible'. But Ireland is where she was born in 1986, and it is where she grew up —— the birthplace of her mother, Odette Rocha. Each year she travels to Hong Kong to spend time with the family. Her memories of childhood rituals and ceremonies, from both places, are at the root of her work: 'Ireland to me is home, and home is where the heart is. Hong Kong is family far away but always by my side.'[17]

As expats, Bourgeois and Rocha experienced homesickness for their native countries. During lockdown, Rocha, isolated in London, felt herself yearning for Ireland:

> "I've been thinking about it a lot, the people, the smell —— of the wet ground, of hops —— the sense of humour but also the narratives that come from the craft, the techniques and the history. My Great-Uncle Barney passed away a few days ago and the funeral tradition of Ireland is so amazing. It's such a moment of coming together, of family. It's always uplifting and ceremonial."[18]
>
> SIMONE ROCHA

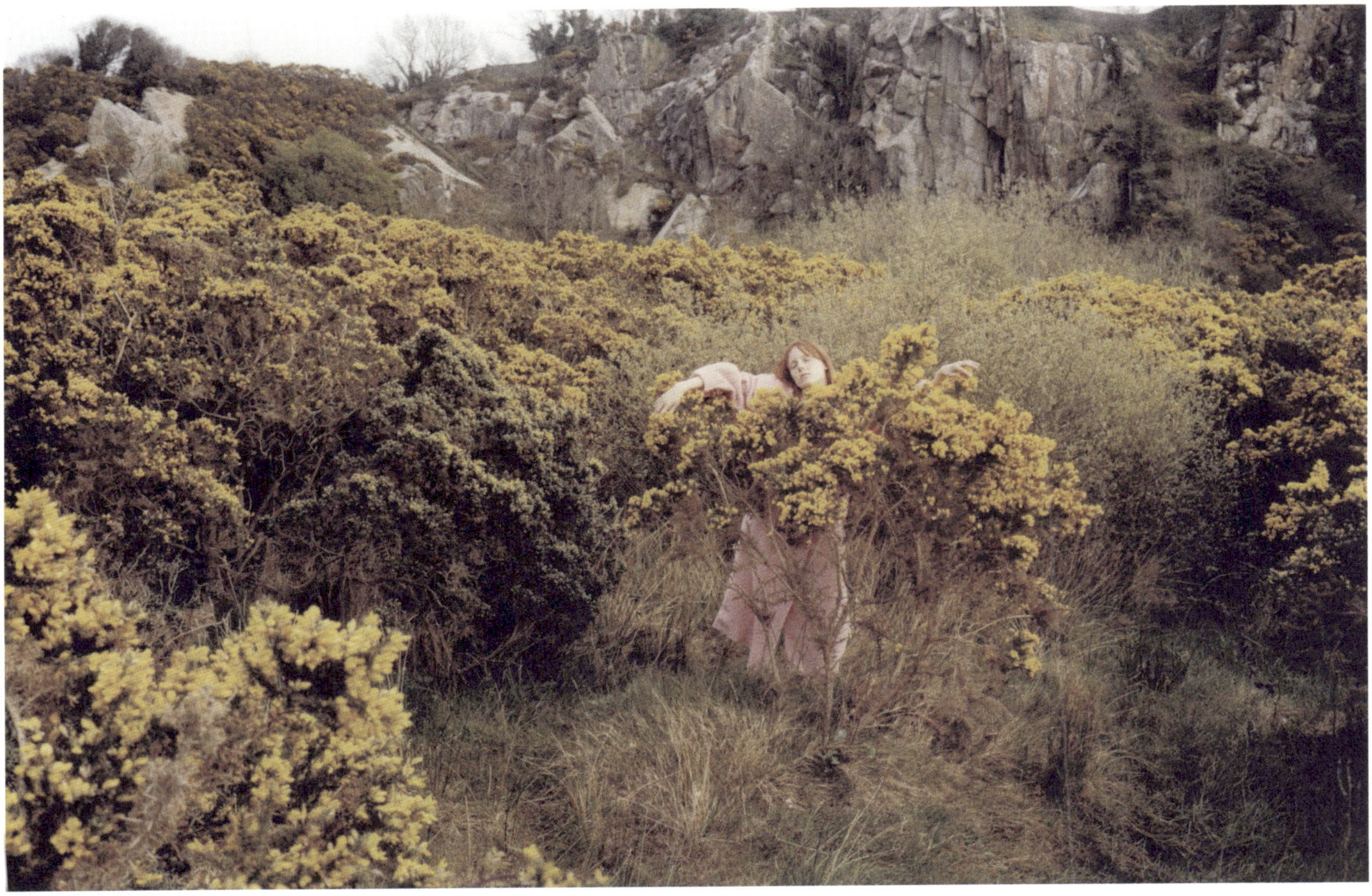

SIMONE ROCHA
Autumn-Winter 2016–17

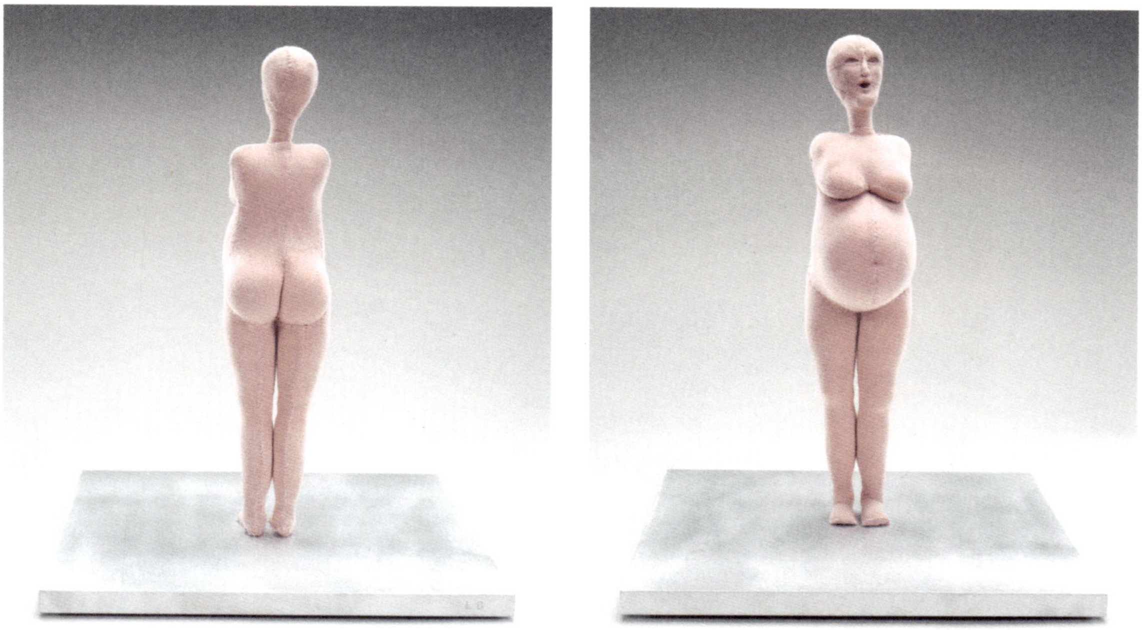

LOUISE BOURGEOIS
Pregnant Woman, 2003

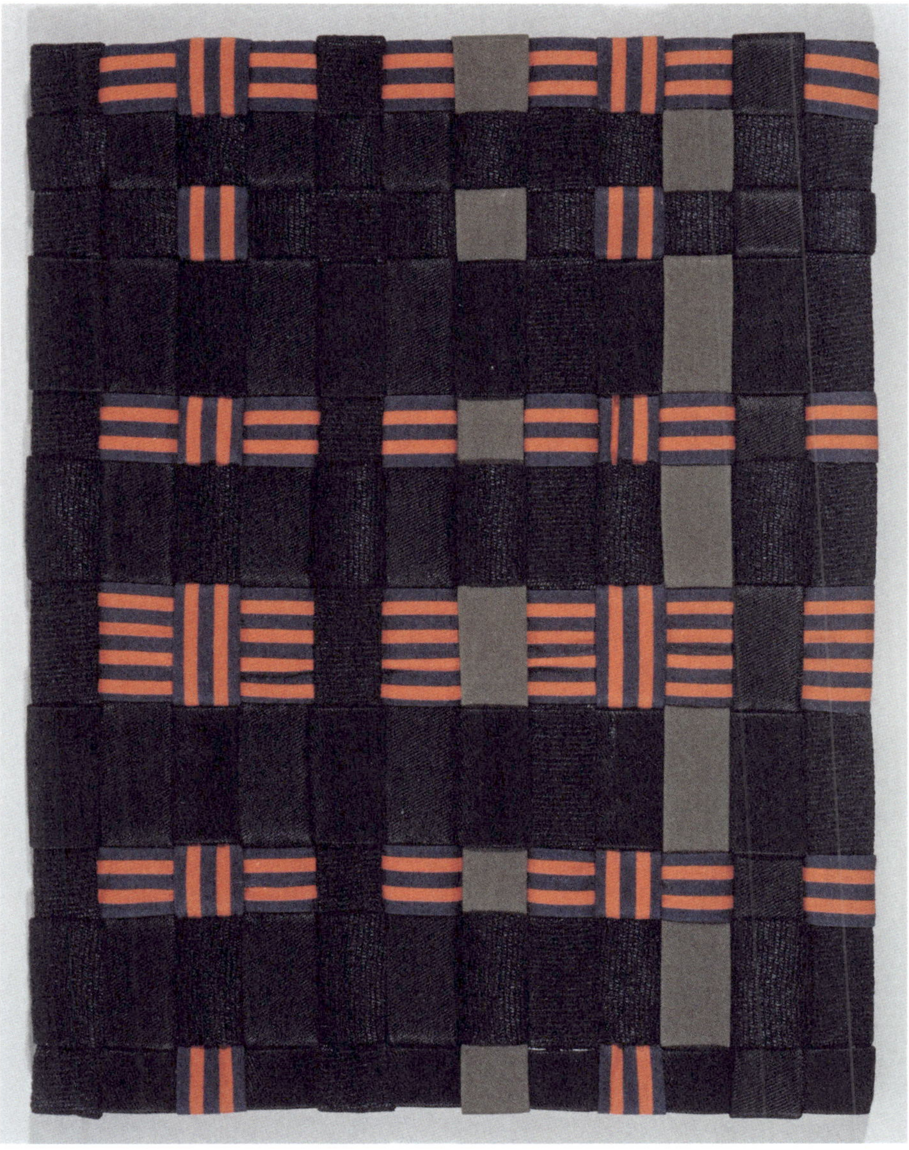

Louise Bourgeois
Untitled, 2002

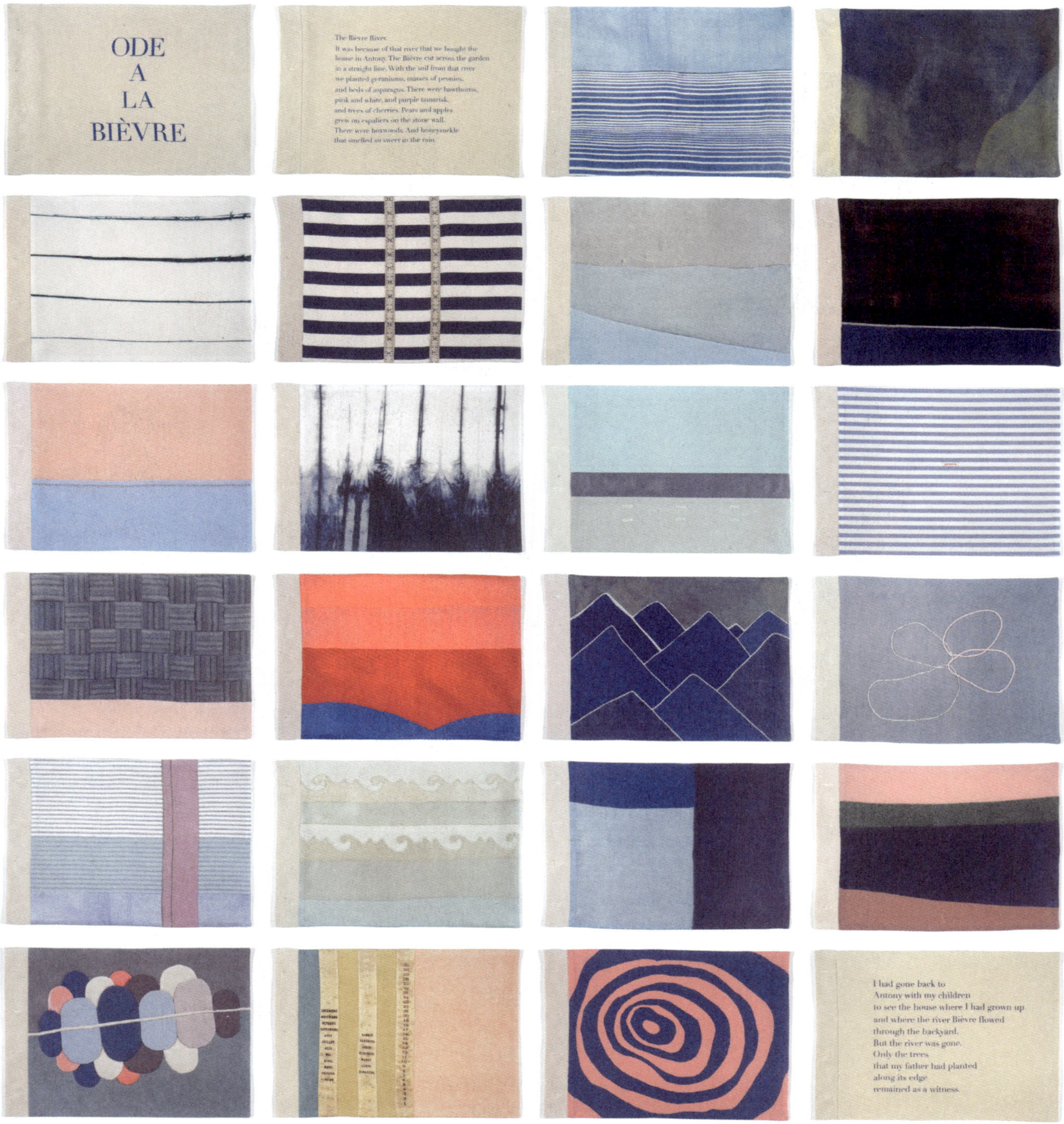

Louise Bourgeois
Ode à la Bièvre, 2007

Bourgeois immigrated to New York City with her husband, American art historian and scholar Robert Goldwater, in 1938. She often dreamt about going back to France and her family home in Antony, which she inherited after her mother's death.[19]

> All day sitting in a chair
> I could not lift a feather
> nor make a phone call
> depression...
> dream of Antony.[20]
>
> LOUISE BOURGEOIS

Sigmund Freud described homesickness as 'the saddening loss of childhood' and consequently the loss of the mother. In his view, homeland nostalgics more fundamentally longed for their childhood homes, the warmth of their mothers' wombs, a stable context tailored to the satisfactions of their desires.[22] One of Bourgeois's fabric books, *Ode à la Bièvre* (2007), tells the story of revisiting the river where tapestries were soaked and wrung out next to her childhood home in Antony and finding that it had dried up. It had been a kind river to her family: rich in tannin, which enhances the dyeing of fabric. The river also symbolised a feeling of loss, because it was where she tried to drown herself when her mother died and was rescued by her father. *Ode à la Bièvre* symbolises the passage of time, and the continuing power of the past within her psychic life in the present. This relationship between nostalgia, time and personal memory was identified early on and most evocatively by Immanuel Kant when he wrote that when people who are homesick revisit the places of their youth, 'they are greatly disappointed in their expectations and consequently cured. Though they think this is because everything has changed there, it is really because they cannot relive their youth there'.[23] Childhood nostalgia is inseparable from memories of the mother. Although childhoods are deeply personal and unique, there is a universality in looking back and in witnessing powerlessly how time moves on. Clothing and fabrics form the tactile remains of our childhoods, and they can take us back to our roots.

Bourgeois was an internationally celebrated artist when she died in 2010. However, for a long time she had struggled to be recognised as an artist in a male-dominated world. She brought the subjects of motherhood and domestic life into her art. A drawing depicting her small boys playing in the bath evokes domestic moments of closeness and intimacy. In her famous *Femme Maison* paintings from the late 1940s, female figures are trapped inside different types of houses. In these works, the house becomes the symbol of the mother: *mother* is homebound —— a feeling of being cribbed, cabined, confined derives from them. Bourgeois's psychoanalysis with Dr Henry Lowenfeld, which began in 1952 and lasted more than thirty years, was precipitated by the sudden passing of her father in 1951. Unbearable feelings of loneliness and isolation had also surfaced previously, in the 1940s, as she struggled to balance her duties as a housewife and mother. During the first decade of her analysis, Bourgeois retreated from the art world and only made sculpture intermittently. The relationship between motherhood (or parenthood) and art, and the practical and psychological difficulty of juggling these two aspects of life, forms a struggle for many artists. Sylvia Plath writes in *Ariel* (1965) about working at dawn before 'the child's cry / melts in the wall': the wall between art and life which, with one cry, melts away.[24] However autobiographical, the work and writings of Bourgeois encapsulate the universal highs and lows of motherhood. They speak to her love for her children but also the fear of being erased as a woman, as an artist.

The exhibition *ECHO. Wrapped in Memory* opens where life begins: in the crib. It explores the tactile, mental and clothed realities of early motherhood and babyhood.[25] The initial days postpartum are often spent horizontally, in limbo between sofa and bed. Feelings of love and euphoria merge with exhaustion and existential anxiety. There are the fragmented nights and rushed showers, the muslin swaddle blankets, the tiny baby socks, the leaking breasts, the wet sheets and damp clothes, the smell of milk —— a hint of sour sweetness —— and the toothless, piercing cries. The mother's body, clothes, selfhood, identity —— her interests and focus —— are altered. Life after birth bathes in a haze of slow domesticity, a world away from the outside, inside the madness of your own creation. For the new parent, the days are long and the nights are short. As you nurture new life, the world outside passes you by.

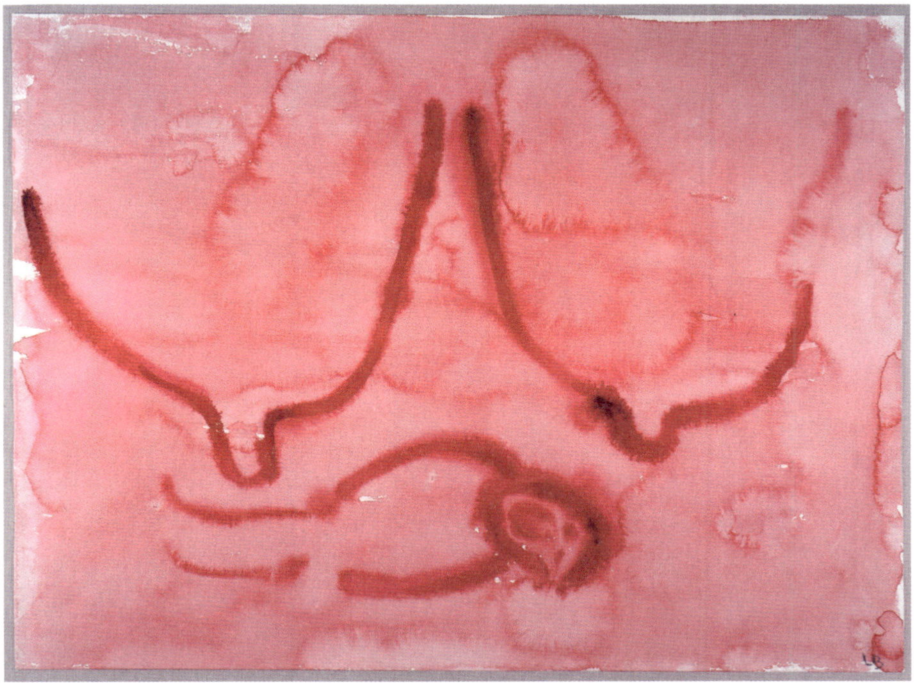

Bourgeois was initially concerned that she would not be able to conceive. During a brief visit to France in 1939, she and Goldwater adopted a French orphan, Michel. Shortly after, Bourgeois gave birth to two more sons: Jean-Louis in 1940 and Alain a year later in 1941. In conversation with Deborah Wye in 1979, Bourgeois was asked about the idea of still experiencing anxiety around infertility after her sons were born:

> "Yes, because you're always afraid of losing them! The anxiety persisted after conception. This is not something which disappears. For instance, when the children are much older you are afraid of something else. You are afraid of losing them; you are afraid of being abandoned; you are afraid of becoming aggressive; you are afraid of lots of things. So it is not a thing which stops once they are born. It diminishes, but it does not stop."[26]
>
> LOUISE BOURGEOIS

LOUISE BOURGEOIS
The Feeding, 2007

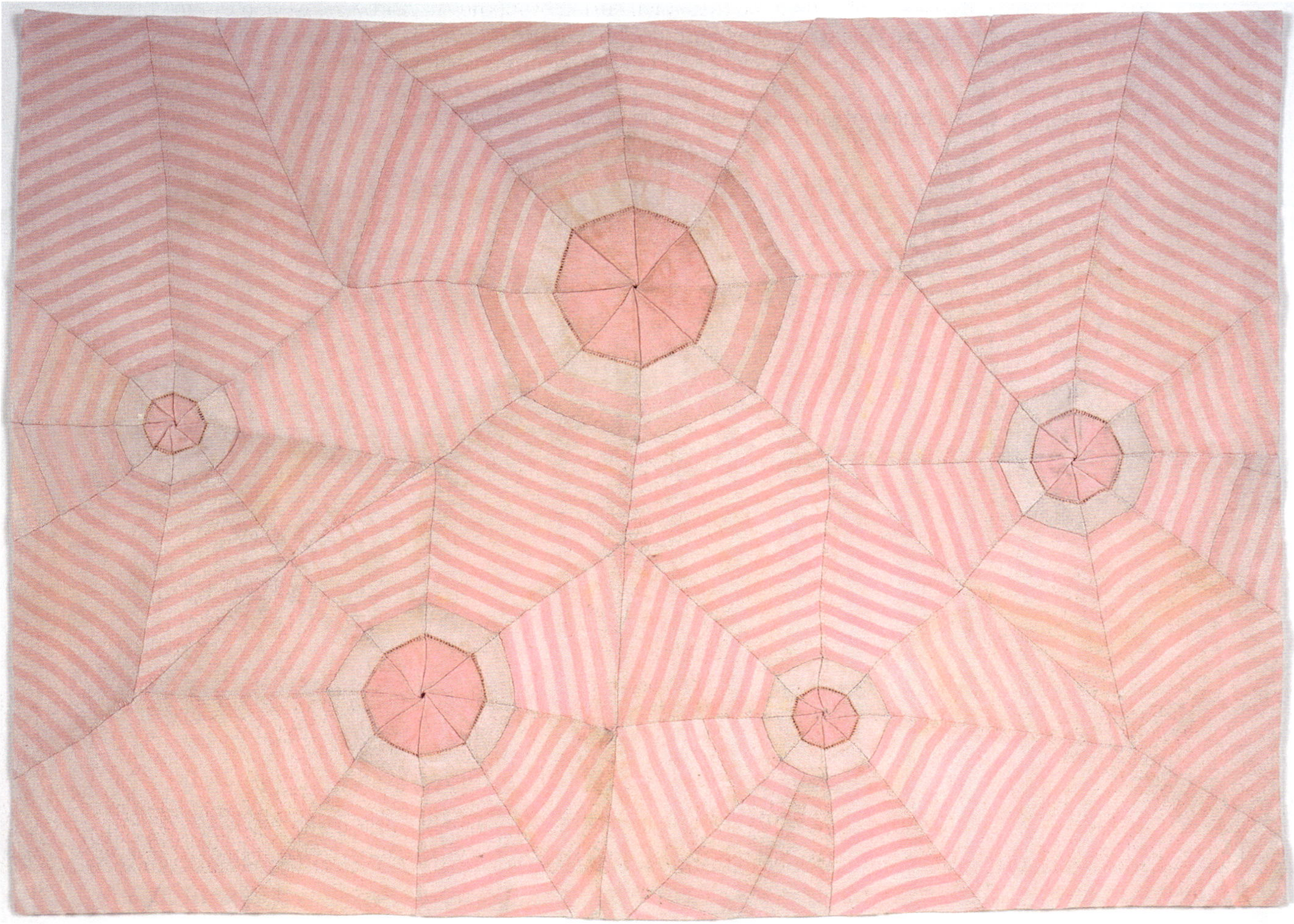

LOUISE BOURGEOIS
Untitled, 2007

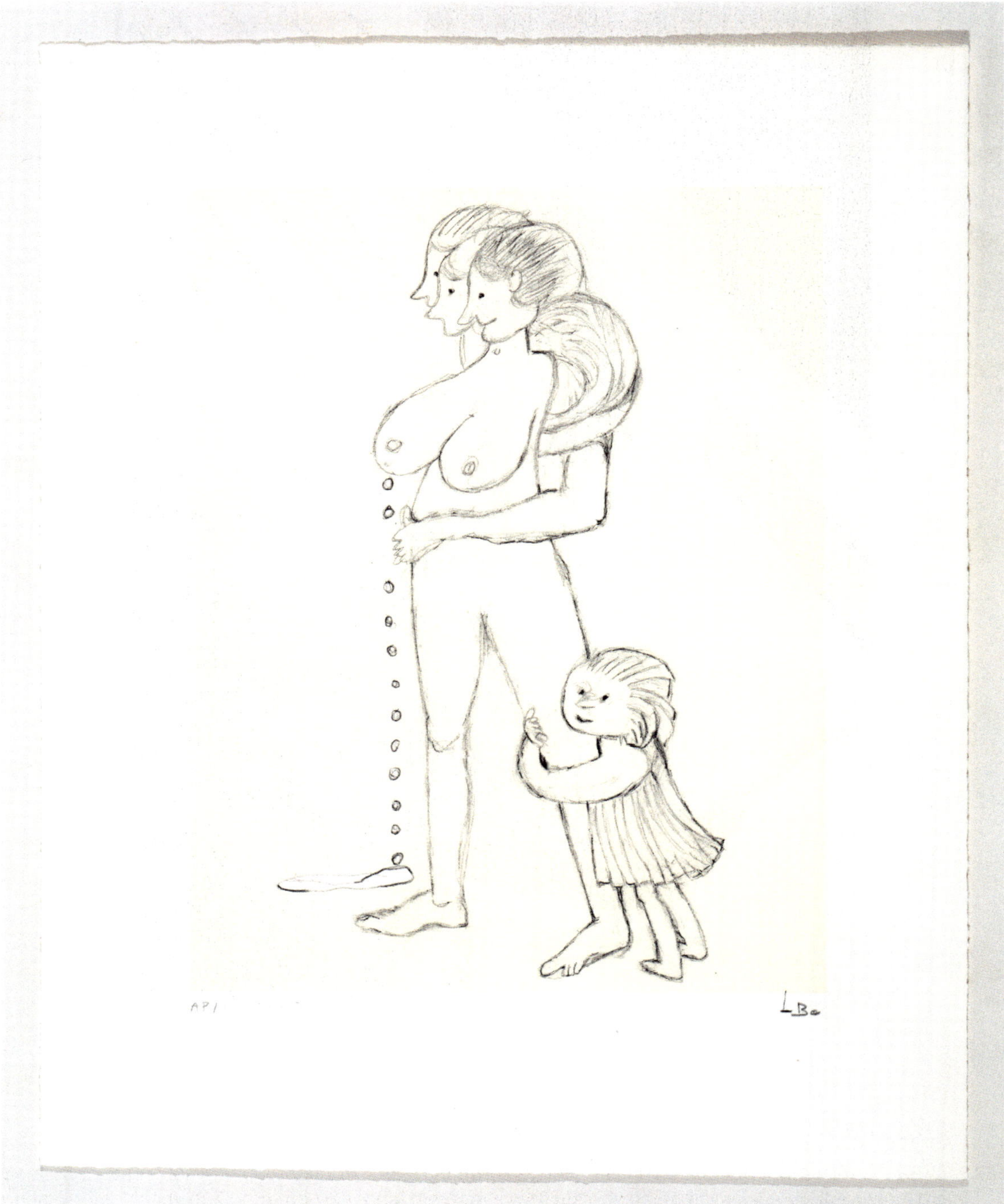

Louise Bourgeois
The Bad Mother, 1998

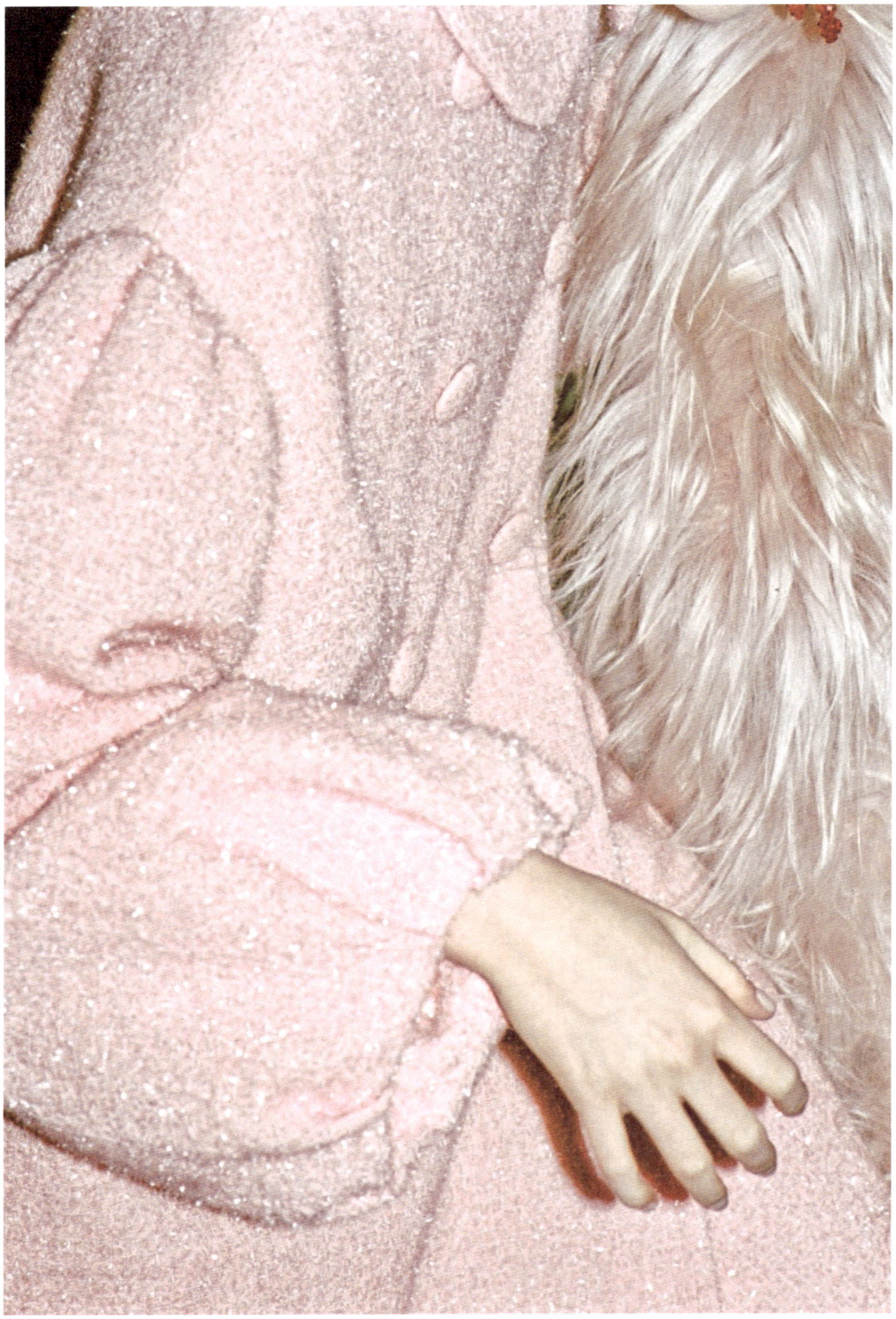

Simone Rocha
Autumn-Winter 2016-17

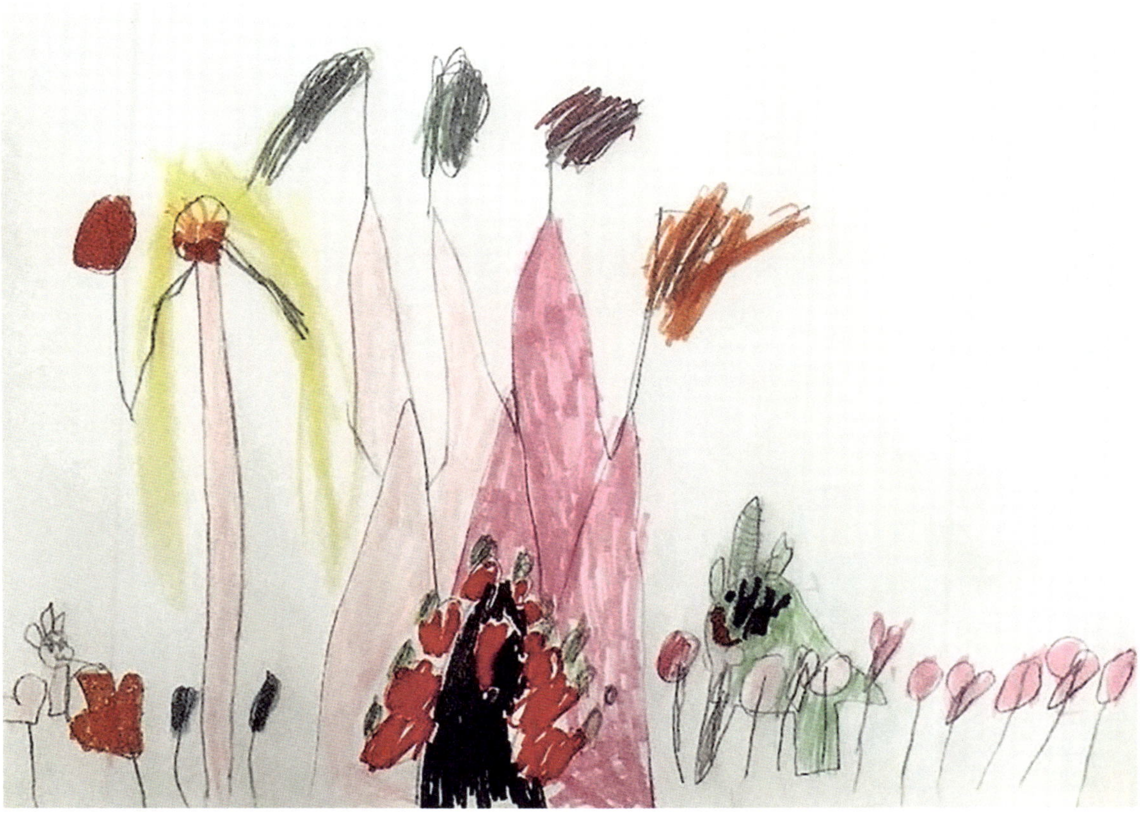

Drawing by Valentine Ming, Simone Rocha's daughter

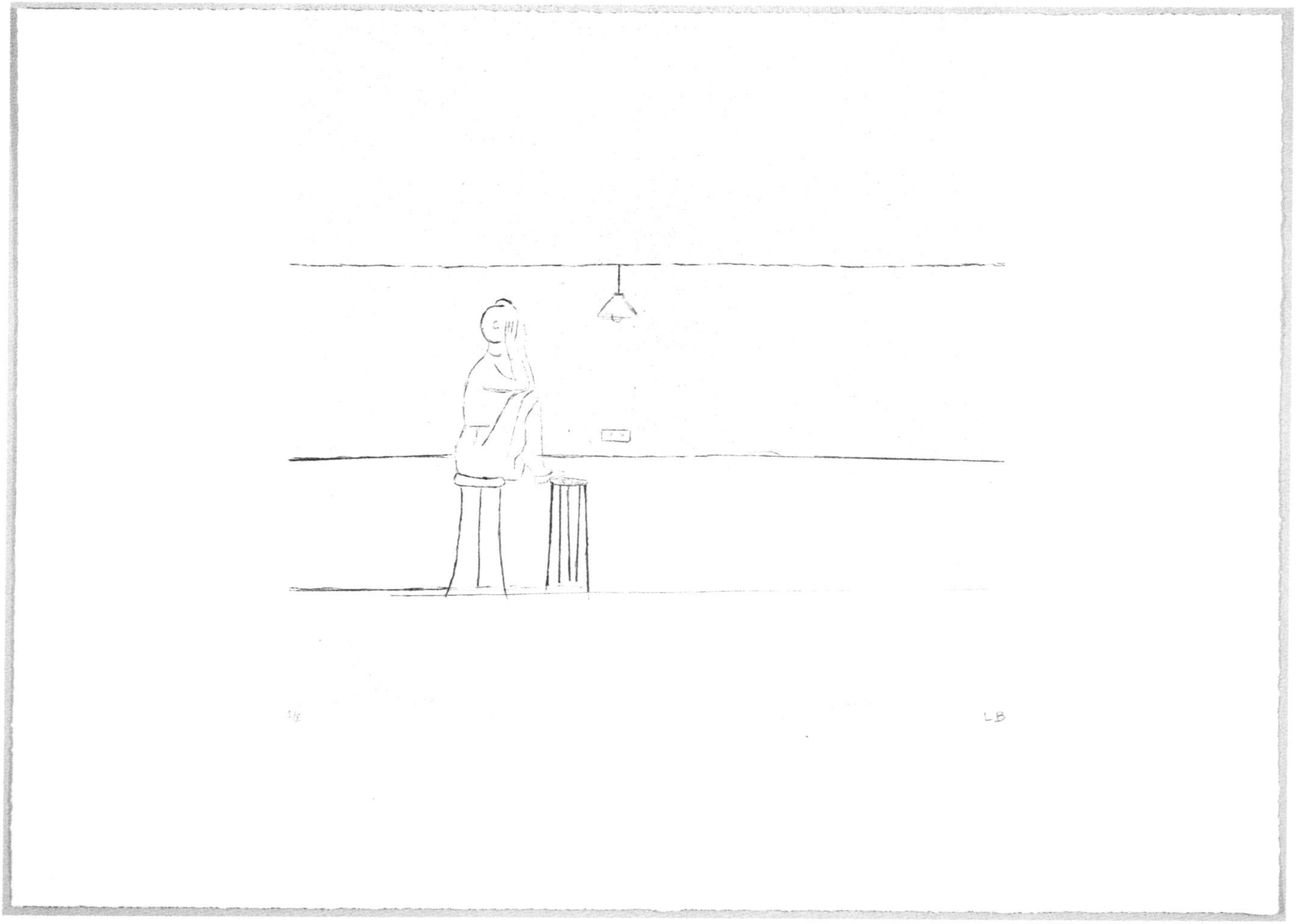

Louise Bourgeois
Empty Nest, from the portfolio *Autobiographical Series*, 1994

In 1994, as part of the print portfolio *Autobiographical Series*, Bourgeois created a drypoint print titled *Empty Nest*. It depicts a mother sitting on a stool, legs bent, feet up, her face resting in her hands. The mother's figure is hardly visible. She sits quietly in an empty space. There is a sense of loneliness, suffering and abandonment. It unites Bourgeois's biggest fears. The work depicts the emptiness and pain of being separated from one's child. Based on drawings she made in the 1940s about her early life in New York, Bourgeois developed the portfolio in the four years following the death of her eldest son, Michel.

Bourgeois relived the birthing experience in her art —— her own birth and that of her sons —— and never more so than in the last decade of her life, when she made many red gouaches with graphic representations of nursing and pregnant bodies, nipples and babies floating in utero attached to umbilical cords. The birthing experience, and the trauma and physicality of it, is also processed by Rocha in two of her postpartum collections. The Autumn-Winter 2016-17 collection was presented three months after she gave birth to her eldest daughter, Valentine Ming. The psychological turmoil and her altered reality as a new mother can be felt in the wrapping and swaddling of stoles, subtle references to the lilac surgical aprons and the pale colours that suggest sickness and nausea. The comfortable cuts of the garments showed a tenderness towards the birthing body; it needs to be caressed and not restricted. There is a sense of the physical trauma of birth that I have not seen evoked by other fashion designers, but labour and birth had equally inspired her and added new depth and layers to her work. Five years later came her Spring-Summer 2022 collection titled *Baby Teeth*, right after the birth of her second daughter, Noah Roses. It was presented as a playfully dark tale about the naivety and reality of the first weeks at home with a newborn, and the ceremony of childhood, from baptism to communion. Some dresses referenced traditional christening robes and homespun baby blankets, and there were tiny porcelain teeth earrings, blood-drip crystals, large knitted underpants and embellished supportive nursing bras. Rocha loved the polarising effect of the latter garment: 'in one way, a nursing bra is very provocative, but it's also very practical and nurturing'.[27] Dresses opened both front and back to allow nursing. From her own experience, Rocha had 'wanted to support the breasts... and to release the hips'.[28] The styling and cropped knitwear looked as if children had playfully created their own outfits. Crisp bedsheets seemed to blend into nightdresses, which was her own way of poetically evoking a sleep-deprived state and demanding night feeds, a time of 'falling out of bed and taking the sheets with you'.[29]

"Your work reflects your experiences. You go through insomnia —— that was a huge influence on the *Baby Teeth* collection, because I was going through it, so I thought I'd bring it to the table. We even got the models to walk slower, to represent that feeling. Because the truth is, it can be really challenging, a new baby, but then there is the huge thing, of a new life, that feels monumental. It was a balance between the everyday and the ceremony of it all."[30]

SIMONE ROCHA

Becoming a parent and working in the performing arts can be disproportionately hard. The physicality of pregnancy and birth is perhaps the biggest challenge and career obstacle for dancers. Anne Teresa De Keersmaeker gave birth to two children in the mid-1990s:

"To have to combine three things: being creative, being a good partner and being a good mother is not possible; you could combine two, but three seems impossible. I was able to do my work because I had a partner —— the father of my children —— who always supported me. In addition, I was lucky to surround myself with a good team at Rosas. I had the opportunity to organise my life and that of my family so that I could do my work to the full. Most women don't have those resources."[31]

ANNE TERESA DE KEERSMAEKER

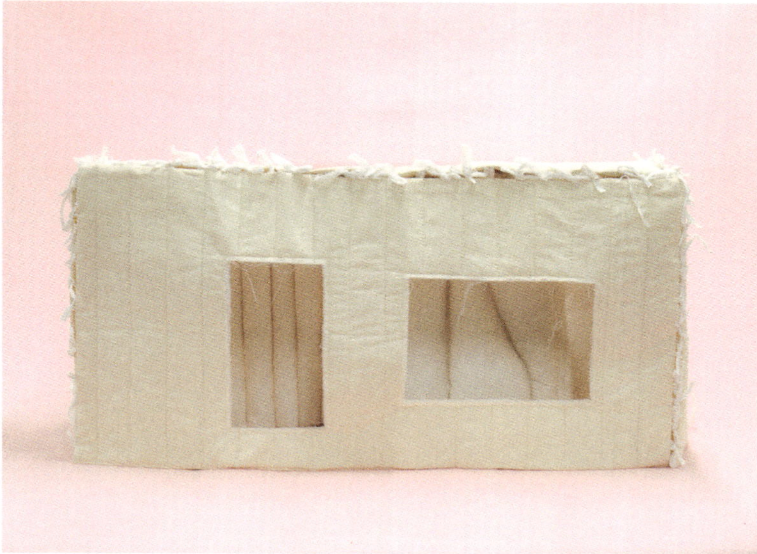

ECHO's set designer, Janina Pedan, a mother of two young girls, and I, a mother of a 15-month-old girl at the time of writing, wanted to open the exhibition with the emotional, sensorial and clothed experiences of motherhood and babyhood. But, importantly, this story is not for mothers or parents only; it is about being nurtured and 'mothering' in a wider sense.

We hope to evoke memories not only by the artworks, clothes and stories on display, but also through the materiality, acoustics and lighting. *ECHO* welcomes you inside intimate installations and allows you to rest your body and reminisce. Bourgeois described how she had her 'blue days and pink days'.[32] On her pink days she felt an intense surge of creativity, optimism, positivity and affirmation, while blue days were days of melancholy, contemplation and withdrawal. The exhibition's mood subtly moves from pink to blue and gives space to these opposing but interconnected forces that shape our memories and everyday experiences. Throughout the show and the pages of this book, you will move from one mental state to another, from conscious to unconscious, from pink to blue.

ECHO. Wrapped in Memory is a conversation between artists of different generations and perspectives. Some of them are well established; others are at the start of their career. Throughout these pages, you will meet them too.[33]

Set design model in calico of *ECHO*'s 'cradle' installation by Janina Pedan

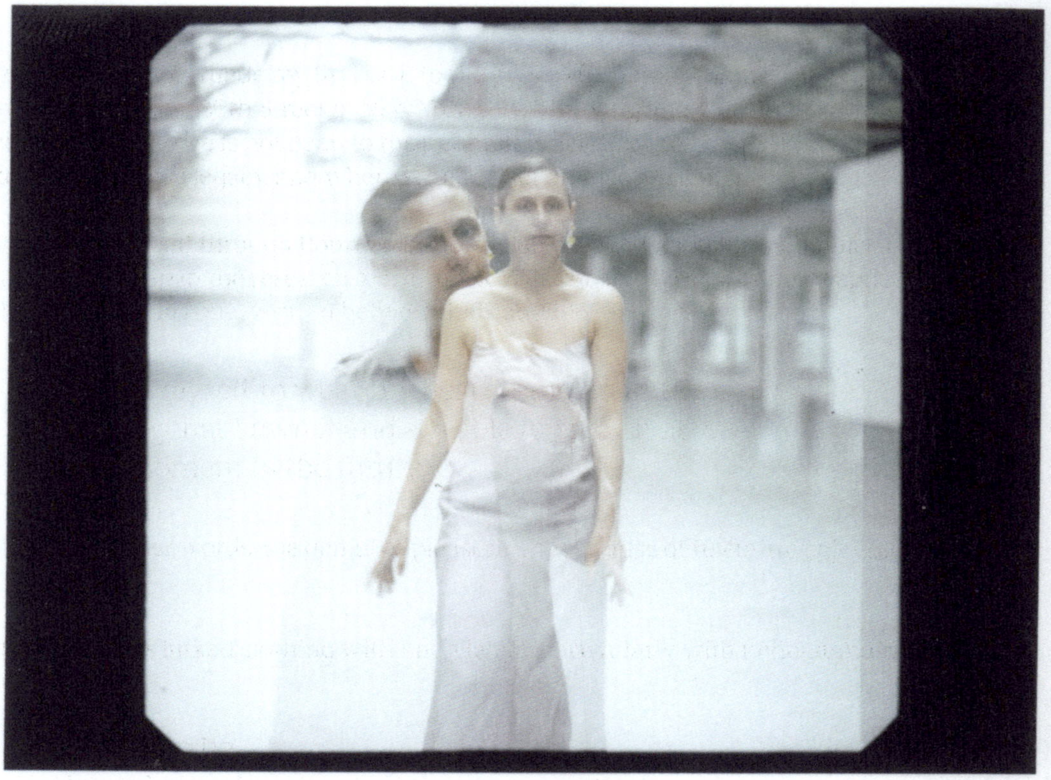

Anne Teresa De Keersmaeker wearing Simone Rocha, 2016

1 'Paulo Herkenhoff in Conversation with Louise Bourgeois', in Paulo Herkenhoff, Allan Schwartzman and Robert Storr, *Louise Bourgeois* (London: Phaidon, 2003), p. 22.
2 This exhibition ran from 4 September 2021 to 23 January 2022 at MoMu Fashion Museum Antwerp. The accompanying book was published by Lannoo Publishers.
3 This exhibition ran from 8 October 2022 to 26 February 2023 at MoMu Fashion Museum Antwerp. *MIRROR MIRROR. Fashion & the Psyche* was an exhibition project by MoMu and the Dr Guislain Museum in Ghent. Each museum curated its own exhibition, and a joint catalogue was published by Hannibal Books.
4 See the complete list of Rosas costume collaborations in Anne Teresa De Keersmaeker's interview in this publication.
5 Interview with Paulo Herkenhoff on 7 March 1997, as quoted in 'Louise Bourgeois, Femme-Temps', in Jerry Gorovoy, Paulo Herkenhoff and Pandora Tabatabai Asbaghi, *Louise Bourgeois: Blue Days and Pink Days* (Milan: Fondazione Prada, 1997), p. 268.
6 As quoted in Charlie Porter, *What Artists Wear* (London: Penguin Books, 2021), p. 19: Louise Bourgeois, loose sheet of writing, c.1963; LB-0202 (Louise Bourgeois Archive/The Easton Foundation, New York; hereafter cited as TEF).
7 An exhibition was recently dedicated to Louise Bourgeois's fabric works: *Louise Bourgeois. The Woven Child* at the Hayward Gallery, London (9 February to 15 May 2022) and traveled to Gropius Bau, Berlin (22 July to 23 October 2022).
8 Isabella Burley, 'Simone Rocha on Louise Bourgeois', *Dazed*, 1 March 2015, https://www.dazeddigital.com/fashion/article/17160/1/exclusive-simone-rocha-vs-louise-bourgeois, accessed 10 January 2023.
9 The Easton Foundation was established by Louise Bourgeois in the 1980s as a non-profit and charitable organisation. Upon her death in 2010, at the age of 98, Bourgeois bequeathed her home and an adjacent townhouse to become the Foundation's centre and donated a substantial collection of her art to its holdings. The foundation is now dedicated to preserving her legacy and promoting the scholarship and awareness of her life and art. As part of this mission, it has established the Louise Bourgeois Archive, a study centre and residency for curators and scholars. http://www.theeastonfoundation.org/foundation, accessed 5 January 2023.
10 Siri Hustvedt, *Mothers, Fathers and Others* (London: Hodder & Stoughton Ltd, 2021), p. 203.
11 https://www.randkrant.be/nl/news/4070/anne-teresa-de-keers-maeker-over-haar-jeugd-in-wemmel, accessed 10 February 2023.
12 https://www.rosas.be/en/news/687-flipping-the-hourglass, accessed 9 February 2023.
13 An D'Huys in conversation with curator Elisa De Wyngaert on 5 May 2023.
14 Ibid.
15 Gorovoy, *et al.* 1997, p. 14.
16 Alice Newbold, 'Simone Rocha —— "I'm Not Making Garments for Garments' Sake"', *British Vogue*, 9 May 2018, https://www.vogue.co.uk/article/simone-rocha-on-motherhood, accessed 15 January 2023.
17 Dan Thawley and Blake Abbie (eds.), *A Magazine Curated By Simone Rocha* (Paris: Evence-Charles Coppée, 2019), p. 31.
18 Sophie Bew, 'Simone Rocha on How Ireland Inspires Her', *AnOther*, 26 March 2021, https://www.anothermag.com/fashion-beauty/13206/simone-rocha-on-how-ireland-inspires-her-interview-2021, accessed 13 February 2023.
19 "The Case of LB" by Philip Larratt-Smith, in Larratt-Smith and Juliet Mitchell, *Louise Bourgeois, Freud's Daughter* (New Haven and London: Yale University Press, 2021), p. 104.
20 As quoted in Larratt-Smith and Mitchell, ibid., p. 102: Bourgeois, diary entry, 5 November 1951 (TEF).
21 Sigmund Freud, 'The Uncanny', in James Strachey (ed.), *The Standard Edition of the Complete Psychological Works of Sigmund Freud*, Volume XVII (London: The Hogarth Press, 1918), pp. 219–53, p. 245.
22 Ibid.
23 Immanuel Kant, *Anthropology from a Pragmatic Point of View* (Cambridge University Press, 2006), as discussed by Amy Kenyon, author of *Dreaming Suburbia* (Detroit: Wayne State University Press, 2004), during the 'Nostalgia Today' conference at the Freud Museum, London, 9 March 2019.
24 Sylvia Plath, *Ariel* (London: Faber & Faber, 2015), pp. 28–9. *Ariel*, first published in 1965, contains many of Plath's poems, written just before her death in 1963.
25 Motherhood in the context of *ECHO. Wrapped in Memory* is not about sex or gender or even about childbearing. It is about one person nurturing another.
26 Quoted in "Two Conversations with Deborah Wye", in Marie-Laure Bernadac and Hans Ulrich Obrist (eds.), *Louise Bourgeois, Destruction of the Father, Reconstruction of the Father: Writings and Interviews 1923–1997* (London: Violette Editions, 1998), p. 125.
27 https://www.vogue.co.uk/news/gallery/simone-rocha-ss22, accessed 7 May 2023.
28 Sarah Mower, 'Simone Rocha: Spring 2022 Ready-To-Wear', *Vogue Runway*, 20 September 2021, https://www.vogue.com/fashion-shows/spring-2022-ready-to-wear/simone-rocha#review, accessed 23 February 2023.
29 September 2021, https://www.vogue.co.uk/news/gallery/simone-rocha-ss22, accessed 23 February 2023.
30 Simone Rocha, quote from the interview by Lou Stoppard in the current publication.
31 Interview with Elisa De Wyngaert on 8 June 2023.
32 Philip Larratt-Smith, *Louise Bourgeois. Les têtes bleues et les femmes rouges* (Brussels: Xavier Hufkens, 2015), pp. 9–16.
33 In no specific order: Maya Barrera, Laila Gohar, Liz Magor, Martin Margiela, Cassi Namoda, Harley Weir, Cathy Wilkes, and Billie Zangewa. A special gratitude goes to The Easton Foundation and Xavier Hufkens. Louise Bourgeois's work would not have played such a key role in the exhibition without their trust and advice. It is a true honour to share her legacy in MoMu's spaces and on the pages of this book. This exhibition would equally not have been possible without the time, help and thoughtful generosity of the teams at Simone Rocha and Rosas. I am immensely grateful to everyone involved.

CATHY WILKES

Untitled, 2017

Cathy Wilkes (Northern Ireland, Belfast, °1966) is known for her installations that evoke poetic visions and places of loss or transformation. Her installations include found objects and reclaimed materials that speak through their associative and material presence. Her work draws from personal experiences and touches upon notions of loss, domesticity, motherhood and the female experience, yet remains veiled in a delicate subtlety and mystery. Here, three children seem to float above the ground. They protect each other, showing love and companionship in their shared suffering. Wrapped in bath towels, they appear to have just been lifted out of the bath, a caring act of a parent who is no longer present. Below them is a white plinth, another consciousness, a place of loss and longing: close but not within reach.

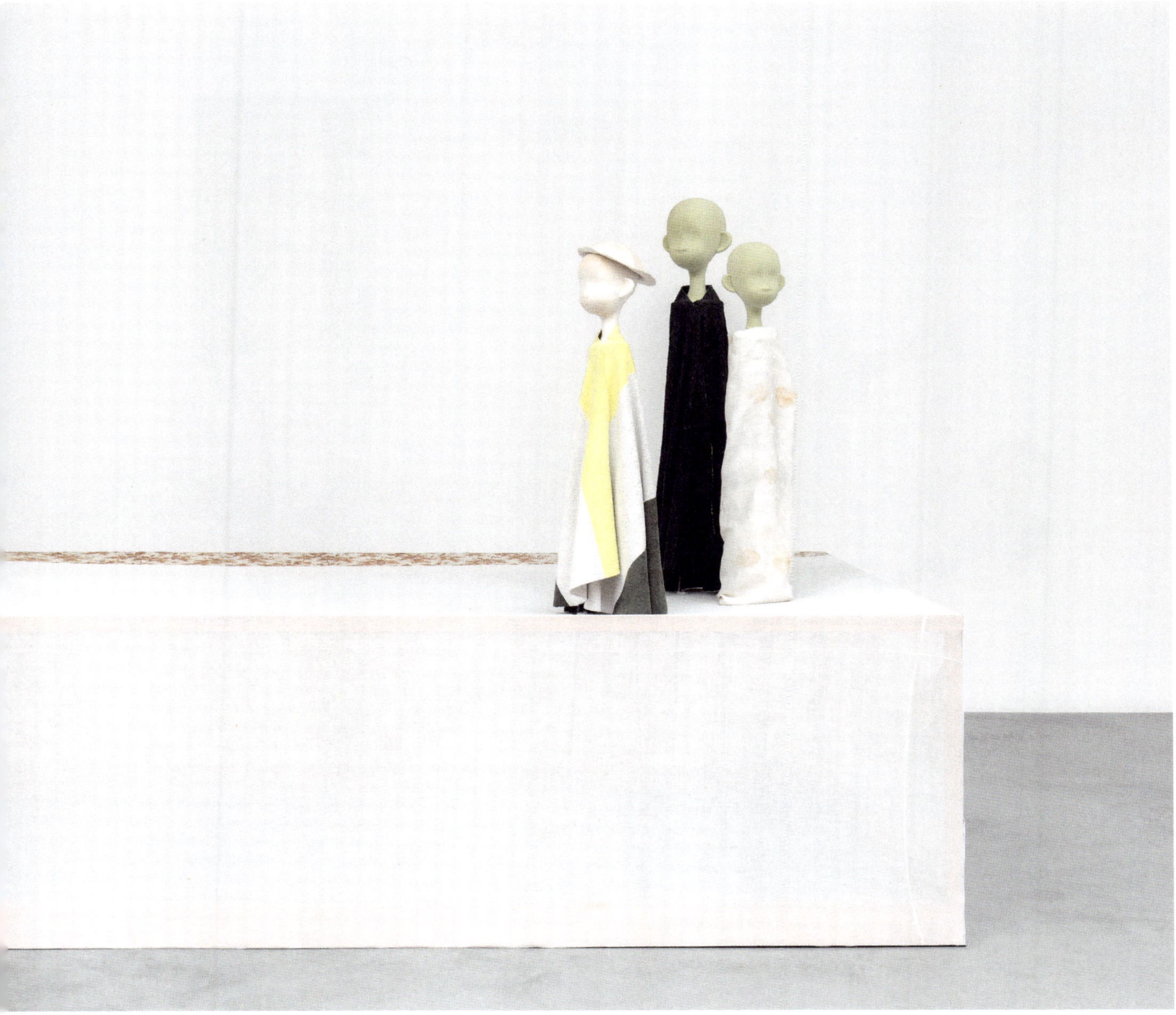

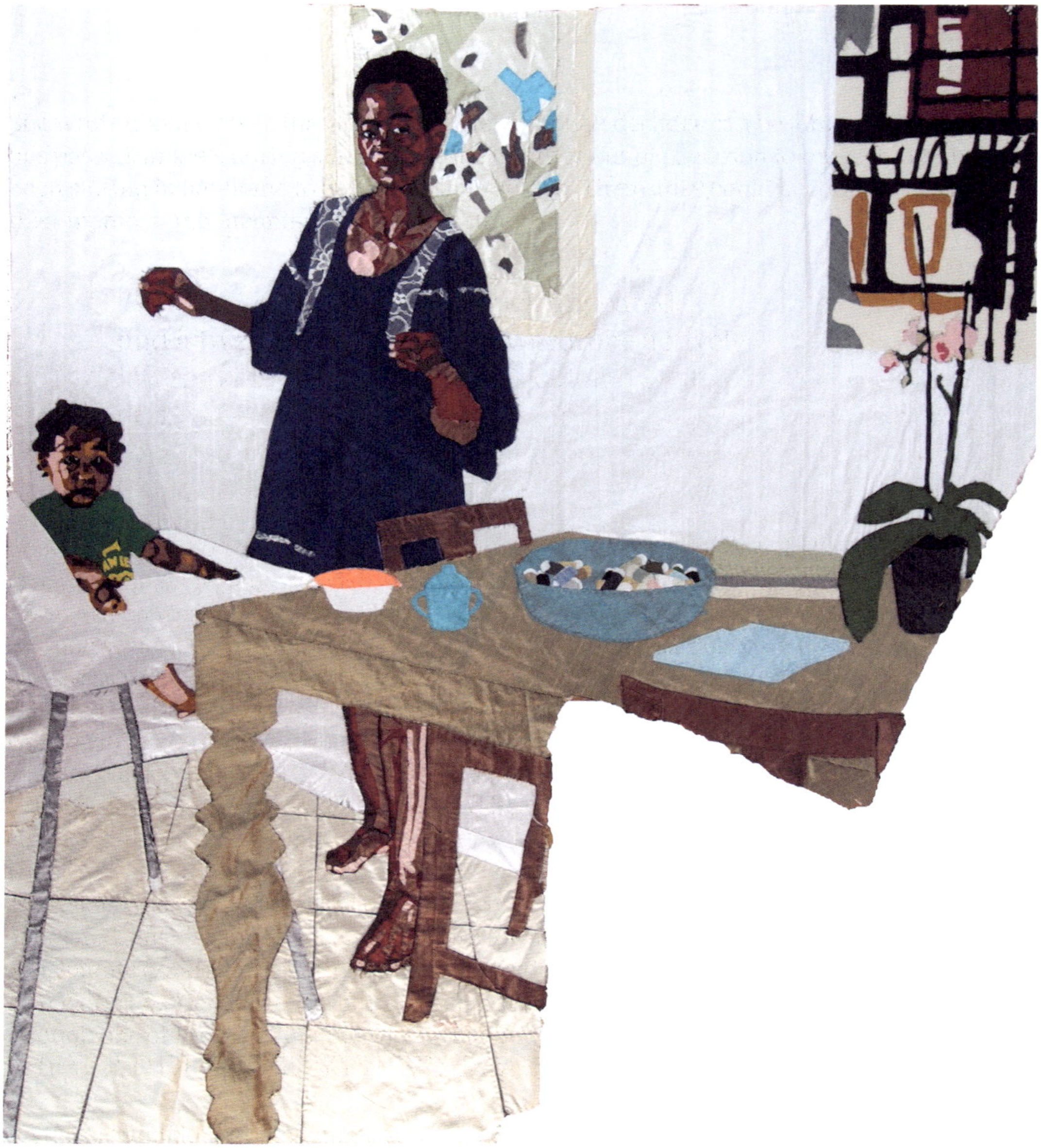

BILLIE ZANGEWA

Mother and Child, 2015

After the birth of her son, Billie Zangewa (Malawi, Blantyre, °1973) began making her well-known silk paintings of domestic interiors to explore the shift in focus from self-examination and femininity to motherhood and the home. Often referencing scenes or experiences from everyday life, Zangewa has stated that she is interested in depicting the work done by women that keeps society running smoothly, but which is often overlooked, undervalued or ignored. Zangewa refers to this as 'daily feminism'. In her work, the domestic sphere becomes a pretext for asking questions around gender stereotypes and racial prejudice.

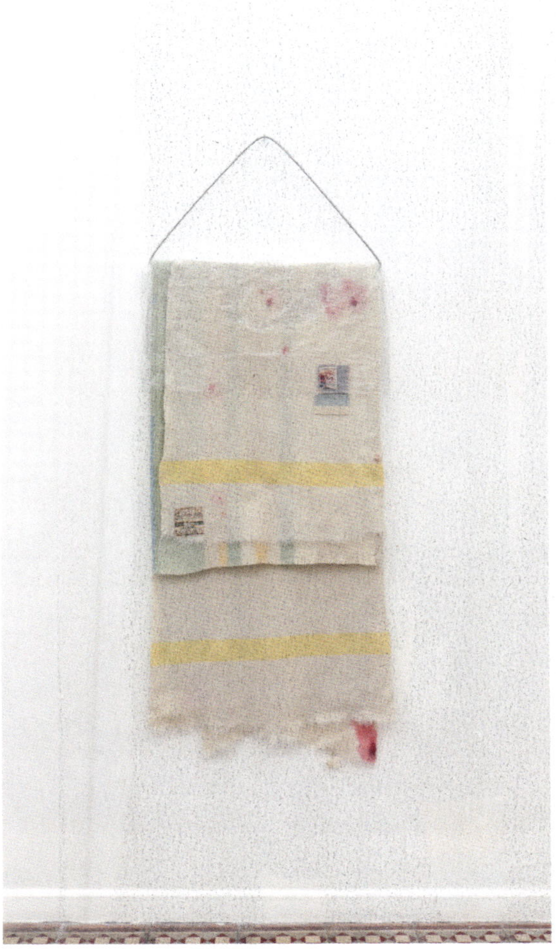

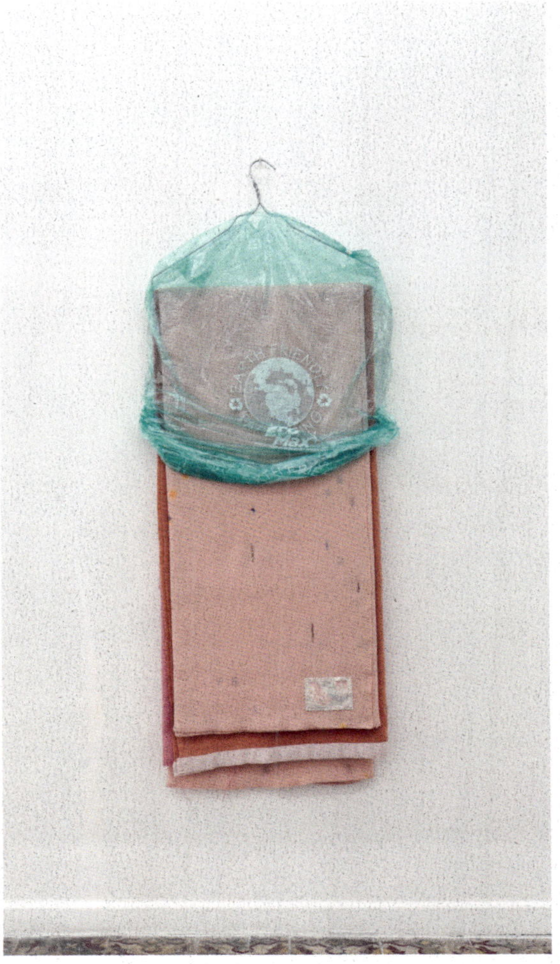

LIZ MAGOR

Alberta/Quebec, 2013 (*left*)
Phoenix, 2013 (*right*)

Liz Magor's (Canada, Vancouver, °1948) work deals with the ordinary and the familiar and questions the physical and emotional relationships we maintain with the objects that surround us. *Alberta/Quebec* and *Phoenix* are part of a series made from second-hand blankets damaged by time and use. Magor leaves her marks on these textiles by mending their tears, and highlighting stains and burns without distorting the memory of the society and people that created, used and then discarded them.

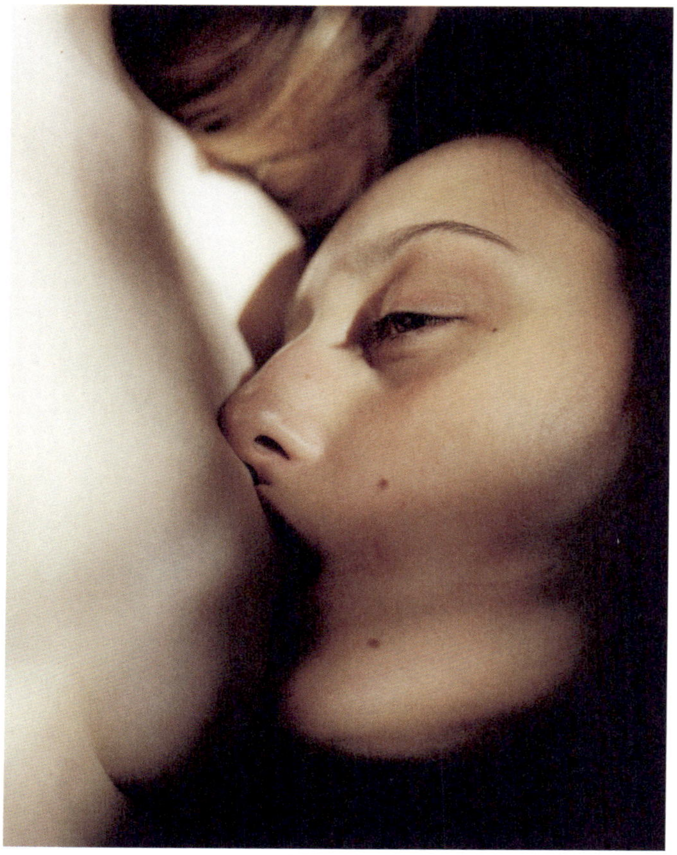

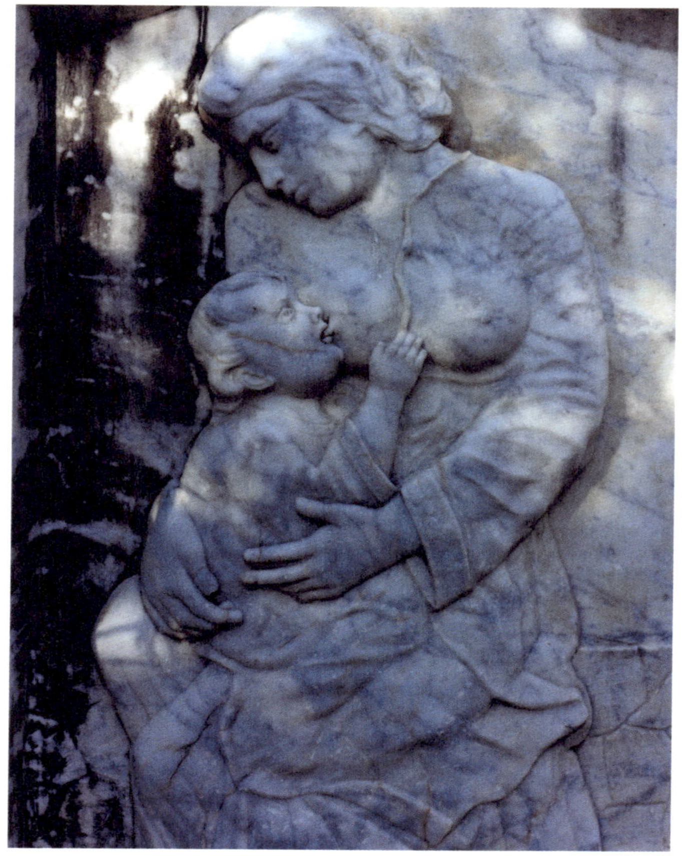

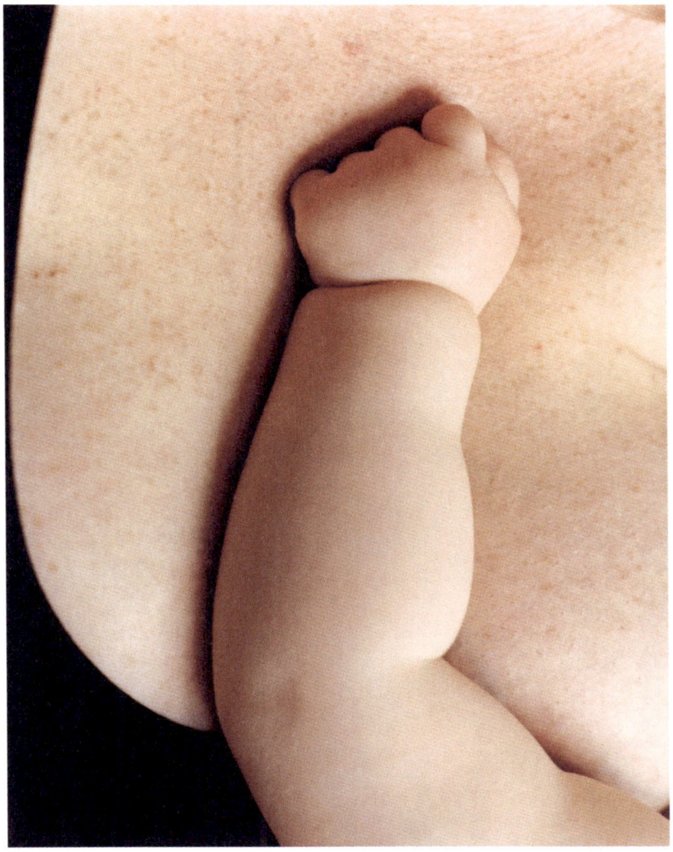

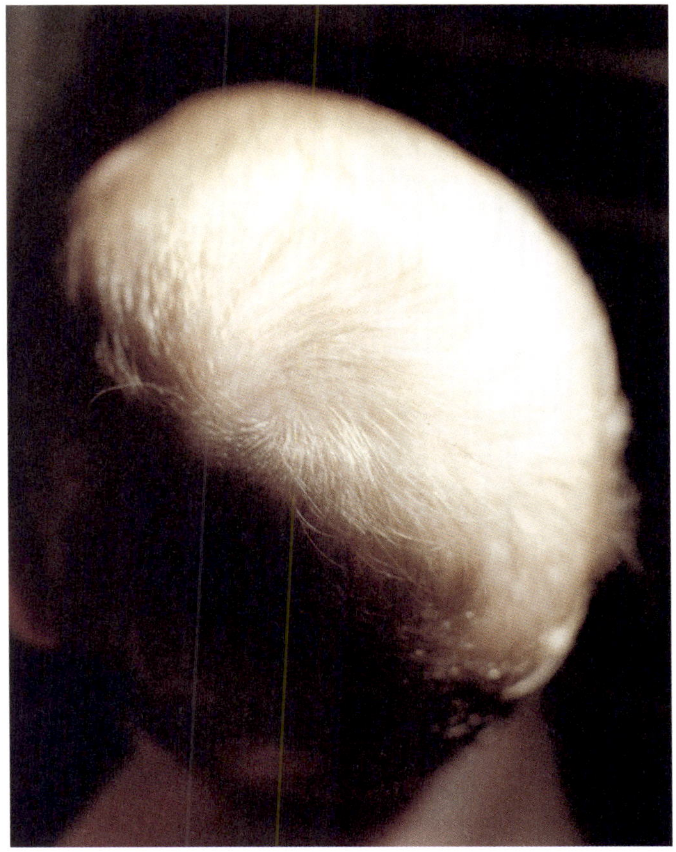

HARLEY WEIR

Baron: Function, 2018

Harley Weir's (United Kingdom, London, °1988) *Function* series explores the female body through its biological functions and how these are mediated in a patriarchal, capitalist society. The female nipple, for example, is both an erogenous zone and a feeding station, and as such, engenders desire and disgust. Weir's childhood friends and their children feature in diptychs as Mary and Child evoking Christian iconography.

MAYA BARRERA

Ego, 2022
Stacked, 2022
Ended Somewhere Else, 2022

By building her sculptures with thin overlapping layers, Maya Barrera's (USA, New York City, °1987) pieces are wrought with traces of her touch, each symbolising an idea, a train of thought. The titles function like diary entries, expressing memories and experiences. The parallel between art making and human making is granular to a new series, which she produced during her recent pregnancy. *Ego* evokes the bleeding, or not bleeding, of menstruation and labour. Its intense redness functions as a totem form of female peacocking, in which pregnancy, fertility and bleeding feel large and visible. *Stacked* symbolises how the physical weight changed on her frame and how fascia and soft tissue created new shapes. The different grid systems in *Ended Somewhere Else* allude to the planning and dreaming she was doing in preparation for motherhood.

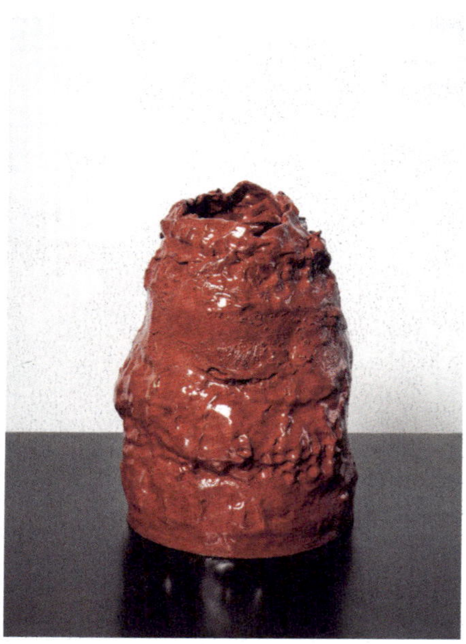

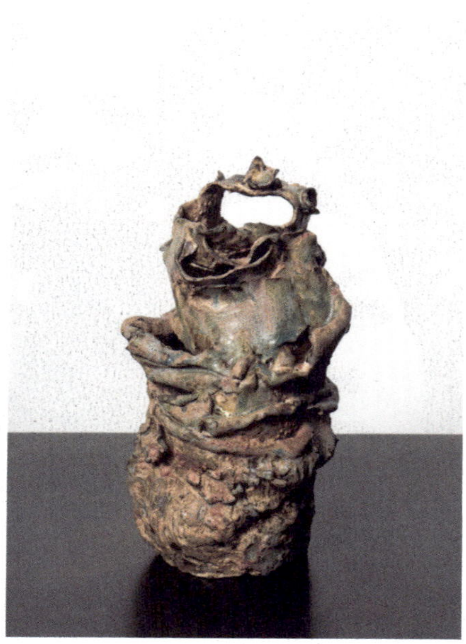

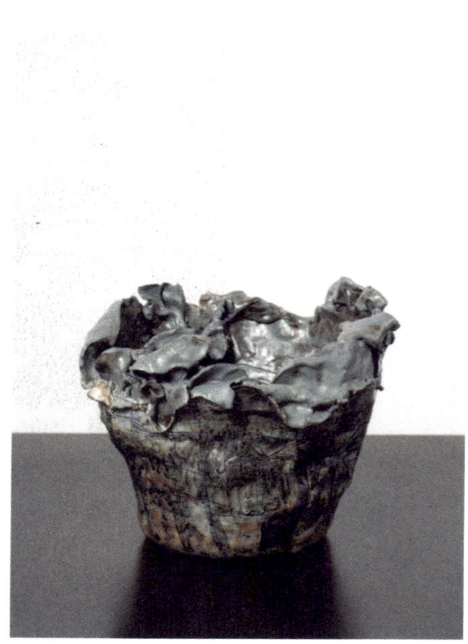

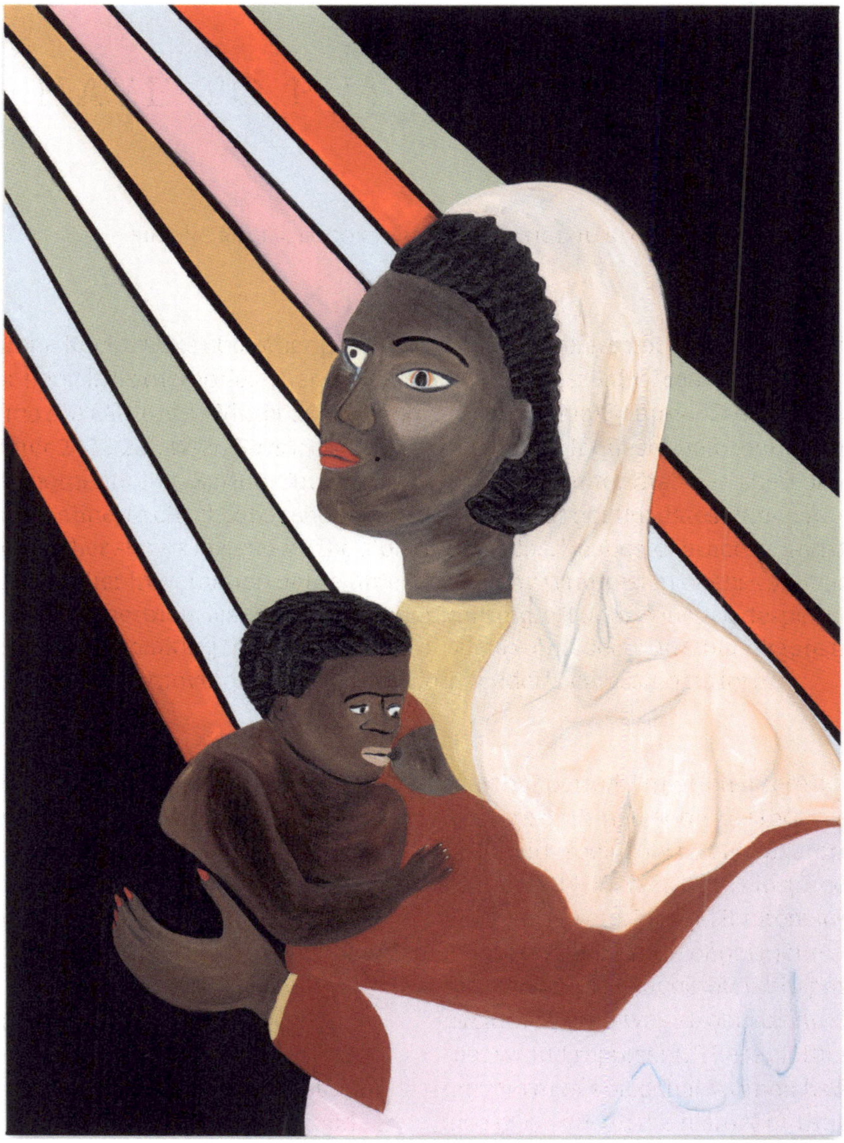

CASSI NAMODA

High Malaria: Maria's Respite, 2022

Cassi Namoda's (Mozambique, Maputo, °1988) paintings explore the intricacies and intimacies of everyday life under postcolonialism. Combining personal memories with historical references, she creates works that attempt to access emotional interiority and communicate human experience in all its subtlety. Her figures cry, embrace, suffer and love. She explores the duality between past and present, Africa and Europe, spiritual traditions and a globalised world. *High Malaria: Maria's Respite* references women's experiences and Mozambique's history of the introduction of Christianity as the majority religion by the Portuguese colonisers.

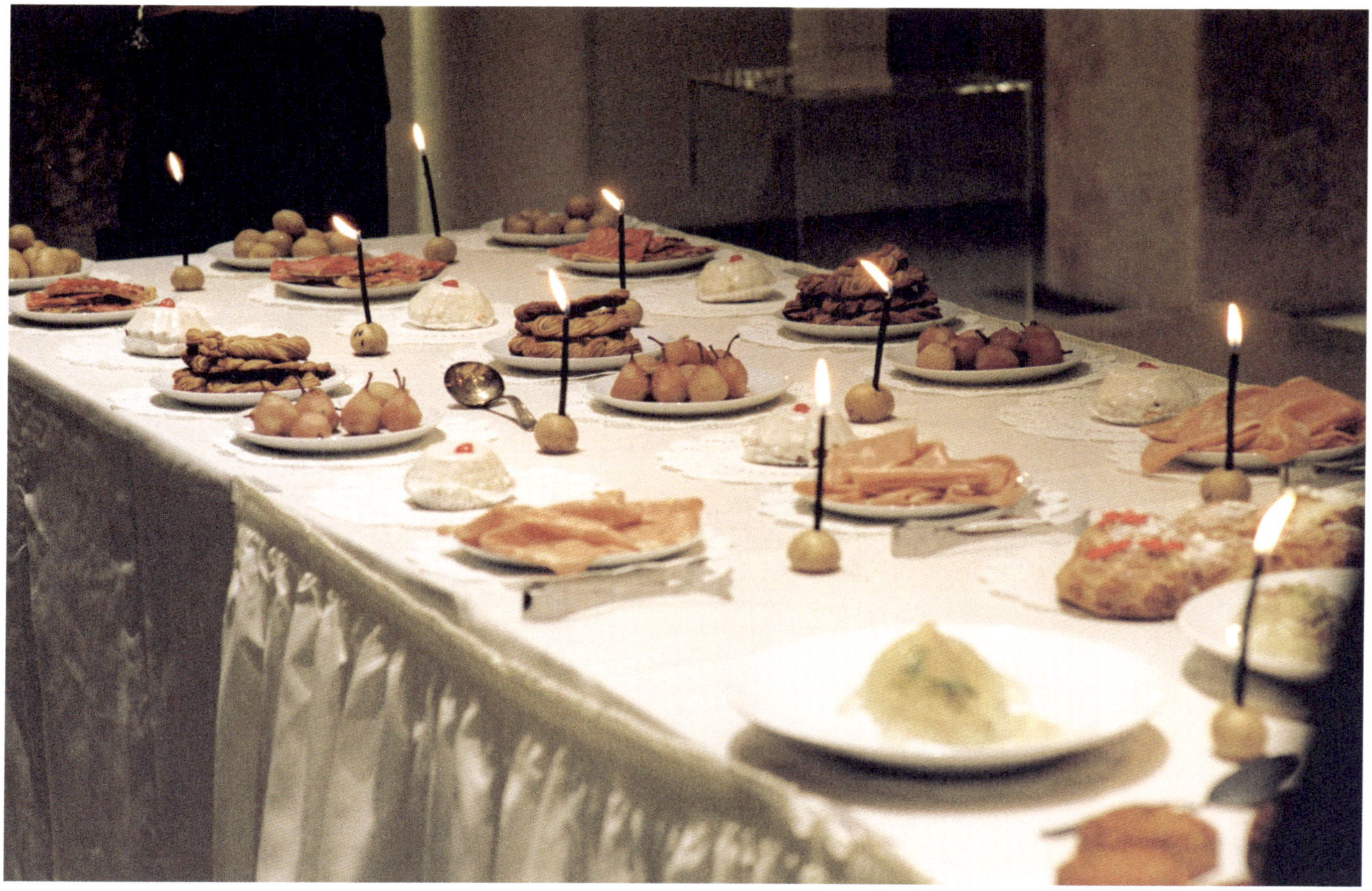

LAILA GOHAR

Installation for Simone Rocha, 2018

Laila Gohar (Egypt, °1988) uses food as her creative medium for visual storytelling. This edible art installation was a festive celebration for Simone Rocha's brand and evoked a sense of fertility, sexuality, femininity, and perversion.

MARTIN MARGIELA

Vanitas, 2019

In Martin Margiela's (Belgium, Genk, °1957) *Vanitas*, the hair on five spheres ages from the youthful blondness of a child to the darker hair of adulthood and into the grey tones of an elderly person. The work is a portrait of a woman and the bodily traces left by the passage of time. These five heads symbolising the different life stages not only function as a *memento mori*, but also embrace the beauty and fragility of each chapter of one's life.

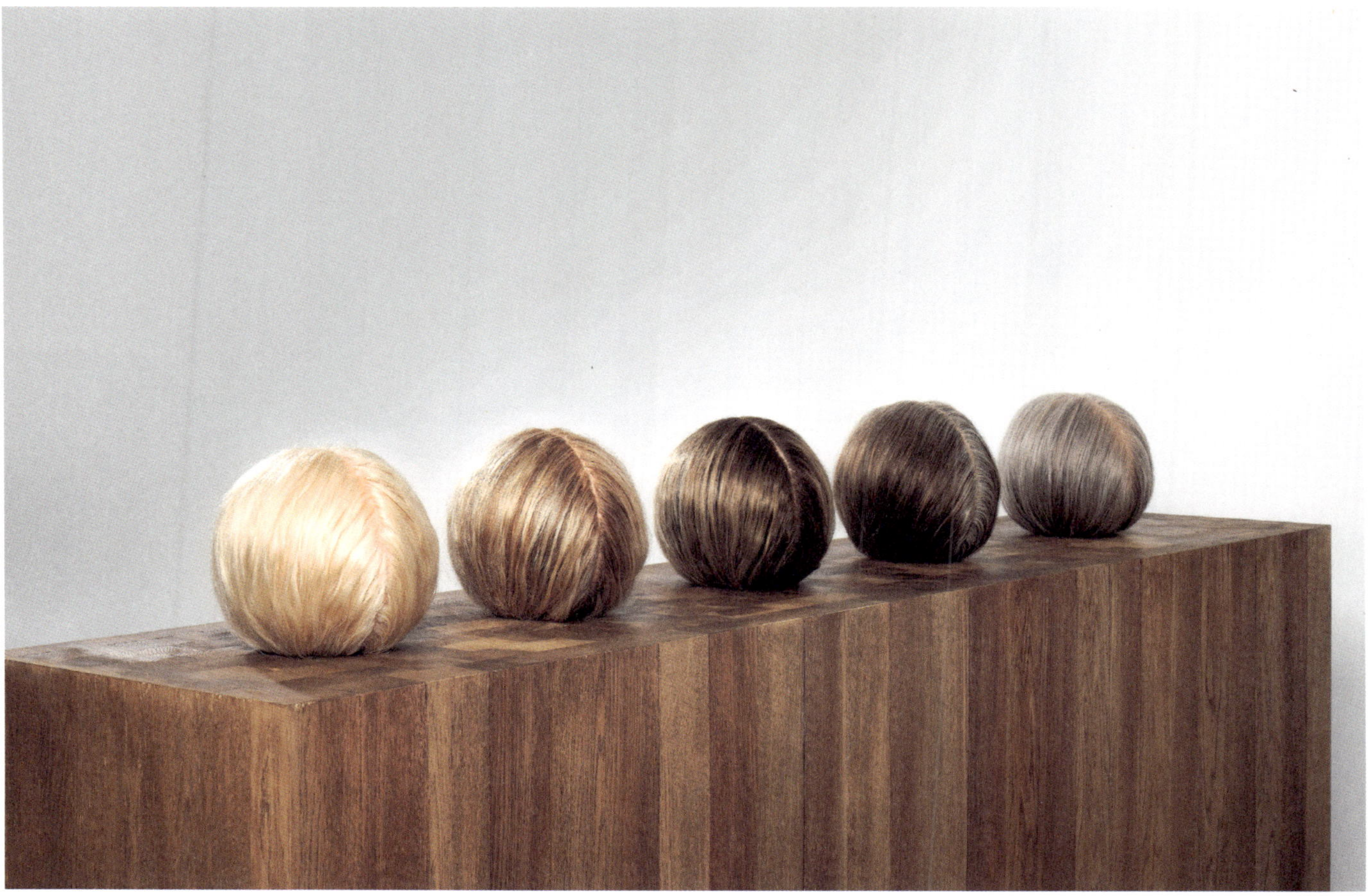

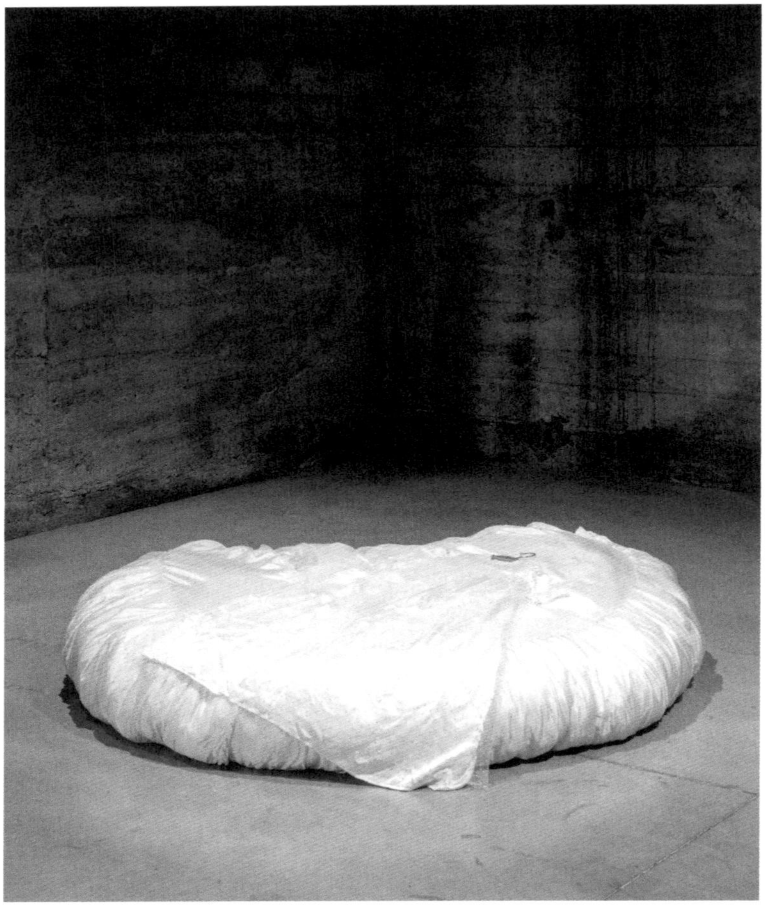

MARIANNE BERENHAUT

Le Pouf (Vie Privée Series), 1993

For more than six decades, Marianne Berenhaut (Belgium, Brussels, °1934) has been working on an impressive oeuvre, which, for a long time, did not get the recognition it deserved. She lost her family during World War II, a loss that deeply influenced her work. Berenhaut is drawn to abandoned objects such as old furniture, clothing and toys. An aura of mystery, sadness, loss and poignancy permeates her sculptures and installations, and is also present in this white, gleaming pouf with christening dress. Her works embody her personal traumas and memories, but above all invite the viewer's own associations.

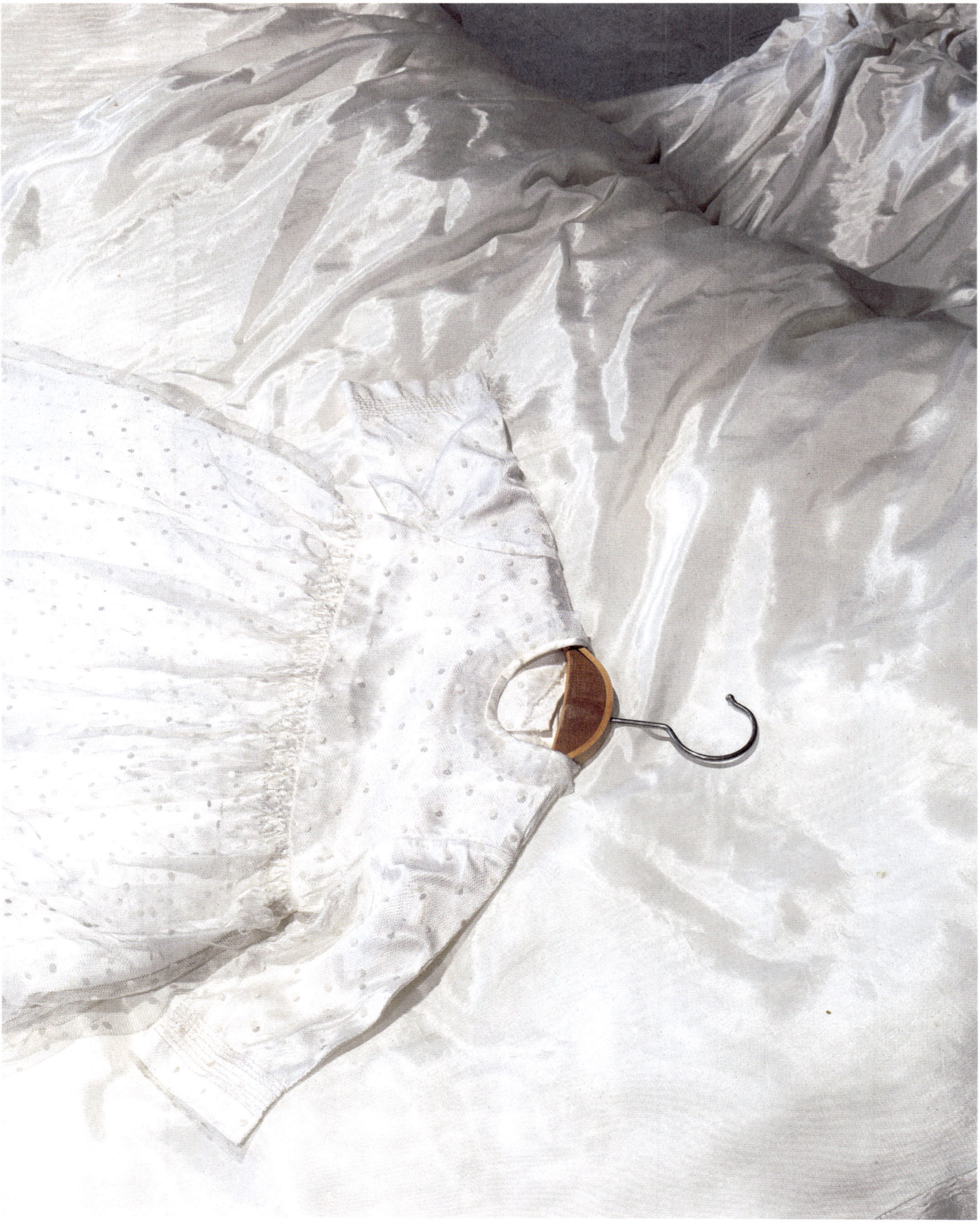

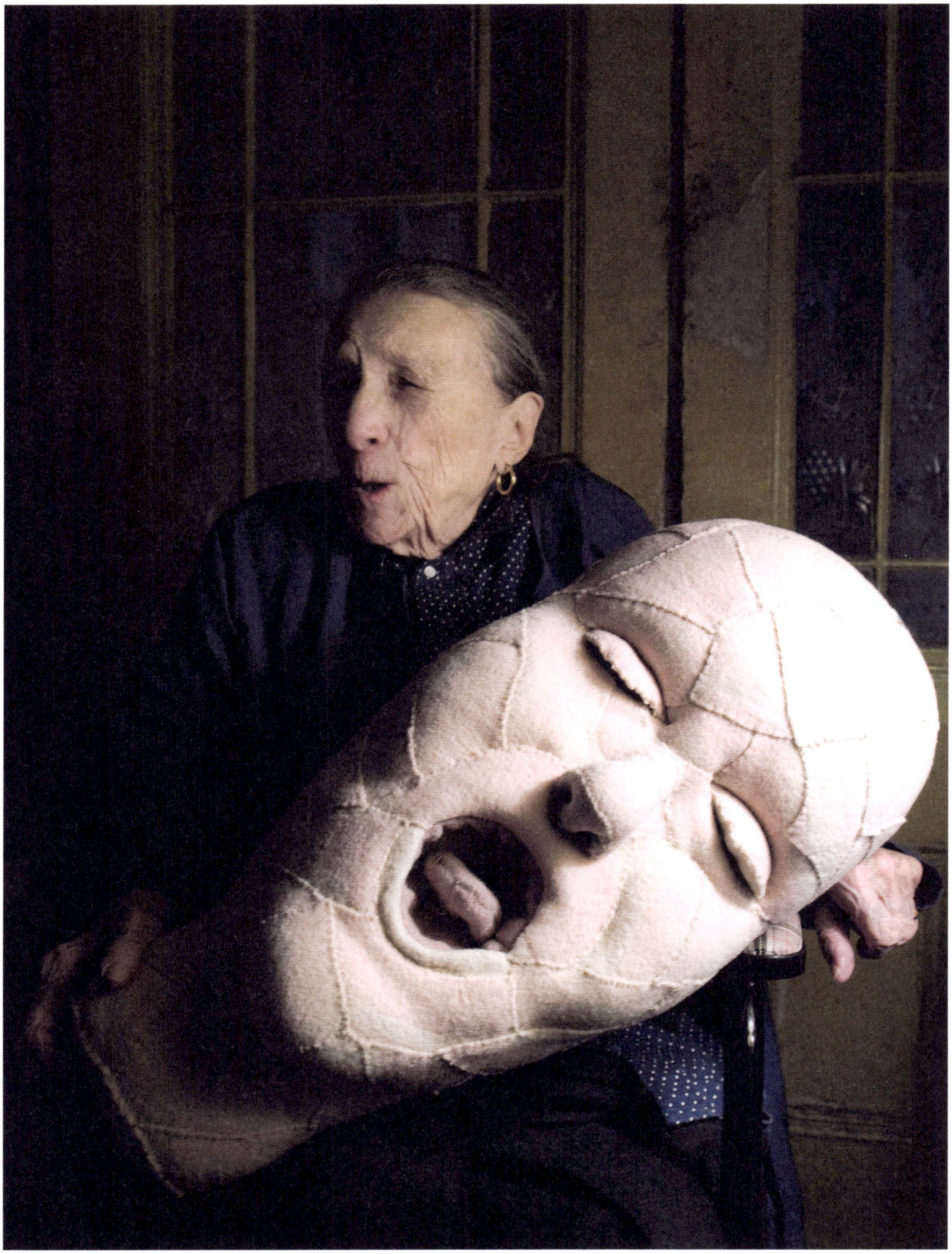

Louise Bourgeois holding one of her large fabric sculptures in 2009
© Alex Van Gelder, from the series *Mumbling Beauty, Louise Bourgeois, 2008-2010*

CHAPTER II

Louise Bourgeois and the Engagement with Clothes

CHARLIE PORTER

Louise Bourgeois spent a lifetime engaging with her clothes. This is different from just loving her clothes, or enjoying her clothes. On 2 January 1961, Bourgeois wrote:

> *my garments and*
> *especially my under garments always have been a*
> *source of intolerable suffering because they*
> *hide an intolerable wound——.*[1]

And yet fashion played a huge role in Bourgeois's life and legacy: her own clothes; the garments that appear in her works; her friendship with designer and artist Helmut Lang; the inspiration she has given to twenty-first-century designers such as Simone Rocha.

It may seem contradictory that this source of 'intolerable suffering' for Bourgeois could be so elemental to her work and life. This contradiction is compounded by the language long used by the fashion industry: 'must have'; 'to die for'; 'wish list'; 'most-loved'. This framing of fashion around pleasure and self-gratification cuts out the ambivalence, at best, that many of us feel about our clothes.

Bourgeois's example points to another perspective: clothing, and fashion, are part of living, and inseparable from our experiences, however painful, either triggering or shadowed from our understanding. By engaging more honestly with our garments and the emotions we invest in them, maybe we can begin to shine a light on all that we do not understand.

On 24 October 2017, I made my first visit to the preserved home of Louise Bourgeois. It is a brownstone on West 20th Street in New York City, her living and working quarters spread over three floors. The home is not open to the public. It is neighboured by the foundation that now protects Bourgeois's legacy, and where scans of her archive are stored.

That morning, I read through Bourgeois's notes and diaries, looking for references to clothing. It was the first step in the research for my book *What Artists Wear*. Her notes appear like poems on the page, like this one, written between 1967 and 1969:

> I deny myself to wear my best spring dress to day [*sic*]
> I <u>know</u> that I own it and am able to enjoy it at
> any moment in the future.[2]

Such tension in her words: the denial of pleasure, the promise of its future enjoyment.

In 1965 Bourgeois linked clothing with knowledge, particularly with understanding sex and physical desire:

> [...] Try to be
> knowledgeable about clothes to prove that
> I know everything about sex —— clothes means [*sic*]
> sex adjusted + fitted just as sex is not an
> abstract notion but a precise or rather
> tangible one ——[3]

Another note showed the narrative given to garments by those who wear them, though Bourgeois finished the note on an enigmatic point, as if there were some essential self that remained hidden and separate:

> *Each garment has a*
> *history, a past, a raison-d-être*
> *behind each garment there is a*
> *person not me* [...][4]

I was shown photographs of Bourgeois taken throughout her life. She was born into an affluent Parisian family, her parents gallerists who dealt in tapestries: fabric was there from the beginning.

A black-and-white photograph from 1913 shows Bourgeois aged two, stood on a chair outside. The coat she wears is extraordinary: a white lace collar, over a larger shearling collar, over another even larger collar of what could again be lace, on top of an A-line knee-length coat with front pleats that push its shape out further. The sleeves are puffed, held by cuffs. It is unknown who made the coat.

A later photograph shows Bourgeois, aged 13, wearing Chanel. It is a simple dress, crewneck, T-shirt sleeves, loose through the body, tied at the waist, finishing just above the knee. In the early to mid-1920s, Coco Chanel was experiencing breakout success with both her fashions and her perfume, N°5. Bourgeois was a young witness to this dynamic new chapter in fashion, and its psychological complexities of allure and identity.

At this time, Bourgeois's father, Louis Bourgeois, had begun an affair with the family's live-in English tutor, Sadie Gordon Richmond. To Bourgeois, it was a devastating rupture of trust. The experience and memory of this betrayal by her father would be forever connected to her clothes. However, her mother was ultimately most relevant in Bourgeois's fabric work. A tapestry weaver and expert seamstress, she died when Bourgeois was only twenty years old. It was the artist's late identification with her mother that motivated her work with the clothing she kept, providing her with a physical way of preserving the past.

For Bourgeois, her clothing kept certain memories alive. In 1968 she expressed how keeping garments was like comforting her younger self (the 'Alain' referred to below is her third son):

> *it gives me great pleasure to hold on to my clo*
> *thes my dresses, my stockings, I have never thrown away a pair*
> *of shoes of mine in 20 years. I cannot separate*
> *myself from my clothes nor from Alain's —— The pretext*
> *is that they are still good —— it's my past and as*
> *rotten as it was I would like to take it and*
> *hold it tight in my arms*[5]

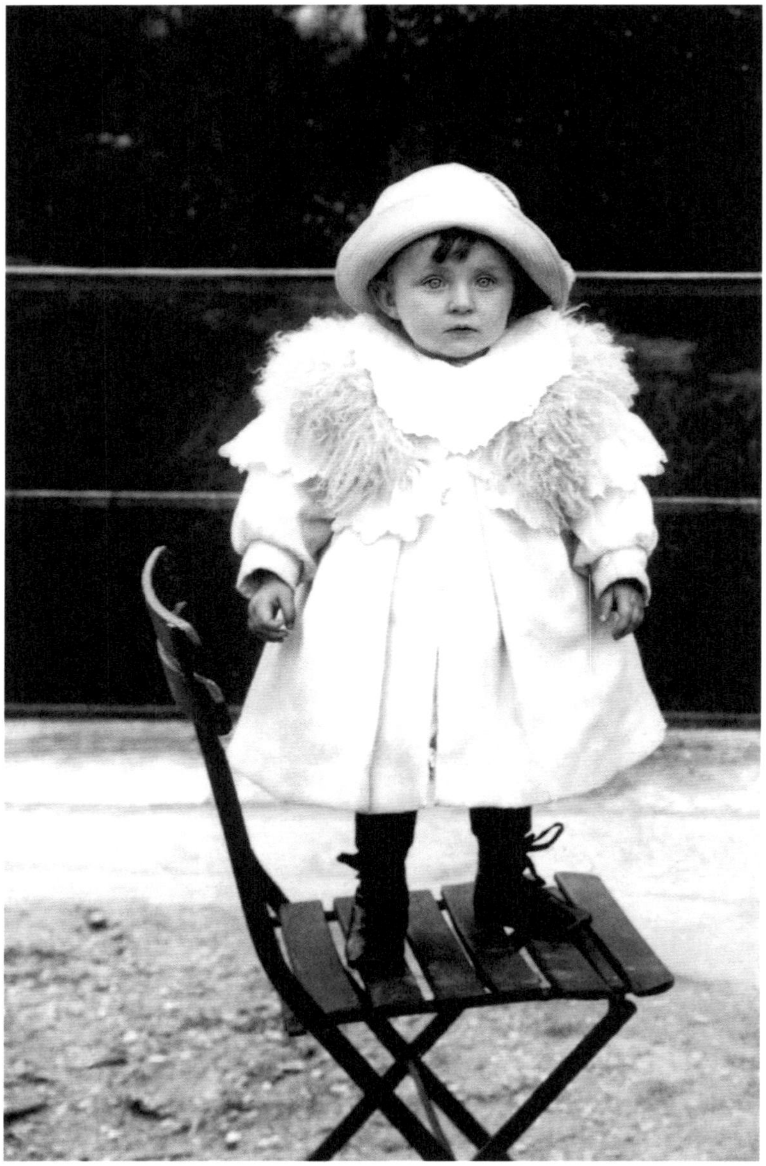

Louise Bourgeois in 1913

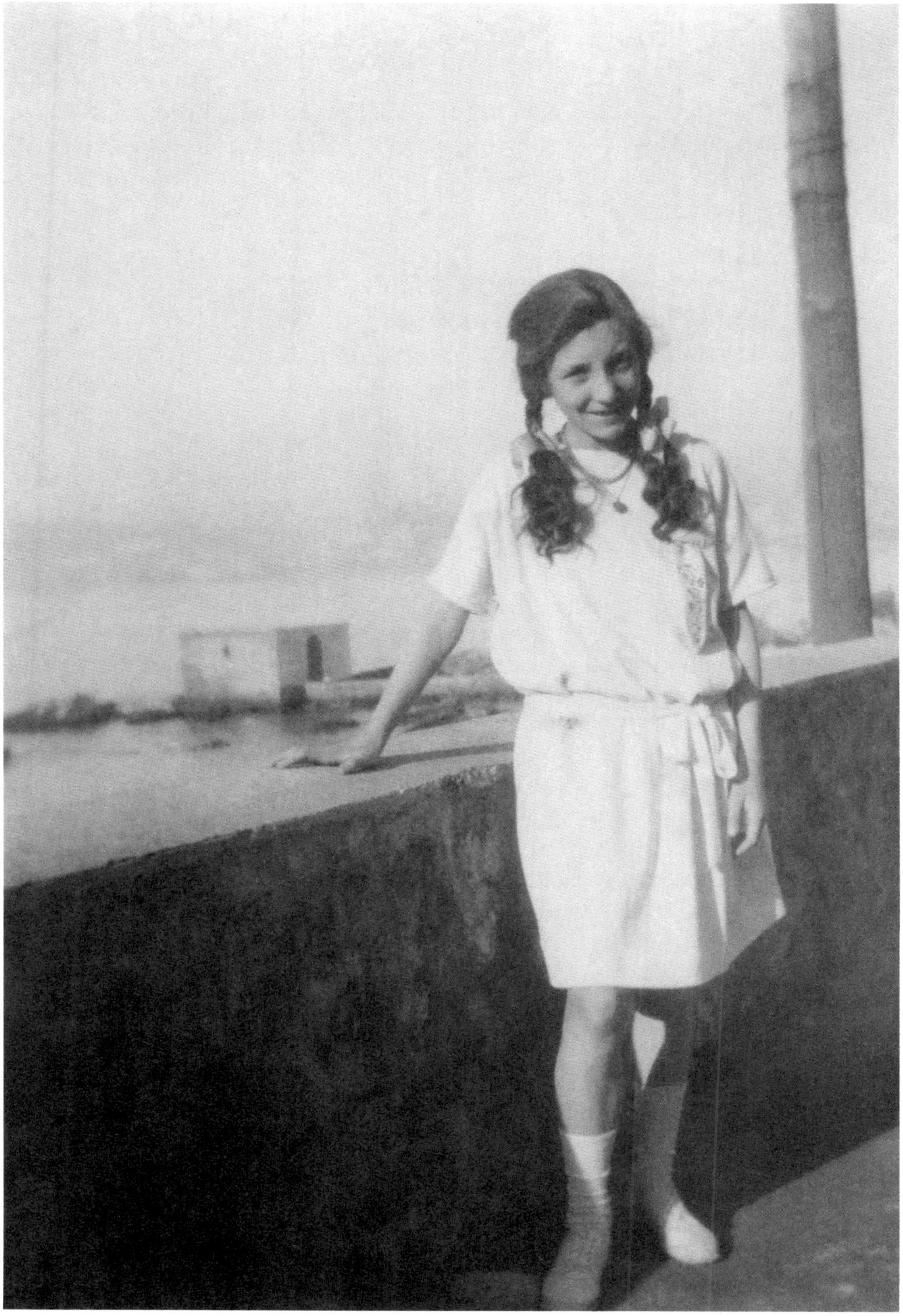

Louise Bourgeois wearing Chanel, aged 13

She wrote about clothes throughout her life. Although decades can be jumped, it is as if only a day has passed. In 1995, during a heatwave, she wrote of her big decision to move the clothes she had been storing in her home to her studio in Brooklyn. There, they could become pieces in her art, their memory and meaning escaping erasure:

> *The shock* came when the truck appeared
> and a twenty year preserved wardrobe actively
> left my sight —— the cord was cut and I felt
> dizzy ——
> The history of the wardrobe started ——[6]

Bourgeois first showed her large-scale sculptures, known as the *Cells*, in 1991. In 1992 she created *Precious Liquids*, a giant, wooden, self-contained cylindrical room, originally a cedar-wood water tower, which was removed from the roof of Bourgeois's studio in Brooklyn. It has two doors through which its contents can be seen. Inside are four metal pole structures, each holding multiple glass vessels, all empty. There is a bed frame with a drain, which is shut, and there is a puddle of water on the bed. Two pairs of balls are placed at the perimeter, flanking an alabaster sculpture, *Le Trani Episode* (1970–71), which is lit from within. One pair is made of black rubber, and above it hangs a black trench coat, over a white shirt. Embroidered vertically down the shirt, on either side of the buttons, are two words: MERCI. MERCY. Stand back, and the coat, shirt and two black balls look like an erect penis.

Bourgeois was 80. Garments bring to her work not only bodily presence, as if the sculptures are populated, but also the chance to play with form. *Cell (Clothes)* (1996) makes a room from a circle of disparate doors, many with glass panes. Inside, some garments are hung on hangers, as if ready for a wardrobe. Others are stuffed or stretched over hangers to create extreme shapes. Visible through one of the doors are the words that Bourgeois embroidered on the back of a white coat: THE COLD OF ANXIETY IS VERY REAL.

On the ground floor of the foundation in New York, a passageway has been cut through the wall into Bourgeois's home. On the other side is a first rail of her clothes, just as she left them. Many are on wire hangers.

There is a mix of high fashion and the everyday. On one hanger is a knitted and padded shawl by Bourgeois's friend Helmut Lang. They became close in 1997, after he invited her to take part in an exhibition. Next to it, a little velvet jacket by the US mass-brand Lord & Taylor. By that, a pink plastic poncho. At the end of the rail, a fitted tweed jacket, full of moth holes.

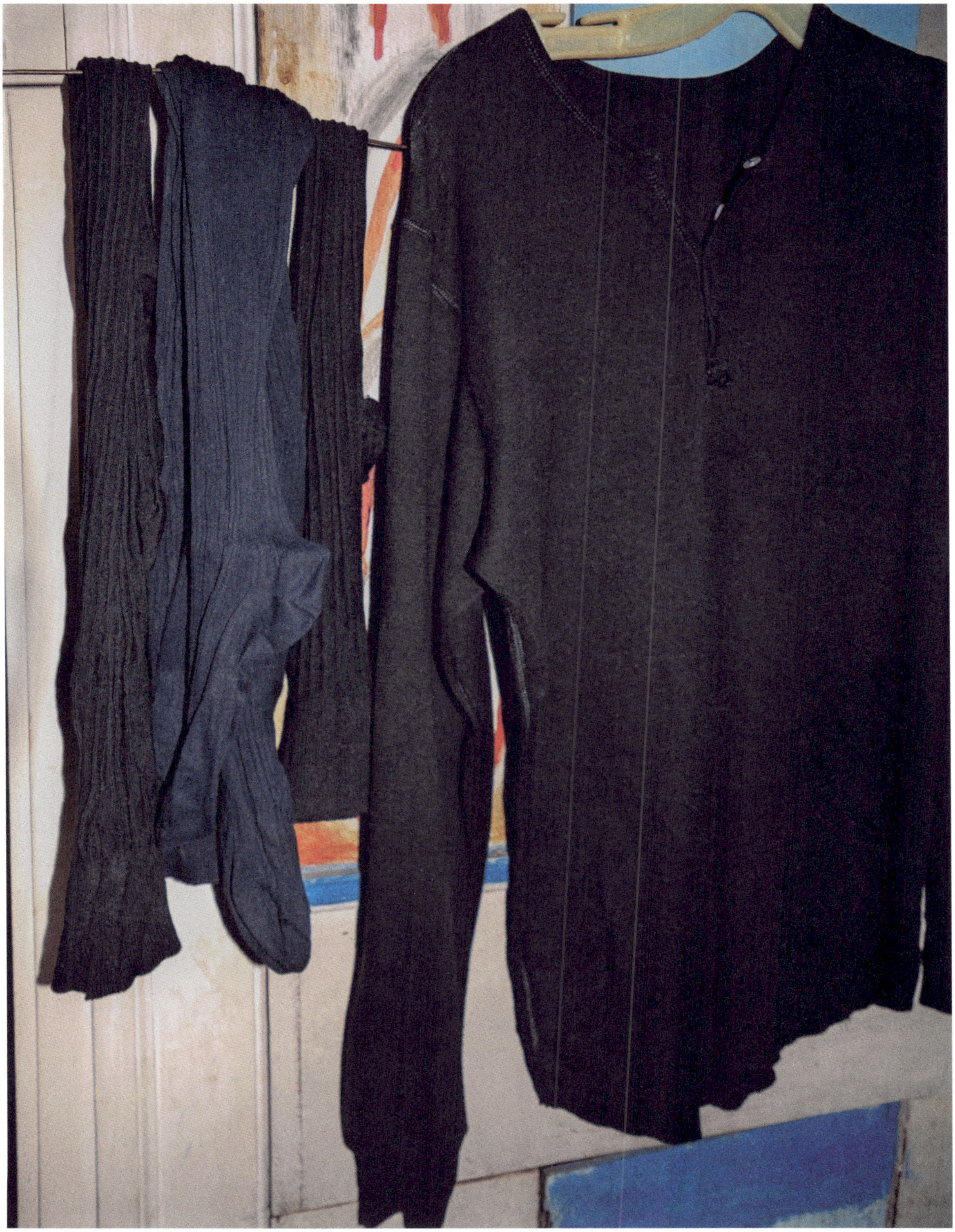

Louise Bourgeois's clothing in her home on 20th Street, New York
© Alex Van Gelder, from the series *Mumbling Beauty, Louise Bourgeois, 2008-2010*

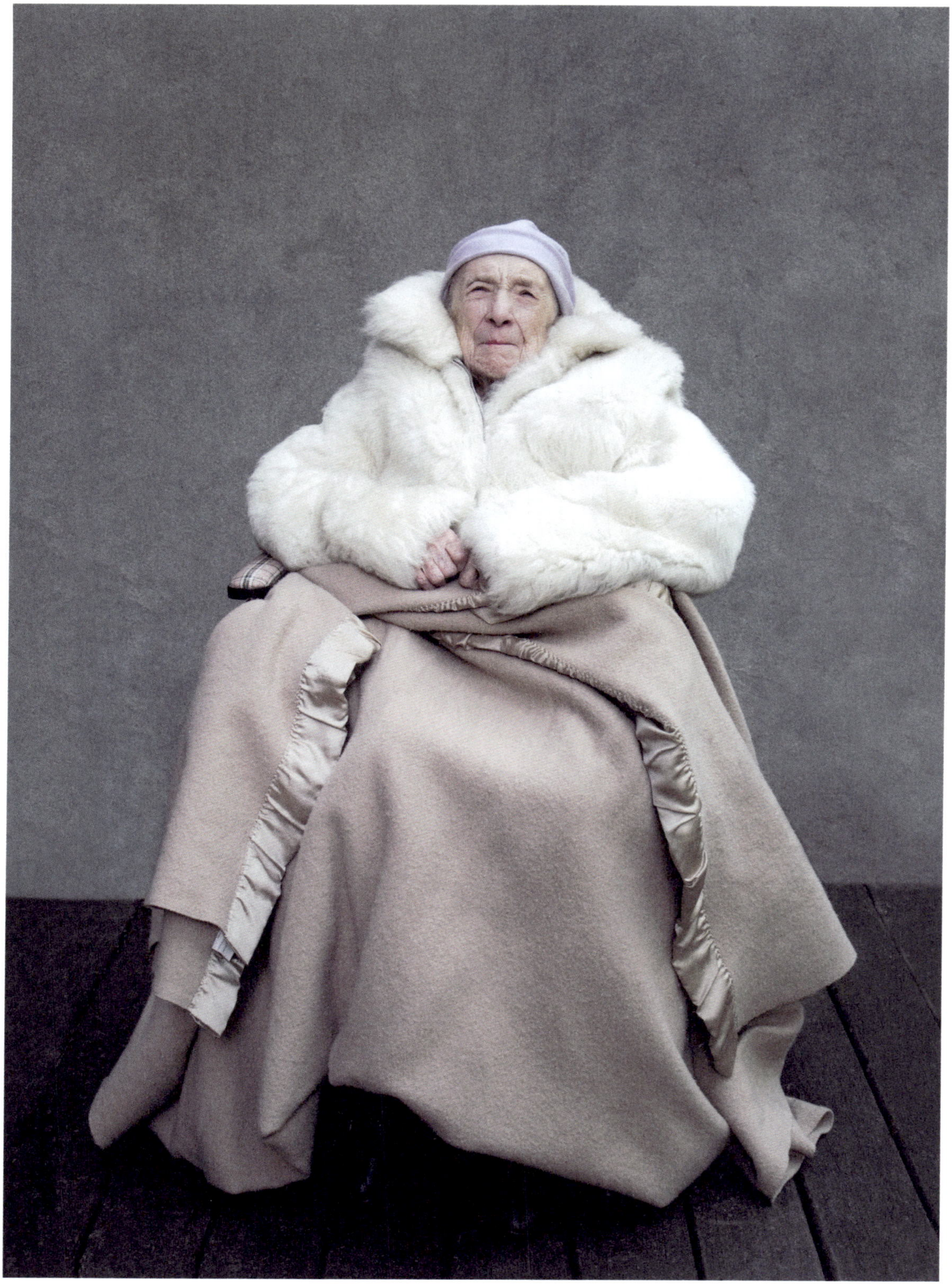

Louise Bourgeois in her home on 20th Street, New York, wearing her Helmut Lang coat, 2009
© Alex Van Gelder, from the series *Mumbling Beauty, Louise Bourgeois, 2008-2010*

In the next room there are stacks of plastic storage boxes filled with folded cloth, much of it brought back from her Brooklyn studio after that building was demolished. The space is full of fabric and plaster models, some small-scale try-outs of future works, a Singer sewing machine as if she might start working there again right now. Bourgeois did her own sewing, until old age meant she required a seamstress. On the back of a door leading to an adjacent hallway hangs a long knitted dress, with a label that reads UNIQUE, and a little denim apron.

Up one flight are Bourgeois's living area and a front office, though the whole house was used as a studio. Connecting the two rooms is a tiny kitchen, with a fierce gas stove more suited to a restaurant, and a closet reconfigured as a passageway between the kitchen and the office. In this small space there is a second rail of clothes. On it is hung a version of the black monkey fur coat she wore in her portrait by Robert Mapplethorpe; she gave the other version, the one in the photo, to her friend Gary Indiana.

Near it is a white sheepskin coat by Helmut Lang. Its shape is strict yet playful: exacting tailored lines pumped up by the thick fluff of the pile. Bourgeois can be seen wearing it in several photos from her final years. This is where her lifelong engagement with clothing led her: actively choosing, in her 90s, to wear garments of rigorous, subversive thinking.

This is the example that she sets, encouraging us to reconsider our own engagement with fashion and clothes. It is possible to live a life in deep and serious connection with our clothing without getting caught in the trap of fashion cycles and systems. It can give us insights into, and even release from, subconscious or deep-buried trauma. For many, clothing remains about conformity. Conformity is often about countering fear. Bourgeois shows us that, if we choose to wear something different, if we engage with clothing differently, we know not where it will lead.

1 Louise Bourgeois, loose sheet of writing, 2 January 1961; LB-0053 (Louise Bourgeois Archive/The Easton Foundation, New York; hereafter cited as TEF). Note: Bourgeois often wrote in a hybrid of English and French. Italics used here and in later quotations indicate passages translated from her original French.

2 Bourgeois, loose sheet of writing, c.1967-69; LB-0055 (TEF).
3 Bourgeois, loose sheet of writing, c.1965; LB-0331 (TEF).
4 Bourgeois, loose sheet of writing, c.1995; LB-0782 (TEF).
5 Bourgeois, loose sheet of writing, c.1963; LB-0202 (TEF).
6 Bourgeois, loose sheet of writing, 27 July 1995; LB-0769 (TEF).

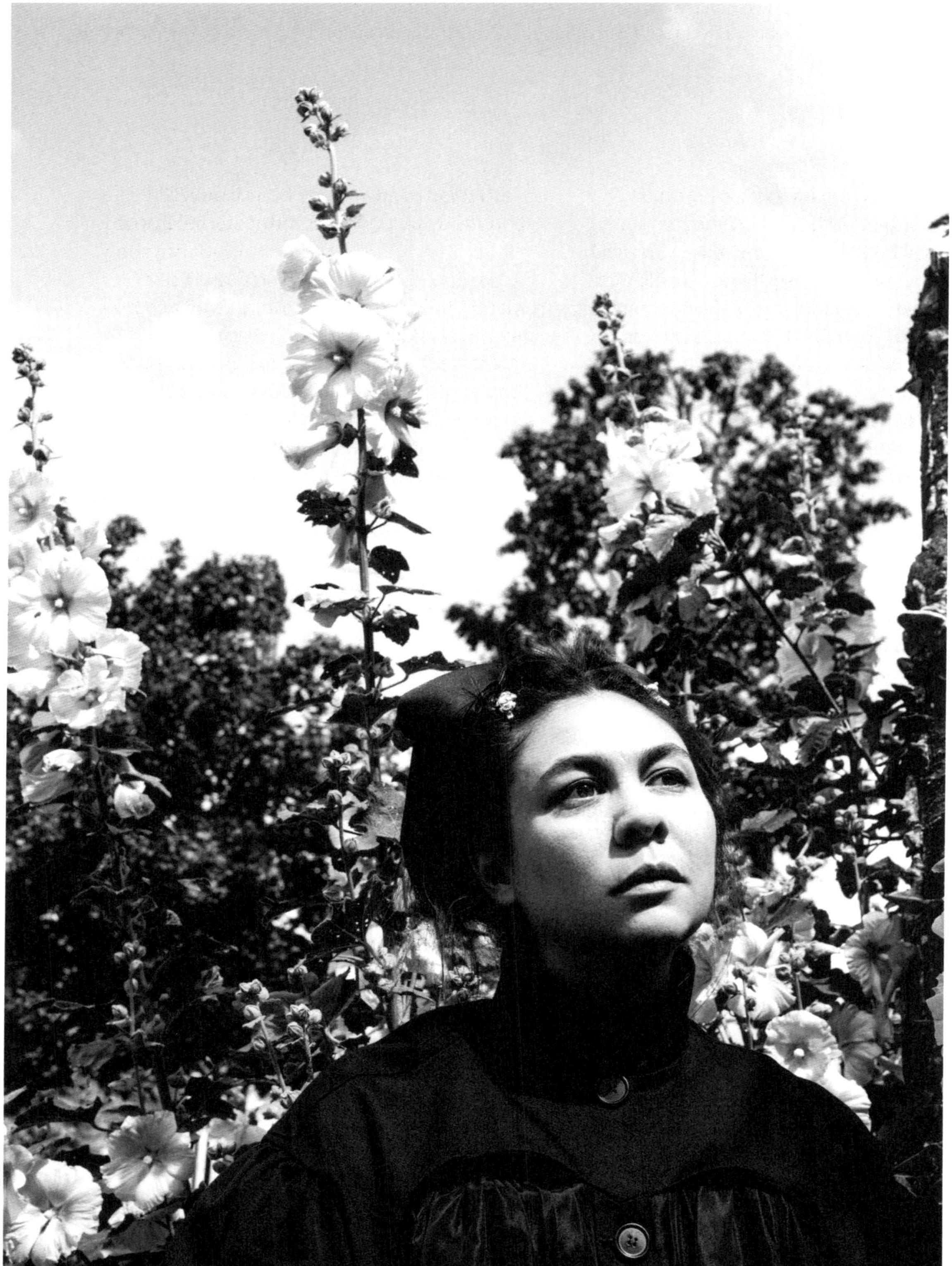

Simone Rocha photographed by William Waterworth, 2022

CHAPTER III

"I HAVE TO PUT MYSELF INTO IT."

SIMONE ROCHA IN CONVERSATION WITH LOU STOPPARD

When Simone Rocha talks about her past collections, she refers not to seasons but to names, used more for herself, as memories, than as formal public titles: *Baby Teeth* (Spring-Summer 2022), *Riders to the Sea* (Autumn-Winter 2020-21), *Red Dolls* (Spring-Summer 2018), *Children of Lir* (Autumn-Winter 2022-23), *Wren Boys* (Spring-Summer 2020). If questioned about particular looks, or catwalk moments —— Spring-Summer this, Autumn-Winter that —— she'll often pull up visuals, online, to check what she made when. 'I never get the dates right', she says. She remembers her shows instead by the stories: the ideas, images, characters and details that were igniting her imagination at the time —— a baby wrapped in cloth; a spot of blood on a bedsheet; a fisherman, lost at sea; a mother knitting; a Tudor courtier, desperate to assert herself without breaking the expectations of silence and decorum that dictate her life; a body moving through time, cloth tenderly caressing its form.

LOU STOPPARD: **First, slightly based on your last show, Autumn-Winter 2023-24, I'd like to talk about the role of history and historical research within your work. You often include details that seem lifted from other eras. Tell me how you draw on the past.**

SIMONE ROCHA: It always starts with a storytelling element, and then a question of where that story is, in time. One of my collections, Spring-Summer 2022, I call it *Baby Teeth*, was built around the time my second daughter was born. Very naturally, I was thinking about the ideas of nursing and swaddling, and then I started to look at the history of swaddling in different eras, and thinking about how that could contribute to some of the manipulation of the garments, in terms of layers or draping. So, it always comes from a storytelling element, and then picking out a period that that story relates to and looking into the dress and costume and customs of the time —— really digging deep into that period. I'm often interested in a mixture of things, some aesthetic, some more to do with social norms. For example, Autumn-Winter 2014-15, which was inspired by the Elizabethan era. I found it interesting looking into the construction of garments, whether in terms of the exaggerated hip panels or the necklines, but I was also fascinated by what that would represent. These clothes were the only form of voice that women had, so that also plays into it: the history of the dress of that time is actually also the dialogue of the female at that time, who might not have had a voice. There's also, within the historical references, always a craft thing —— growing up in Ireland, craft was very present —— I would hand-knit and hand-crochet. I've always been attracted to —— and have felt comforted by —— doing things by hand. I think you see that with the *Riders to the Sea* collection, which was Autumn-Winter 2020-21, which was all about (the Irish playwright) John Millington Synge's play of the same name (1904), in which a mother lost all of her sons and her husband to the sea. The play was set on the Aran Islands, so I started to think about Irish Aran knits, and how different details and weaves would represent different families, and we came up with a knit that was for a fictitious family. It got knitted into these pieces that were almost like bibs or even life jackets. So, you see there, it's a dual thing, of storytelling with the time and place and what certain details represented, and then looking at it in terms of what I want to say within that collection, and how it plays into the garments themselves.

LS: It's really interesting what you say about women and expression through clothing. In some ways, throughout history, clothing can be seen to have restricted women, because of the obsession with the female image and appearance. But on the other hand, it's liberated women because it has, as you say, given them many opportunities to communicate and express themselves, which has actually continued to today.

SR: Even just to take up space in a room, without saying anything. That is always something that I have been intrigued by: taking up space and having a presence, physically, without having to vocalise it. I think there is a real sincerity and a weight to that, because it's not just talk —— it's embodying what you are trying to say.

LS: These forms of communication can be really powerful: gesture, the visual arts, clothing. There's a softer element to them and it provides an opportunity to be much cleverer, much subtler.

SR: Exactly —— and secretly powerful. Like getting under the skin.

"They're all gone now, and there isn't anything more the sea can do to me... I'll have no call now to be up crying and praying when the wind breaks from the south, and you can hear the surf is in the east, and the surf is in the west, making a great stir with the two noises, and they hitting one on the other. I'll have no call now to be going down and getting Holy Water in the dark nights after Samhain, and I won't care what way the sea is when the other women will be keening."

—— John Millington Synge, *Riders to the Sea*, 1904

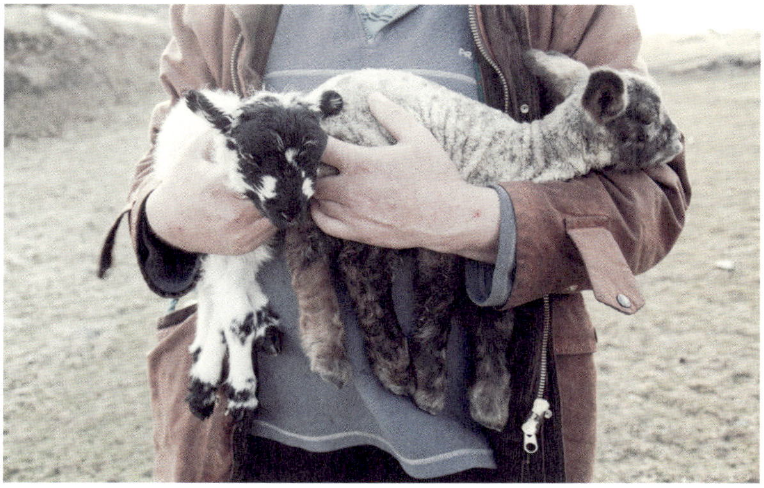

Lambs on Inishark

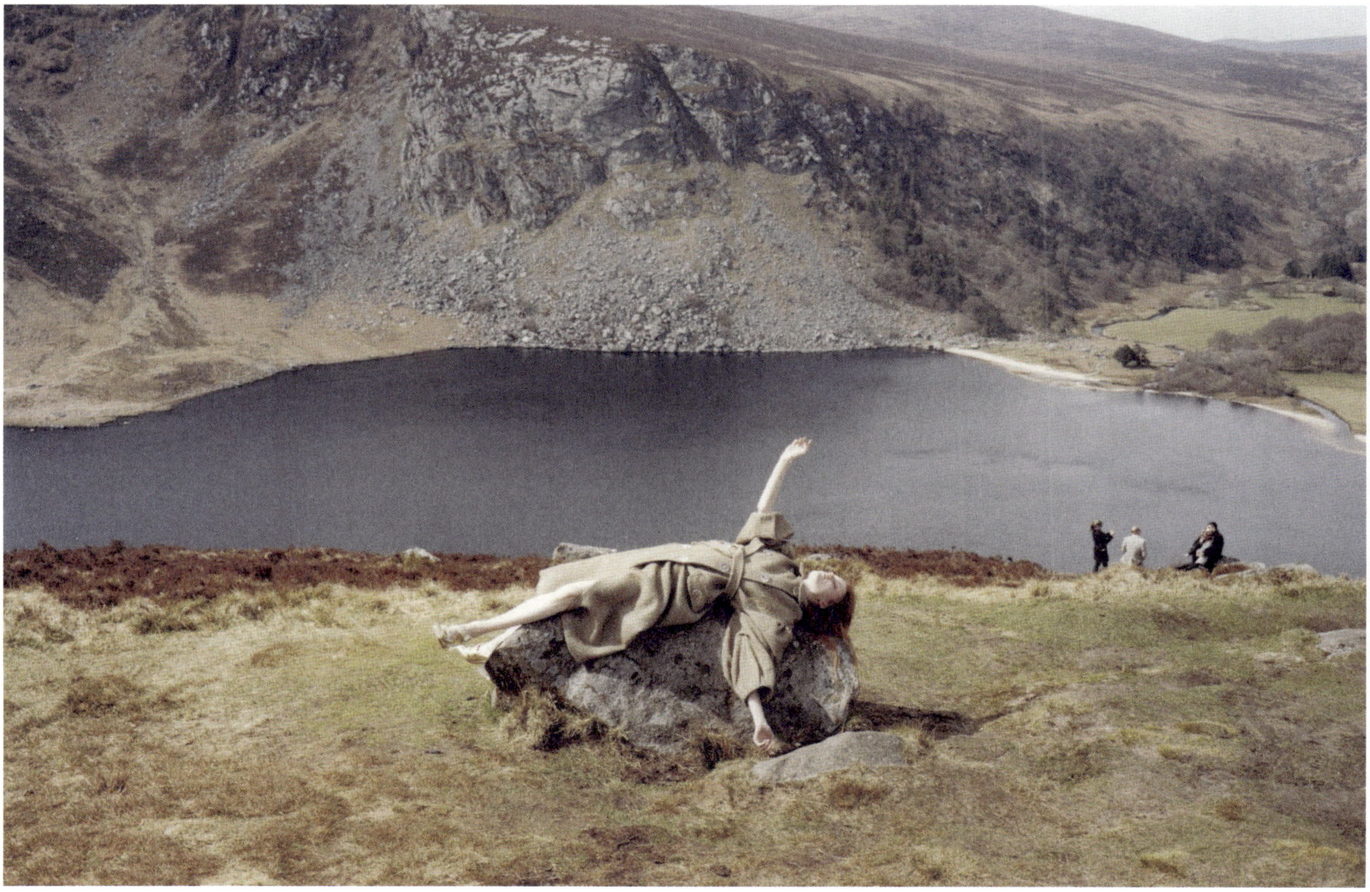

Simone Rocha
Autumn-Winter 2016-17

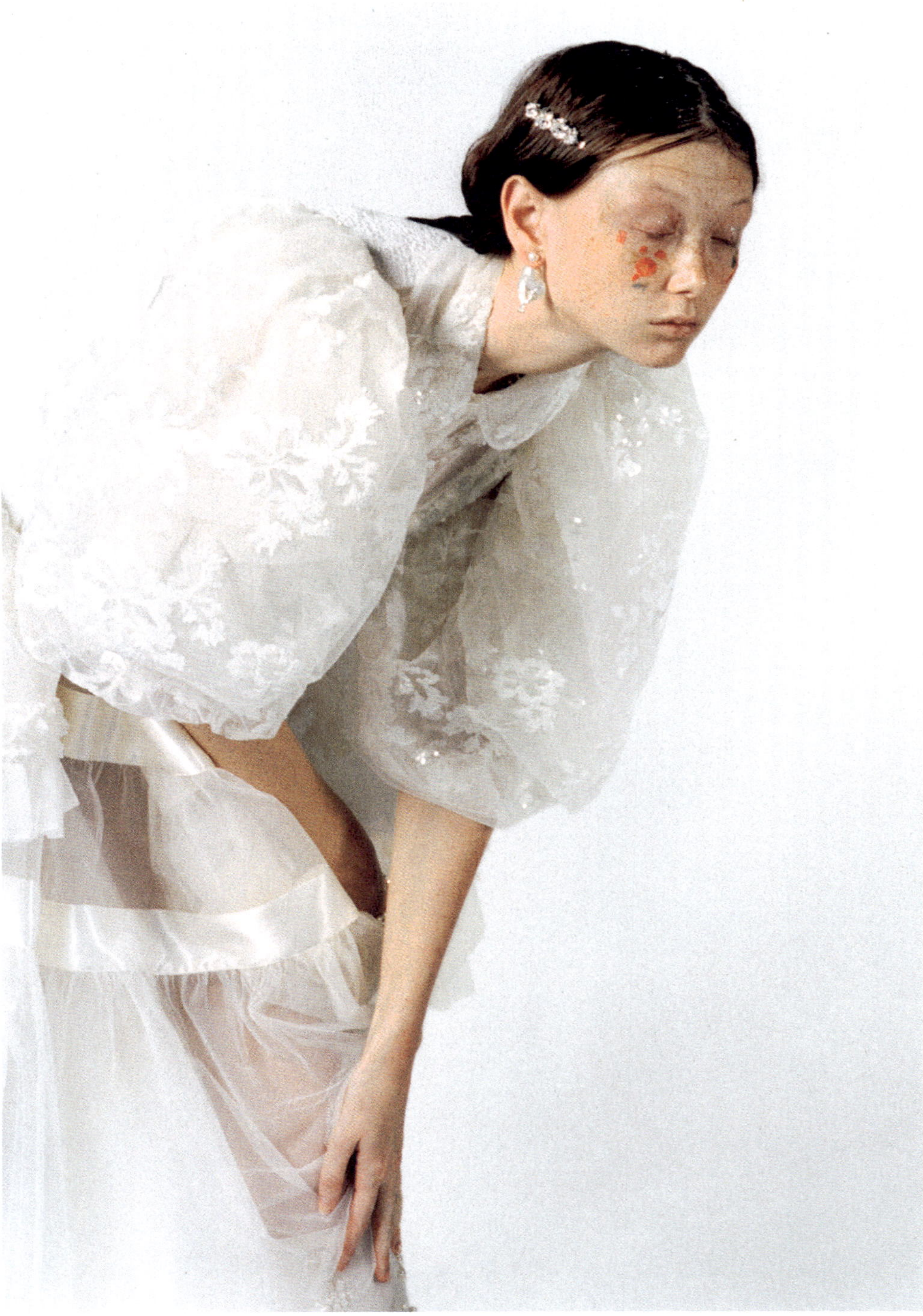

Simone Rocha
Spring-Summer 2022

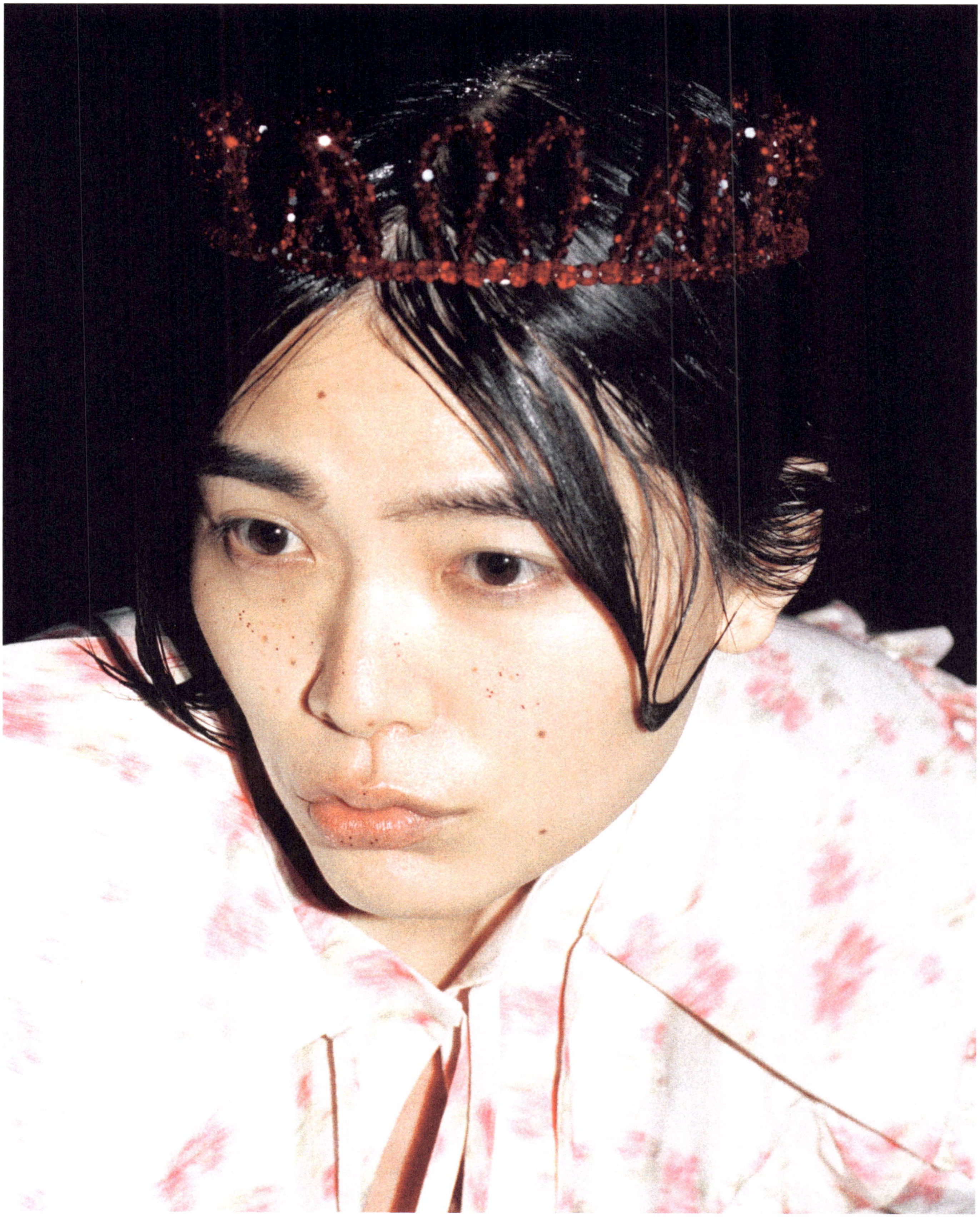

LS: It feels to me that you look at collective history —— for example, the history of Ireland or the history of craft —— but you also look closely at personal histories. Your own childhood memories seem very present in your shows, even if they are used to tell universal stories. Tell me about that.

SR: That balance is exactly what I want. When I'm looking at and designing the collections, I can't not put myself into them. I have to think about how things sit with me, and with me today, because with fashion it is an identity, it's so personal. And for it to feel like my identity, it has to be a story that I feel personally engaged with in some way, or something that still has a resonance or relevance today. It's hard to describe how to balance it, because it's definitely me, within it, within the clothing. But it's also more about how I break down fabrics, or the stories or the shapes, and think about how those feel relevant, more broadly. I've never wanted to make clothes that won't be worn. I want them to be integrated into the way that you feel when you get dressed. I don't want them to just be in a glass box, on a pedestal. I do believe they come alive on the body, but I also think, for that to happen, and for people to feel connected to them emotionally, I have to put a bit of myself into them, even though that can be challenging.

LS: How would you describe your upbringing? And your attitude as a young person and a child? You were growing up across two cultures [Ireland and Hong Kong, where your father was born], and also surrounded by beauty, fashion and art.

SR: I grew up looking. I've always been very reactive. Whether it's growing up between two cultures, as you say, or whether it's growing up somewhere, Ireland, with a really rich sense of narrative and storytelling and guts and earth in it. I've always been sensitive to it all, and engaged in it all. It sounds obvious, but when I look at art, I like to feel something. So, when I first started designing, I knew I wanted people to have that reaction. And I thought that the only way that people would feel something would be if I put something into it that came from me. Whether it was where I grew up, or where I live now, or things that have happened to me in my life. It feels like that's the way I communicate.

LS: And I guess it's about imbuing the clothes with something personal too? Because the relationship that we have with our clothes is very personal, the way that they touch you or cocoon you. It is really intimate, so there is something nice about feeling that the clothes have a personal story from the maker.

SR: Completely. And also to feel that each piece can be about different selves. Sometimes you want to feel super intimate, and maybe show bits of skin, and then other times it can be very coy, with lace. It's so important that all those facets can be put in at different times and in different collections, almost like little secrets. It's very much a narration of being a woman.

LS: You drew a lot as a child, I believe. What do those drawings mean to you now? Do they influence you?

SR: When I was a child, I was very much not a diligent student [laughs]. I would spend all my time doodling and drawing, so I had loads of diaries and notebooks and journals, a mixture of written things and drawings and photos and also a lot of found objects —— a lot of things got stuck into the diaries. Sometimes I would get friends to contribute: give them a page and see what they would do. That was just me as a kid, or a teenager, and I always felt at home doing that. One of the few places I felt very at home at school was in the art room.

LS: It seems that you correlate making, or drawing things, with telling stories. The way you describe getting friends to contribute things, it was almost as if it was a form of chronicling.

SR: Exactly, like documenting time. It's not as if I thought of it as a prolific thing that I was putting forward to the world. It was all about documenting, and almost a release, personally, for me.

LS: Could we talk more about the role that craft plays in your work? I love the homages you pay to traditional 'women's' activities that have often been overlooked in importance in the history of the visual arts —— say weaving or embroidery. Why are these techniques so important to you?

SR: The domesticity aspect is interesting to me: things that are known as a historically female output and that were traditionally made in the home. I always found that interesting, and I think that's why I feel a real kinship with someone like Louise Bourgeois, who grew up in a family that did textiles —— I obviously grew up in a family that did fashion —— and I think there is something inherited there. It's just a huge part of me. Going back to the idea of domesticity, there's something that I find very nurturing and comforting about embroidery and knitting.

LS: Perhaps a sense of home or safety?

SR: Exactly.

"In the beginning, tapestries were indispensable, they were actually movable walls, or partitions in the great halls of castles and manor houses, or the walls of tents. They were a flexible architecture [...] I, myself, have very long associations with tapestries. As children, we used them to hide in. This is one reason I expect them to be so three-dimensional —— why I feel they must be of such height and weight and size that you can wrap yourself in them."

—— Louise Bourgeois, *Craft Horizons*, vol. 29, no. 2, March/April 1969,
quoted by Frances Morris in the exhibition catalogue *Louise Bourgeois: Stitches in Time*
(Dublin: Irish Museum of Modern Art, 2003).

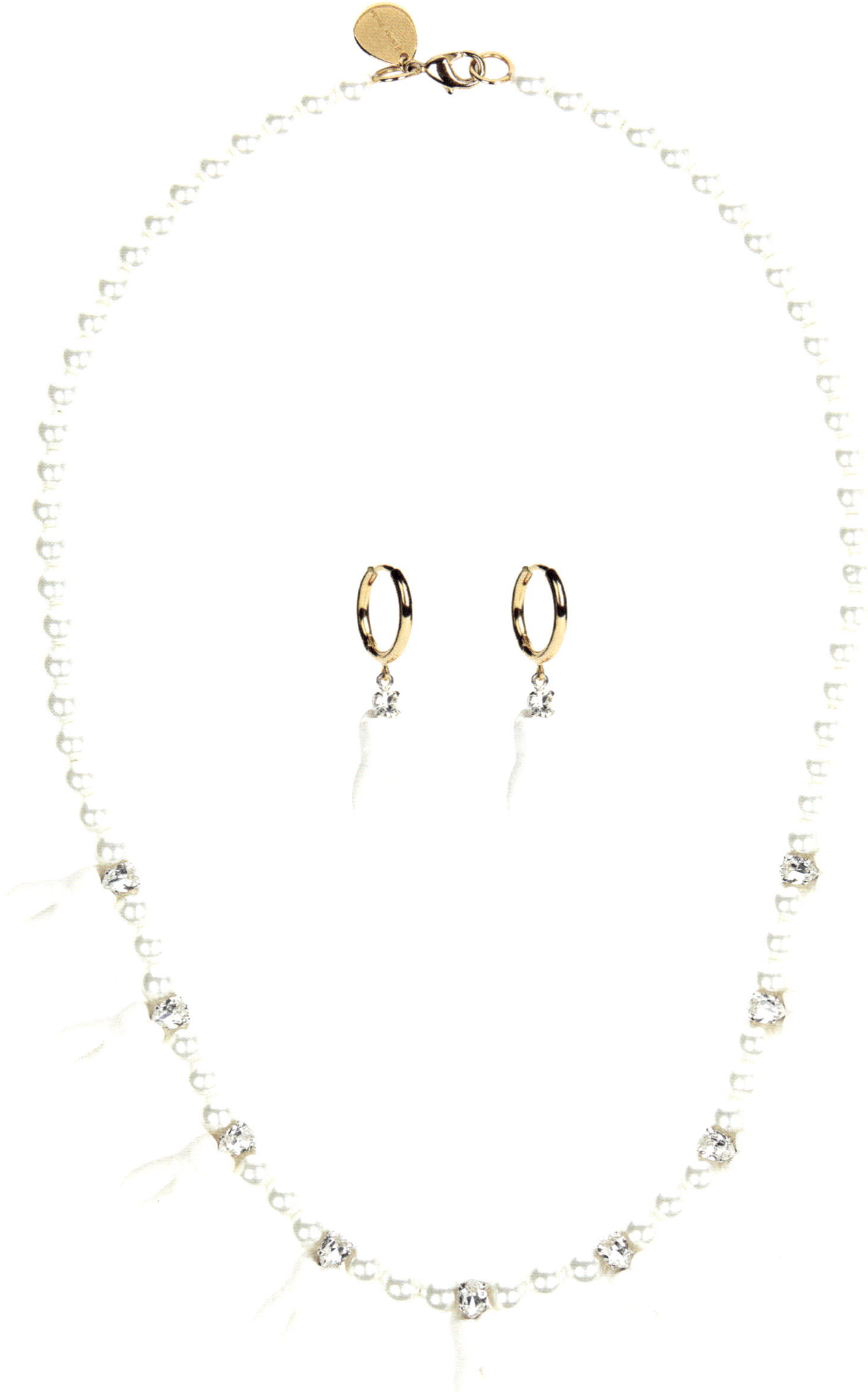

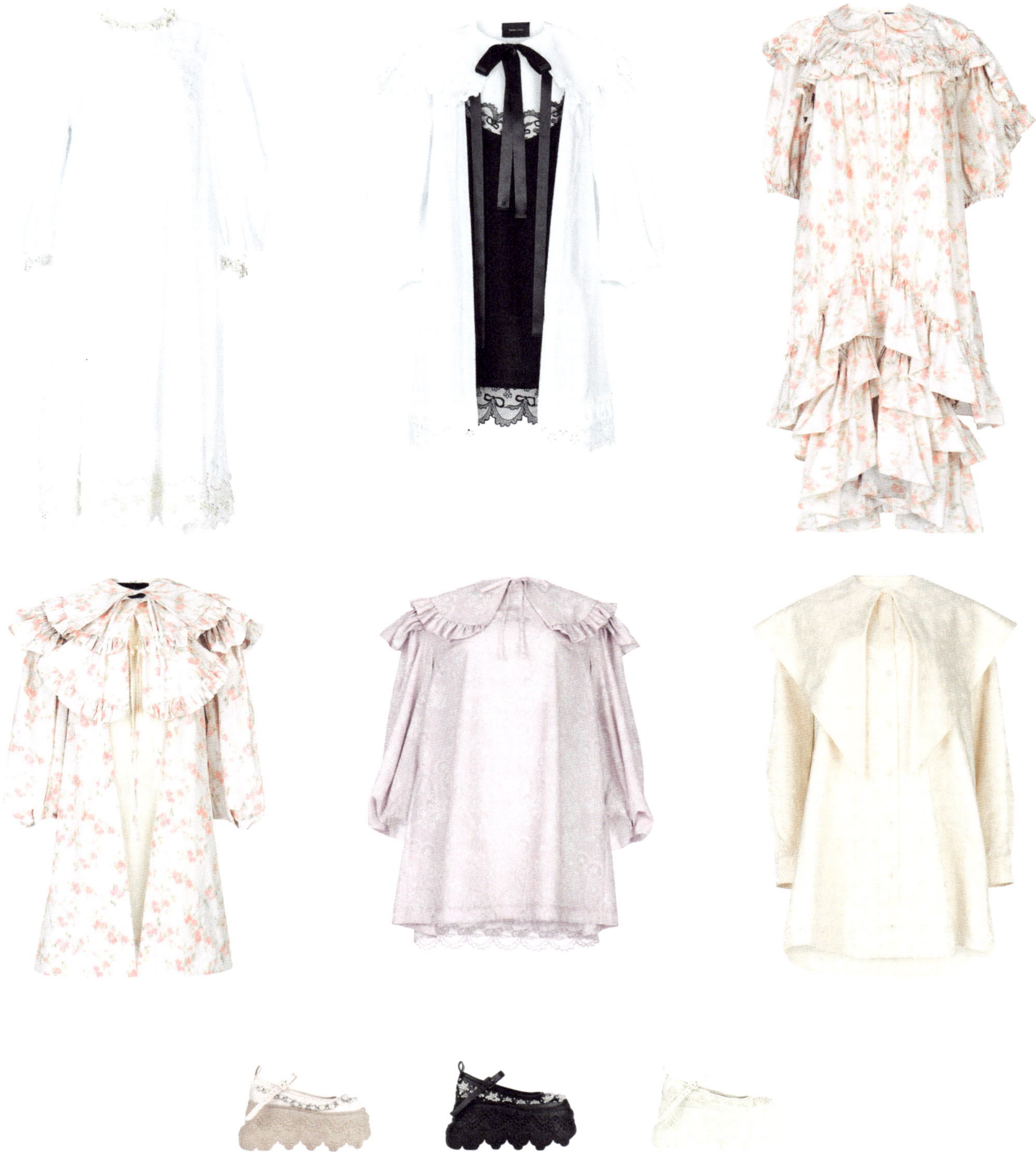

Simone Rocha
Spring-Summer 2022

LS: Domesticity is not something that is mentioned a lot in the world of high fashion, perhaps because it feels too quotidian, or too safe, and I guess because high fashion is meant to be about things that are more daring: dreaming, theatrics. It's interesting that you manage to bring the tenderness of domesticity to the clothing while also offering a sense of escape, or of otherworldliness, or of something slightly 'off' or strange.

SR: I actually had a long conversation with a friend, the artist Daniel Freeman, after the most recent show [Autumn-Winter 2023-24], about the dresses with the hay. We were talking about why I'd wanted to stuff these ornate —— almost perversely ornate —— pieces with something as raw as hay. And he pointed out how twisted it was, because of the fact that hay would be used to stuff chairs, to stuff mattresses —— a really humble material that would be used to create a home, but was then hidden. So, it was twisted to expose it, in the most unhumble, provocative, embellished, handworked way. I liked the idea of something female —— this female domestic thing —— almost being *exposed*. And, as he said, I liked the perverseness of it, because it had all these hand-done sequins on top of it, and I've always found that kind of slight twist stimulating.

LS: That is a word that you use a lot: 'twisting'. It's the idea of subtly revealing things, these little glimpses of things that are subversive or usually hidden. It feels like it's a big part of your work, this kind of quiet subversion.

SR: Exactly. And that's what Robbie Spencer, the stylist I work with on my shows, always says: it's not just pretty dresses for pretty people —— there is so much more beyond that. Some people might only see the prettiness, and that's absolutely fine. But there are so many layers to everything: not everyone has to see them, but they are there, and I know they are there. And all those layers together, that's the proposition. And the thing that often excites me, as with this collection, is juxtaposition. Something hard and something soft. Something adult with something childlike. A very ornate fabrication with the hand-knitted hay.

LS: I often find it frustrating when female designers are endlessly asked about motherhood, because male designers are so rarely asked how they balance work and family life. But you do refer to your daughters, and to mothering, in some of your collections, as we have already discussed. How influential has being a mother been on your work?

SR: Firstly, we should say, there are just so many working mums. Almost half the planet is working mums! But because my work is personal, I find it impossible not to let it influence the work at certain times. But actually, in general, I can put it forward and it can influence a collection, but at the same time, I actually keep it quite separate. I try not to jumble it all together —— I find that stressful. I like to be a mother when I'm at home. And when I'm at work, I don't really feel like a mother, and that's how I can do the work. But then, being a mother will influence a collection, of course. But I try to do it in a way that doesn't put the girls under pressure —— an influence rather than a dedication.

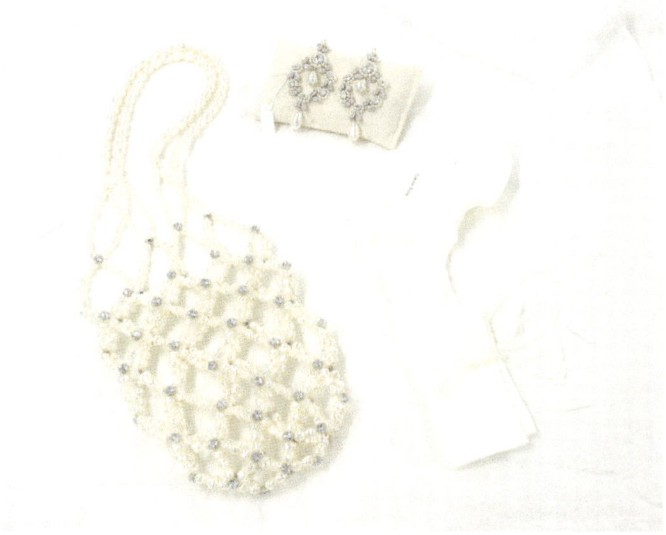

LS: Can we talk more about that Spring-Summer 2022 *Baby Teeth* collection? I know it's a favourite of yours.

SR: Spring-Summer 2022 is one of my favourite collections. Some of them I like, and some of them I don't like so much, when I look back! But with this one, I just think, yes! As I said, we called it *Baby Teeth*, and we made these little porcelain teeth that were actually earrings and embellishments. I had just given birth to my second child, so there was this idea of ceremony and baptism: she's not even baptised, it was just something we did in the collection! And then we softened things with a beautiful broderie anglaise, which is associated with these very small communion dresses. Another big influence was this idea of lack of sleep, and that's where all the bed dresses came in, the dresses that were somewhere between a slip and a negligee, and in part almost sheeting and bedding becoming one with the dress.

I think you really see it with Look 8: the exposed negligee, the sense of insomnia, the underpinnings which almost looked like nursing bras, but we did them in nude to reflect the idea of the skin, and then there were the embroideries that almost looked like blood. But it was also about the beauty of those things: birthing and nursing, mothering, all the cloth, all the washing, all the blankets, the swaddling, all the mountains of fabric. The connotations and also the realities, but still showing them in a slightly ceremonial way. Because the truth is, it can be extremely challenging, a new baby, but then there is the huge thing, of a new life, that feels monumental. It was a balance, between the everyday and the ceremony of it all.

LS: It seems that you look at motherhood in such a way that there is never a spotlight on the girls —— its more about looser ideas, like swaddling, or the sense of new life or changes in bodies. It's a kind of universal inspiration.

SR: Exactly. The influence can be in draping, or tiny little christening outfits influencing the knitwear. Some of the influences are about motherhood in general. But of course there is a personal element too: for me to be pregnant, and have children, and give birth, and keep showing, to then say, now I'm going to do a collection about buildings, it would just be impossible. Your work reflects your experiences. You go through insomnia —— that was a huge influence on the *Baby Teeth* collection, because I was going through it, so I thought I'd bring it to the table. We even got the models to walk slower, to represent that feeling. It's funny, because it's impossible to separate, it's impossible to not let it influence you.

Simone Rocha Spring-Summer 2021
Collection MoMu inv. T22/1918/1, inv. T22/1919/1-22, inv. T22/1925/1-2

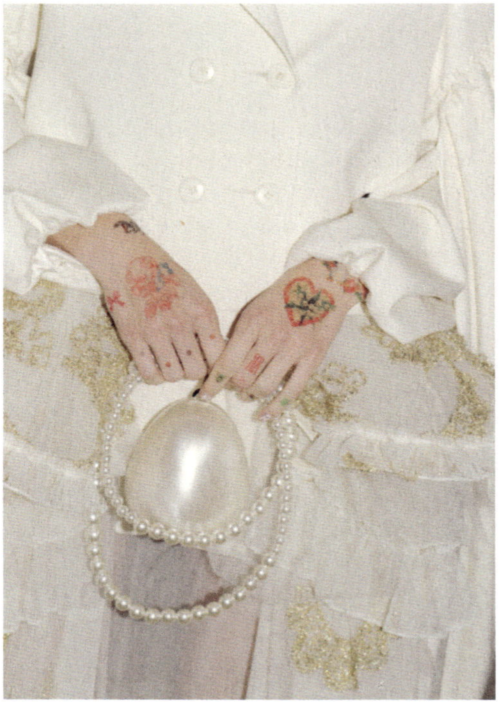

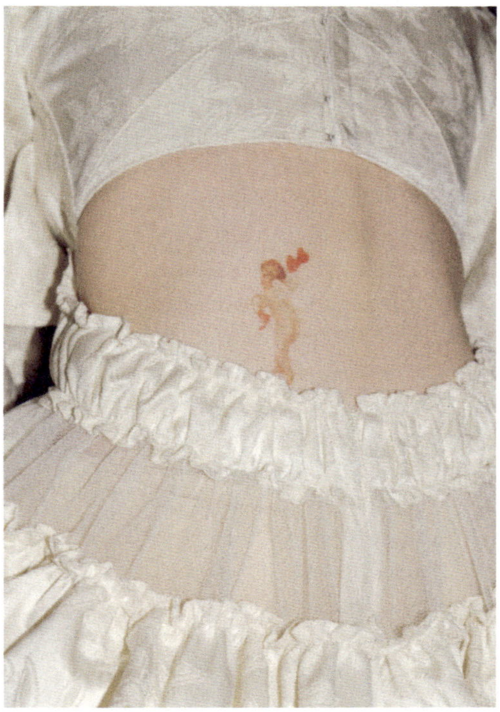

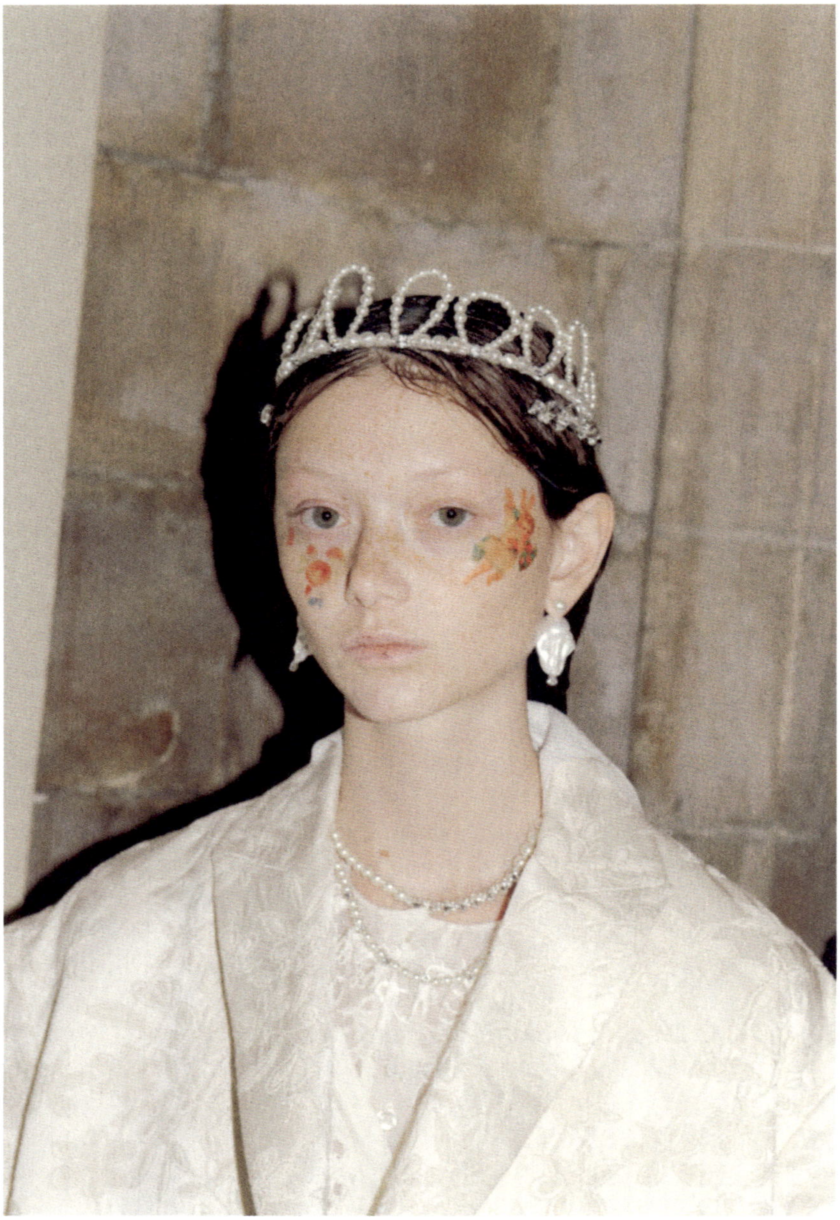

Simone Rocha
Spring-Summer 2022

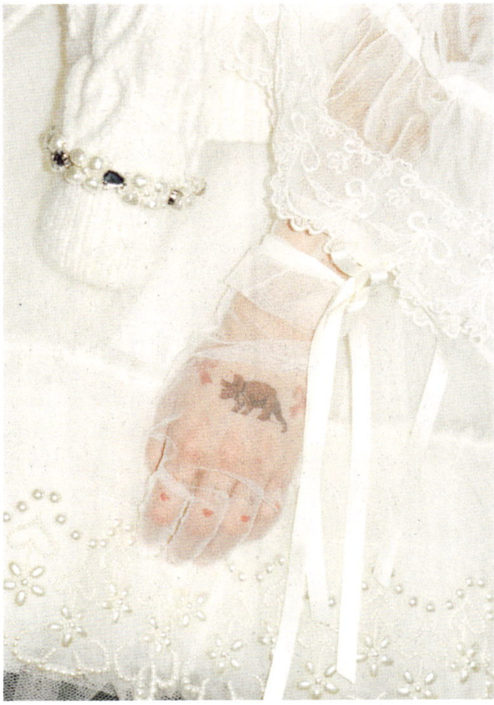

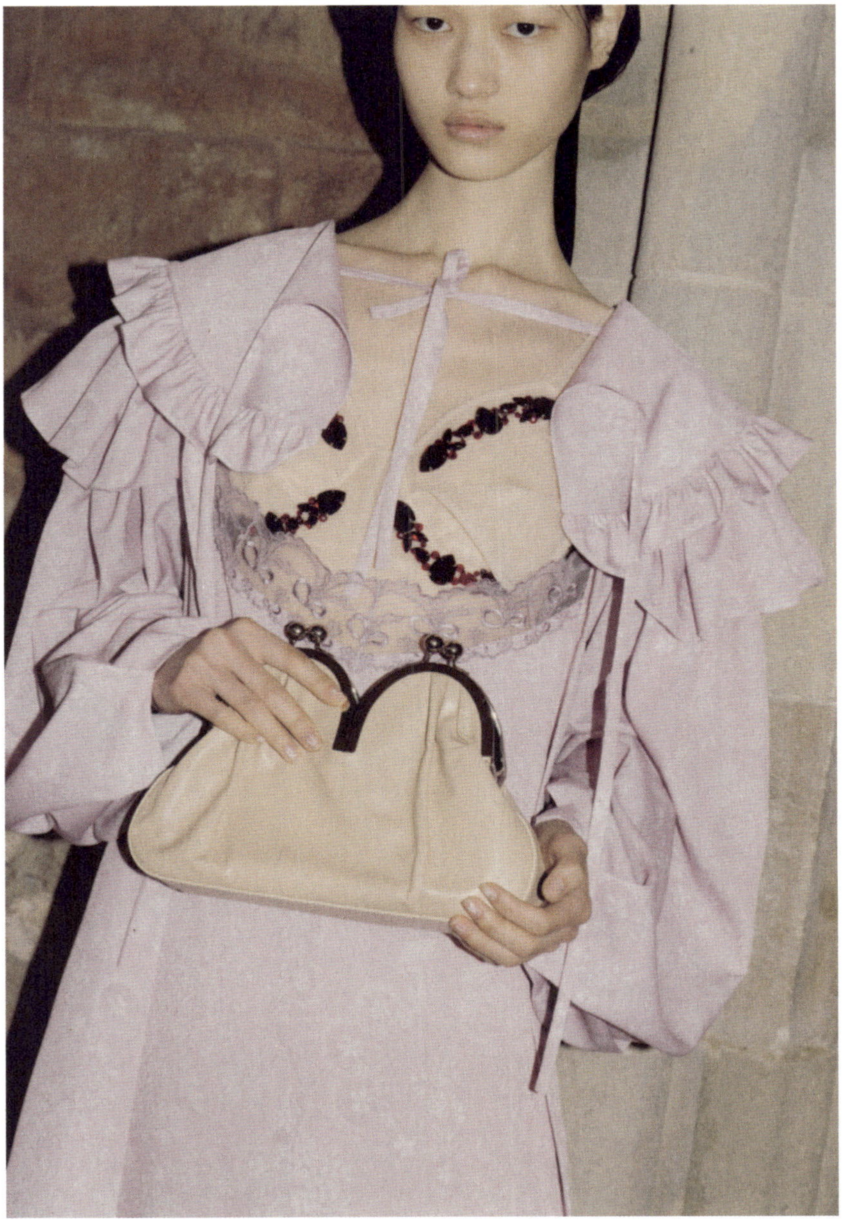

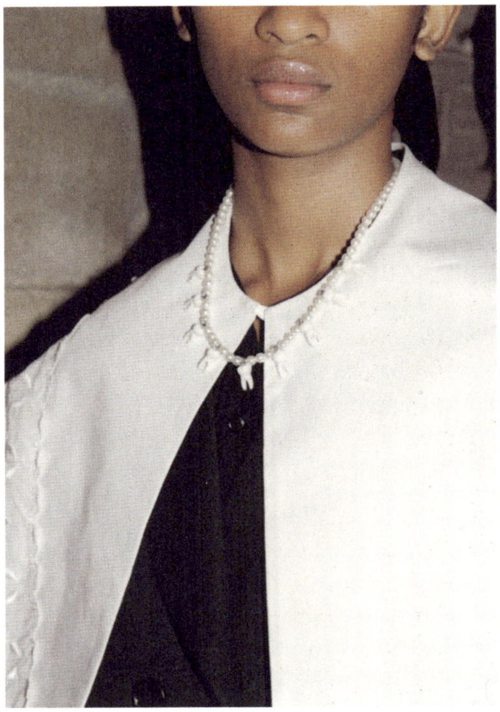

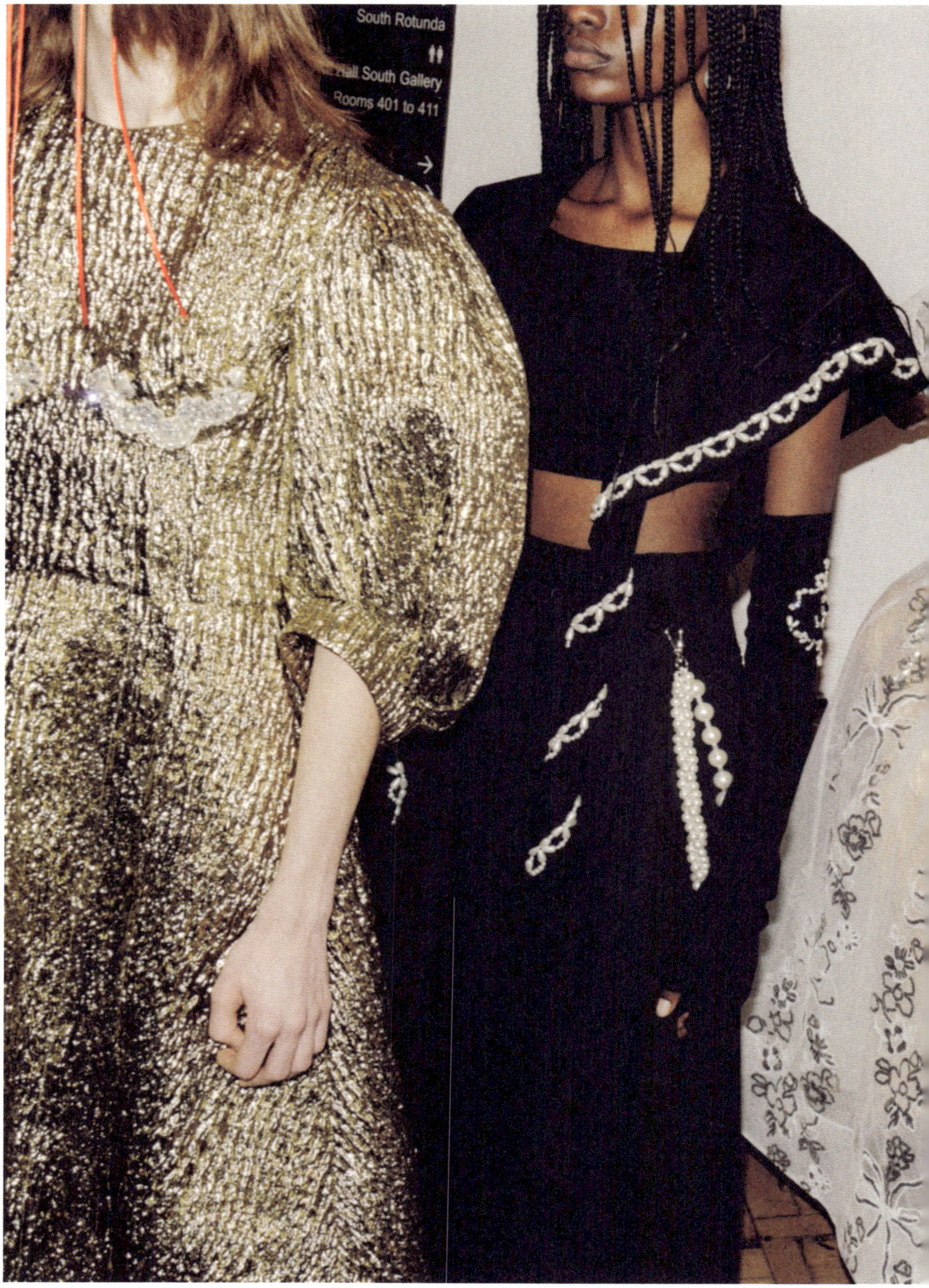
South Rotunda
Hall South Gallery
Rooms 401 to 411

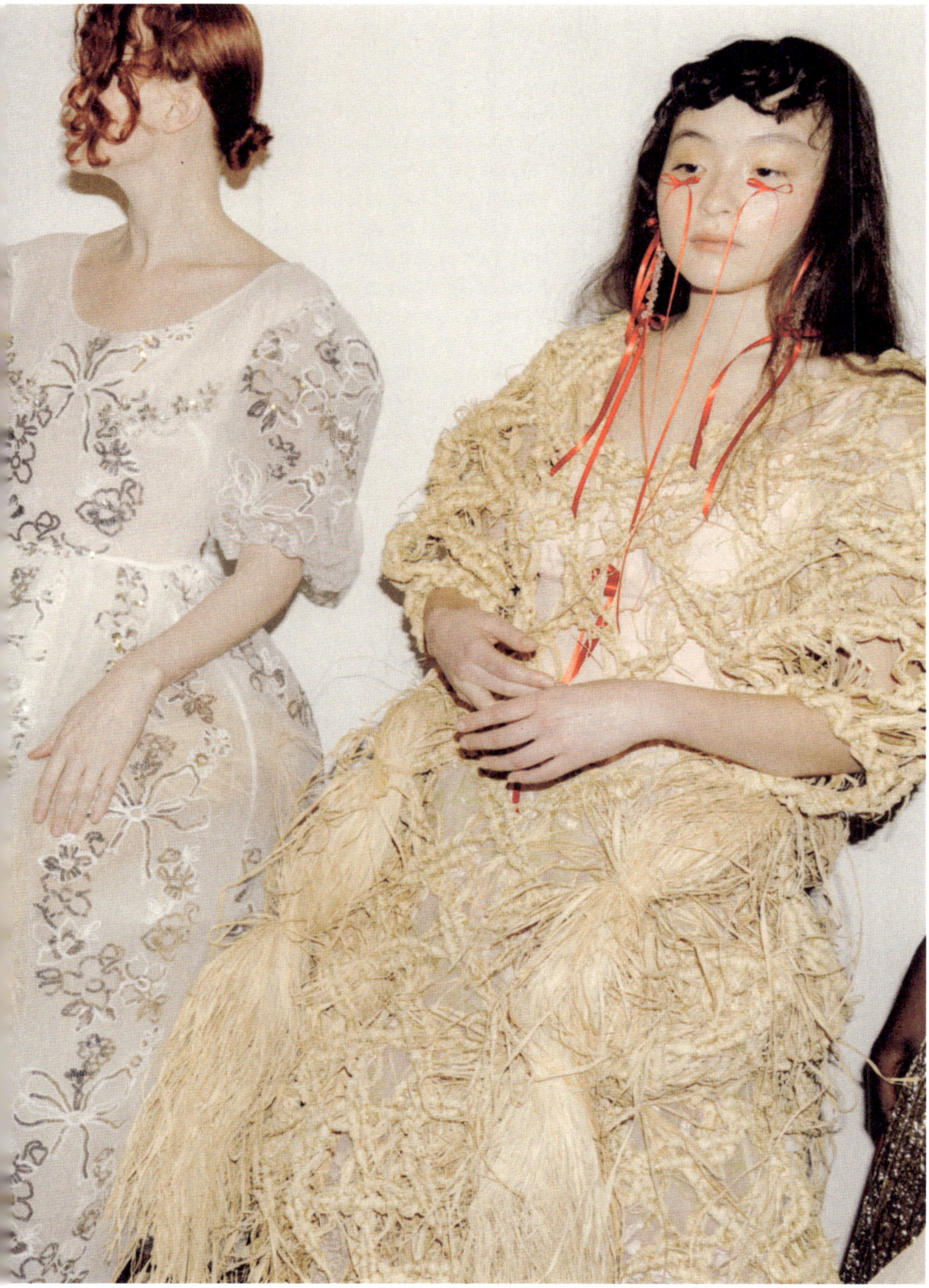

Simone Rocha
Autumn-Winter 2023-24

LS: Who would you say have been the pivotal female influences who have shaped your practice?

SR: There's people like Louise Wilson [Rocha's former tutor at Central Saint Martins], who was a huge influence on me. She completely changed my life and my view on the world, and the work I wanted to do, my output, and reclaiming that, somehow. My mother is a big influence. My team are a big influence —— they are all female, bar two. Then there are so many artists —— obviously Louise Bourgeois. Or Rachel Whiteread, and the presence of her sculptures. Or, similarly, the late Phyllida Barlow. Or people such as Roni Horn, who is a completely different type of artist. Their work is completely theirs. Also, there are people like the designer Rei Kawakubo. I think with all these different figures, what I have always admired is the way their work has to come from them. That's what resonates with me. And that's from established designers and artists through to young designers and artists.

I curated a show recently in Lismore [*girls, girls, girls* ran from April to October 2022 at Lismore Castle and featured Louise Bourgeois, Roni Horn, Alina Szapocznikow, Dorothy Cross, Genieve Figgis, Cindy Sherman, Harley Weir, Francesca Woodman and Luo Yang, among others] and working alongside some of the younger artists, such as Harley Weir, who is representing femininity today, in all its subversions, was really inspiring. For me, what it's about is their identity: it's 100 per cent coming from them. And that's what I think is the power of female designers and artists —— it's coming from within. That's the thing that ties it all together, when you look at the figures whose influence can be seen in my work over the years: it's theirs and they are putting themselves into it. And that's really what I have to do. I have to put myself into it to tell a story.

LS: Can we talk more about Louise Bourgeois, because she's been a constant presence in your work from when you began? What is it about her work that has been so important? I know, for example, that you were very drawn to her fabric works —— why?

SR: When I was a teenager, there was a Louise Bourgeois show at IMMA (the Irish Museum of Modern Art) just before I was about to start art college. IMMA is such a beautiful space —— it's an old barracks and it's all cobbled and it's this brilliant weighted historical building —— and I've always been really attracted to historical buildings. I had just got into the National College of Art and Design, and I didn't know what I wanted to do. I didn't actually want to do fashion at that point, so I thought I'd do a year of all different disciplines.

And I remember walking around IMMA, looking at these terry cloth towel figures hanging within these modern galleries that had been built inside the historical barracks, and feeling totally enamoured. They were art but they were made of fabric, and they were so physical. Once I'd researched into Louise Bourgeois, and learnt, as I said before, that she came from this textile family, I just felt this weird kinship. In her work there was a cheekiness and a playfulness that I felt a connection to, even though it was menacing as well. It felt like how I felt inside —— someone was putting it outside. It was really overwhelming, actually. And then I began looking at the drawings: there was one which was a blue outfit, but it showed the bones inside, and just showing the physicality of a body inside a garment really struck me. That and the fact that she used so many of her own garments in the work —— that's a real personal sacrifice, because it's exposing, telling your story, physically putting yourself into your work. But it was also coming from a place of resourcefulness and, again, domesticity, making use of what you have around you.

Many years later, I was lucky enough to go and visit her house, which has been preserved, and there is her Foundation next door. She'd done all of these tapestry sculptures that are almost like totem poles, influenced by the textiles that she was making in her father's factory. It was such an amazing place —— there were biscuit tins, all towered in the living room. I was dying, I was completely engaged with everything. I think the work was so brave and provocative and exposing. I've always been really attracted to the pink, the red, the baby blue —— it's just a kinship. I sound like an absolute lunatic now, but she used to do a salon, where she would see students and their work, and my dream, as an art student, was to bring my work to her. But she passed away, and it probably never would have happened anyway, but I felt there was a really cathartic thing that I eventually got to bring my work to present to Louise Wilson.

LS: What you are describing is almost like an imagined dialogue that you had with Louise Bourgeois. Is that correct?

SR: Yes —— and essentially, I'm a really big fan [*laughs*]. I just think it's such powerful work. Phyllida Barlow and I actually had this debate when there was the show at the Hayward Gallery [*Louise Bourgeois: The Woven Child* ran from February to May 2022]. She said, 'What I dislike about the work is the textiles' [*laughs*]. She said that the bronzes and the more solid works were the pieces that had all the impact. She felt that the textiles were hiding a layer —— a barrier between the true work, all the amazing brass and bronze. It was one of the most amazing conversations I've ever had in my life, and it also made me question myself as a fan of Louise and look at her work in a different way, because it was totally different to how I saw the work previously. It was a real privilege to have had that conversation.

Simone Rocha: I personally do feel there's humour in the work, like *The Reticent Child* [2003], where it's documenting the birth of one of her sons, and the backdrop is this mirror, where it's kind of distorting the story. To go through childbirth and to actually want to physically put it out there and document it, you have to have a sense of humour [*crowd laughs*]. For real. Otherwise, you'd just be like, I can't even put that into words, let alone physically manifest something. The fact that it's distorted is showing the viewer the sense of humour as well. Personally, I think that in some of the works there is a sense of humour.

Phyllida Barlow: I agree, yes. But for me, that work, I can't get into it at all. But where she's dealing with the visceral, I think that's where I see the change —— I mean, the evolution of her whole work fascinates me. And the change from using the materials themselves, of plaster and clay and things, the really visceral works that were coming out of that, and the fabric works seemed to clean up on that in some way. The childbirth becomes sort of toylike, and I find it quite sickening —— it doesn't seem to touch on my experience at all [*laughs*]. I think there's a sort of particular loss that happens with the fabric works —— not all of them, just some of them —— where the habit of them seems to over-contain something of this incredible spillage that she brings into the work...

Shahidha Bari: There is a question about why she turned to fabric, and whether that is about age, about turning to softer materials at a later stage in your life. Do you have any theories as to why she did that?

PB: Not really. I just wondered whether it was practical. Some of the huge drawings that she did right at the end I think are quite extraordinary, that she wanted to keep that energy going. But whether the fabric provides some way of keeping that intimacy that you're talking about...

SR: Or whether it's —— obviously it's something that she felt at home in, growing up in a textile mill. And maybe potentially later in life, not that you always want to go home, but there's some... not security again, but *familiarity*. Is the fabric mopping up all the other spillages and all the mess, and you're coming back to something that you know, that then you can take all these ideas that you've been exploring your whole life and immortalise them essentially in a way that potentially, at this stage in life, you want people to understand? It could be something like that.

—— Extract from a conversation on Louise Bourgeois between Phyllida Barlow, Simone Rocha and Shahidha Bari, held at the Southbank Centre, London, in March 2022.

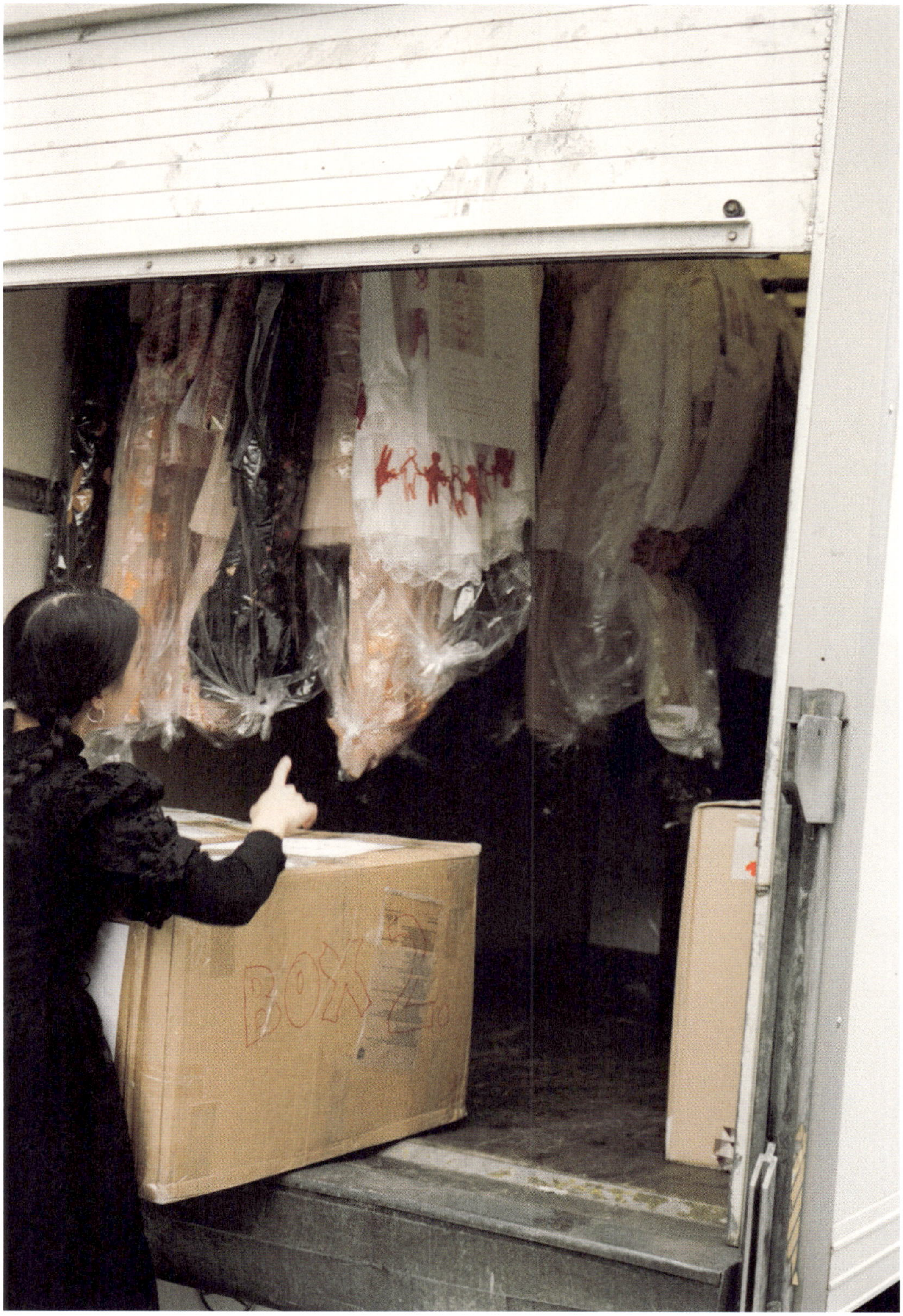

Simone Rocha
Spring-Summer 2018

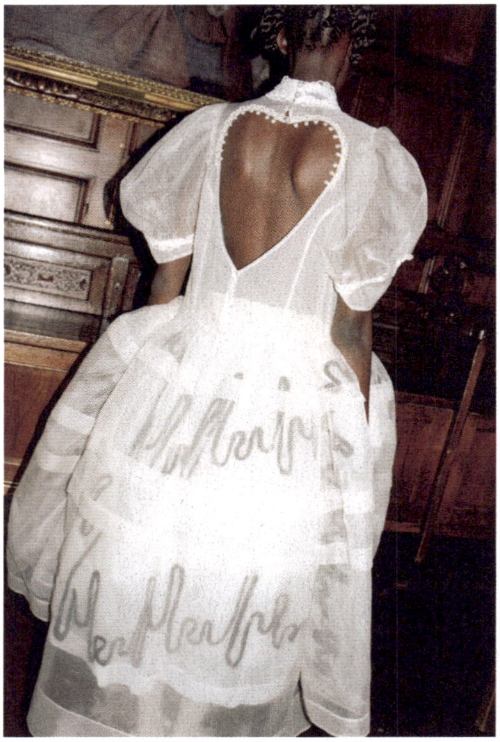

LS: She's there in all your work, as we've said, but your Autumn-Winter 19 collection was particularly Louise Bourgeois focused.

SR: We did it as an official collaboration with her foundation, The Easton Foundation. We did a collaboration across the fabrics, which we co-branded. The fabrics drew on these octagon tapestries of hers, which was a body of work that she had done using her own clothes. We were given permission to reissue those fabrics and we made them into different dresses. It was amazing actually, to officially do some pieces together. And then the collection as a whole took so much influence from her; we did embroideries that were based on her spiderwebbing. We wanted the pieces to have a lot of volume in the room —— a presence —— an idea that was very much influenced by her dusty pink busts piece, *Mamelles.*

LS: A final thought —— menswear! A recent addition to your work. People always associate your work with womanhood and femininity, but somehow you bringing in menswear has felt so natural, like completing a family or world.

SR: I spent a lot of time thinking about the menswear in terms of the role, in comparison to the womenswear. Who is that character, what is the tension and the interaction and the push and pull against it? And to me, what was so interesting was seeing how that could play out, with the menswear having its own identity, and the two of them together also having an identity as one. Now, when I start, I think of the collection itself and then I split it into the man and the woman. So, I'll start and I'll design some menswear and womenswear together, based on the collection's story and themes, and then I'll split and work on the woman and her collection, and then work on the man, but at the end I bring them back together. I think we are working at a time when menswear is more open, more fluid —— more open to the creative process and maybe less traditional —— so it felt like the perfect time to introduce men to the story. And, as you say, it felt like completing the world.

Simone Rocha
Autumn-Winter 2022-23

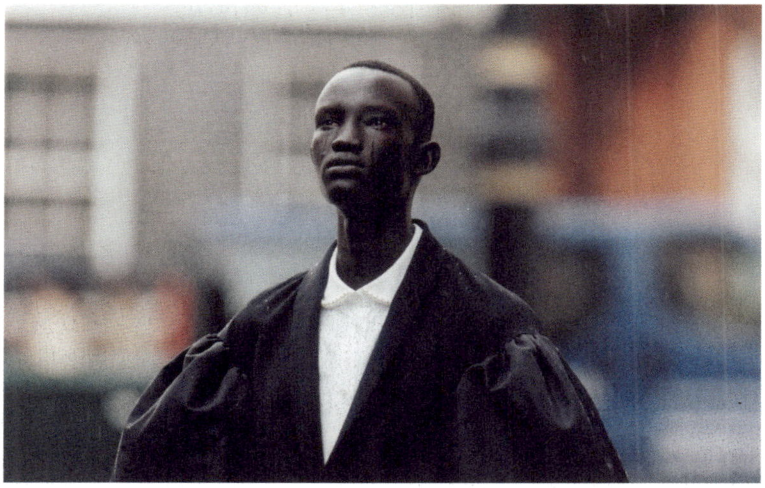

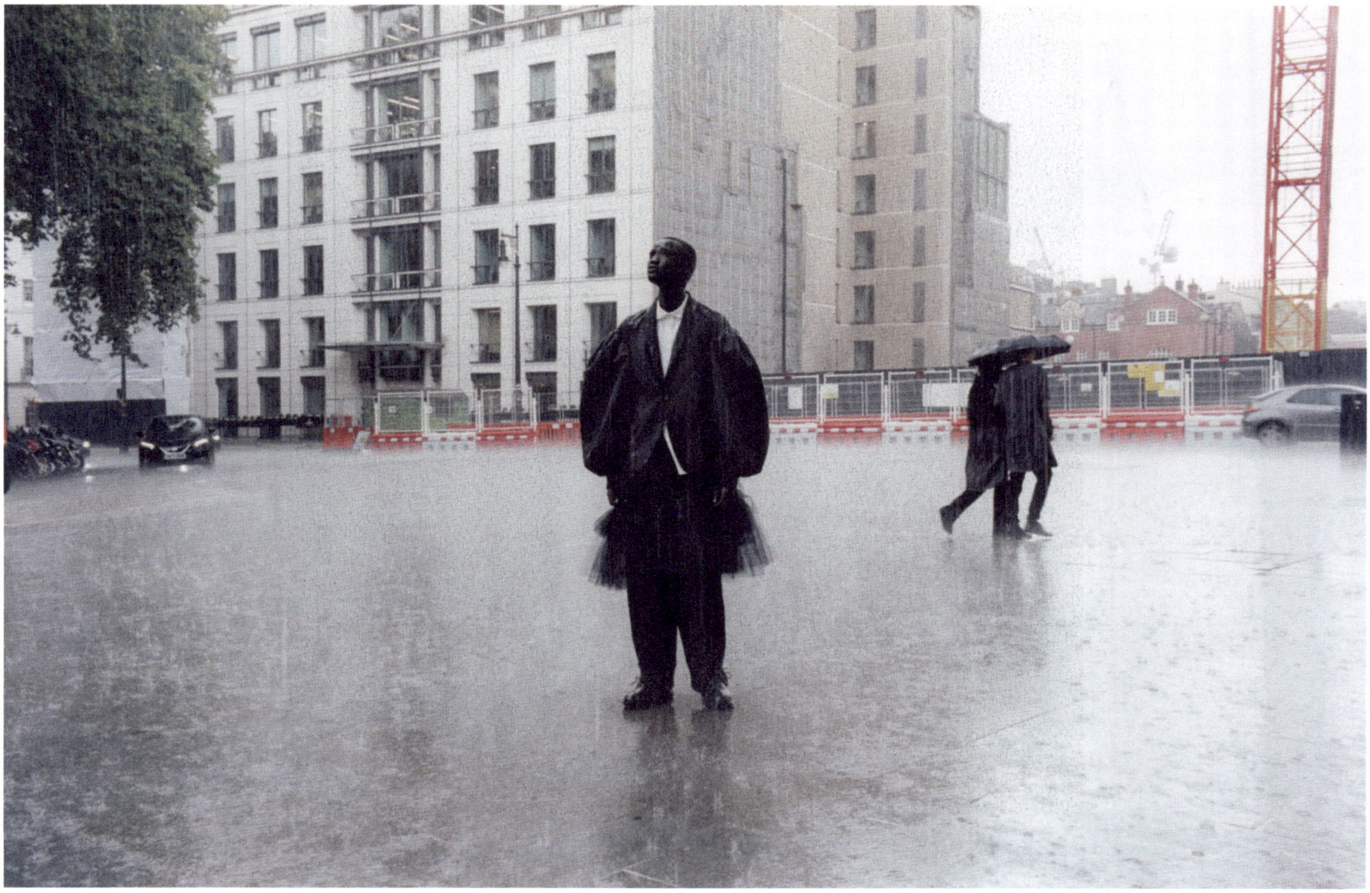

Simone Rocha
Spring-Summer 2023

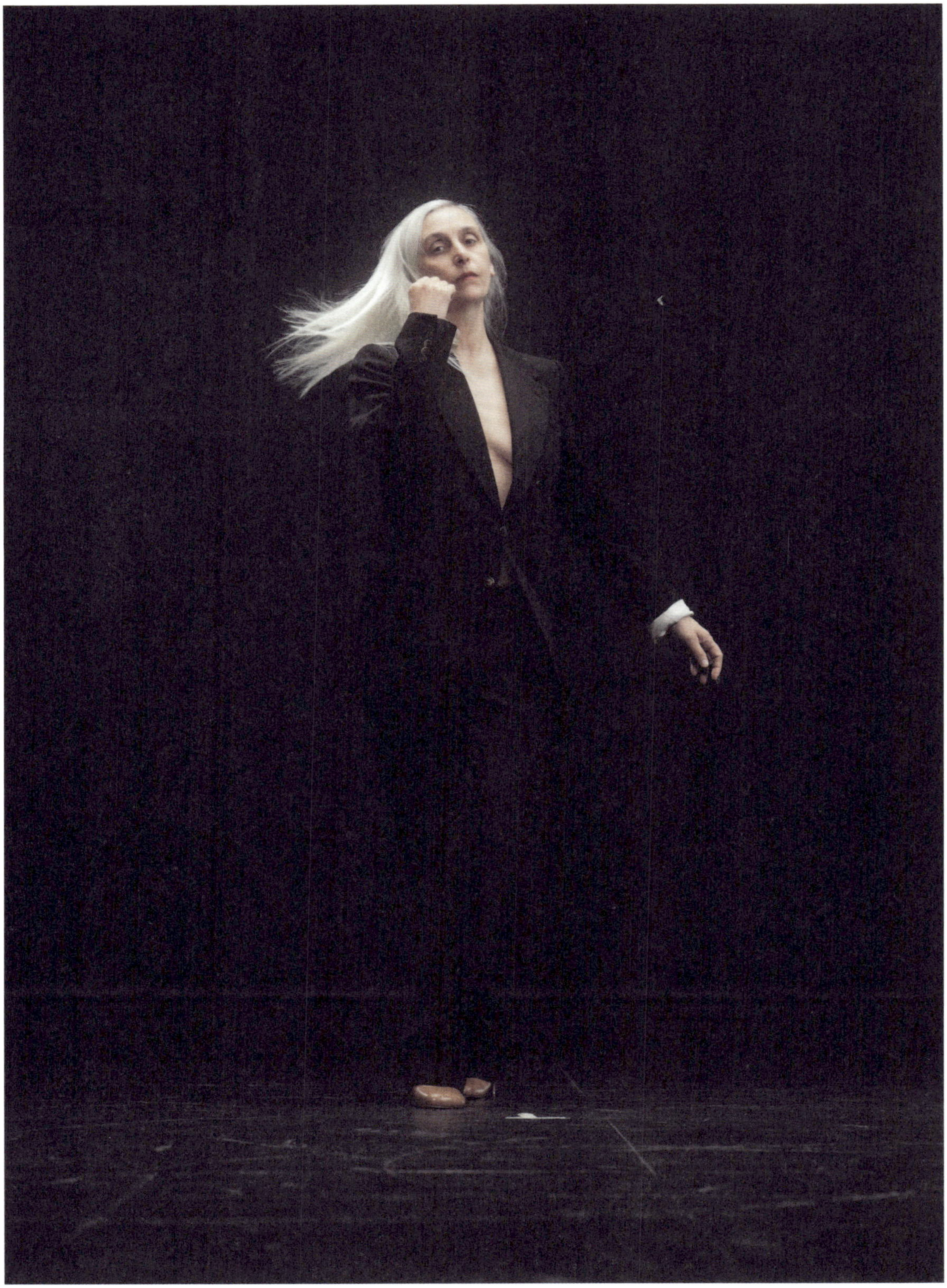

Dries Van Noten's Autumn-Winter 2021-22 collection film,
choreographed by Anne Teresa De Keersmaeker

CHAPTER IV

Clothing is Crucial

A Conversation with Anne Teresa De Keersmaeker

ELISA DE WYNGAERT

In 1983 Anne Teresa De Keersmaeker founded the dance company Rosas in Brussels. In 1995 she set up the dance school P.A.R.T.S. (Performing Arts Research and Training Studios) with De Munt/La Monnaie. While De Keersmaeker is known for taking music as a blueprint for her choreography, her intimate relationship with clothing remains unexplored.

EDW: What does clothing mean to you?

Anne Teresa De Keersmaeker: Clothing is crucial. When I look back over my entire career, particularly the very first productions in which I danced myself, such as *Fase, Four Movements to the Music of Steve Reich* (1982), *Rosas danst Rosas* (1983), *Elena's Aria* (1984) and *Bartók/aantekeningen* (1986), I tended to start with the costume. In fact, the choice of music, and of a dress or pair of trousers, sometimes coincided. I think clothing is important. Look [points to her white shirt with rolled-up sleeves], I like that, the thought of 'rolling up my sleeves' makes me feel good [*laughs*], and I need to feel good in what I am wearing when I move. I've always felt uncomfortable wearing garments that are too tight, which is often the case in classical ballet. But I don't go as far as adopting the 'pyjama culture' that seems ubiquitous in contemporary dance.

EDW: Can a piece of clothing be as decisive as the music for a choreography?

ATDK: For my very first solo, *Violin Phase*, I found a dress that, in combination with the music of Steve Reich, led to a movement vocabulary based on turning and spinning movements. Skirts have continued to be special for me: they exaggerate and intensify rotational motion. A piece of clothing has a certain structure that closely, or not quite, follows the lines of the body. It also has a certain architecture that magnifies, or diminishes, a movement. The readability of the choreography and the visibility of the body's anatomy are also defining concepts.

EDW: So, in those early years, clothing often inspired the choreography.

ATDK: In *Elena's Aria* we explored the very opposite. 'What do you wear when you no longer want to dance?' That led to sleek high heels and body-hugging dresses, and to replicas of a vintage dress recreated in some curtain fabric we happened to find. Then came *Bartók/ aantekeningen* and the black skirts in that old crêpe I love so much. The weight of the fabric and the way it pleats are incredible. When I bought second-hand clothing, the quality of the fabrics, the cut and the detail of the finishing often amazed me.

EDW: Is it necessary to be able to rehearse in the right silhouettes from the start?

ATDK: For me, it's immensely important. I create an entirely different vocabulary depending on whether I dance in a skirt or in trousers. Colour is also decisive. It's often about 'readability': if all the dancers are dressed in black, it's different than if everyone's wearing different colours. I also often explore the energetic value of colours and the sequences of the alchemical process.

EDW: Speaking of colour, in your production *Rain* you wove a dialogue between an unusual transition in the colours of the costumes, the lighting and set design.

ATDK: That experimentation with colour came about through my first collaboration with Dries Van Noten and Jan Versweyveld for *Just Before* (1997). For that production, we started with a palette of black and dark blue, which evolved into greyish light blue to white with a touch of orange at the very end. In *Drumming* (1998) and *Rain* (2001) it was about a quartet: the music of Steve Reich, the costumes of Dries Van Noten, the light and set design of Jan Versweyveld and my choreography. *Drumming* began where *Just Before* ended: with an orange touch. *Rain* took that further, with a colour palette that shifted from beige, to salmon pink, to magenta.

EDW: How did this intense collaboration with Dries Van Noten begin? Did you approach him?

ATDK: I asked him if he'd like to get involved. Through our collaborations, my admiration for Dries grew all the more. He has an astounding wealth of knowledge and craftsmanship. Dries comes from a family that has worked in fashion for generations, and he also has outrageously good taste. I take such pleasure in working with him because he also takes into consideration movement and colour, structure and the various degrees of transparency... and his designs reflect that.

EDW: He must have needed to do a little research, because surely dance costumes have specific technical requirements?

ATDK: Yes, the costumes must always allow sufficient freedom of movement. And when choosing the fabric, you have to consider the weight of the garment and its fluidity, unless the choreography calls for rigidity and weight.

EDW: How important are shoes?

ATDK: Shoes are also fundamental, perhaps even more so. They are your relationship with the floor, the earth. The weight of the footwear is all-important. There's a good reason why: in classical ballet, pointes are like extremely high heels, so they emphasise verticality. It's about the right sole and the right grip. You must be able to fully relax the soles of your feet. The floor is your first partner.

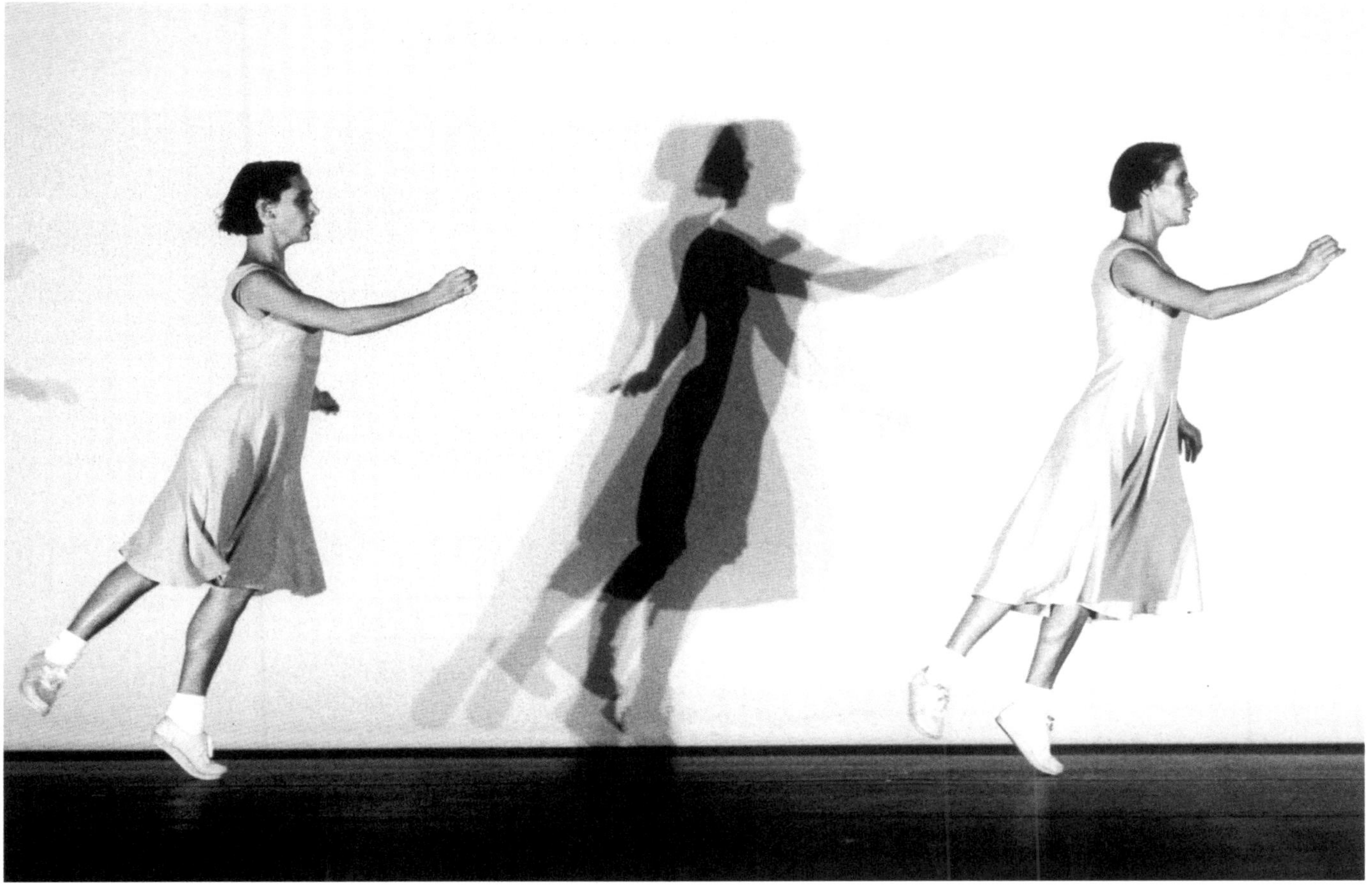

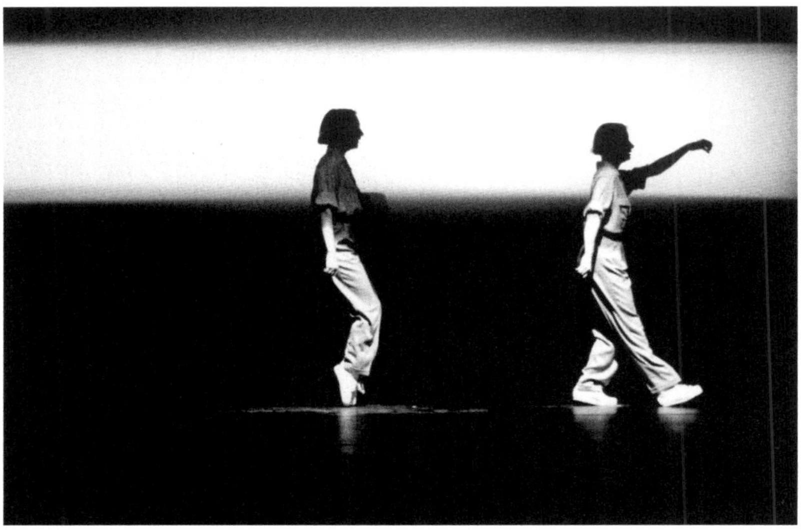

Fase, Four Movements to the Music of Steve Reich, 1982
Anne Teresa De Keersmaeker, Michèle Anne De Mey

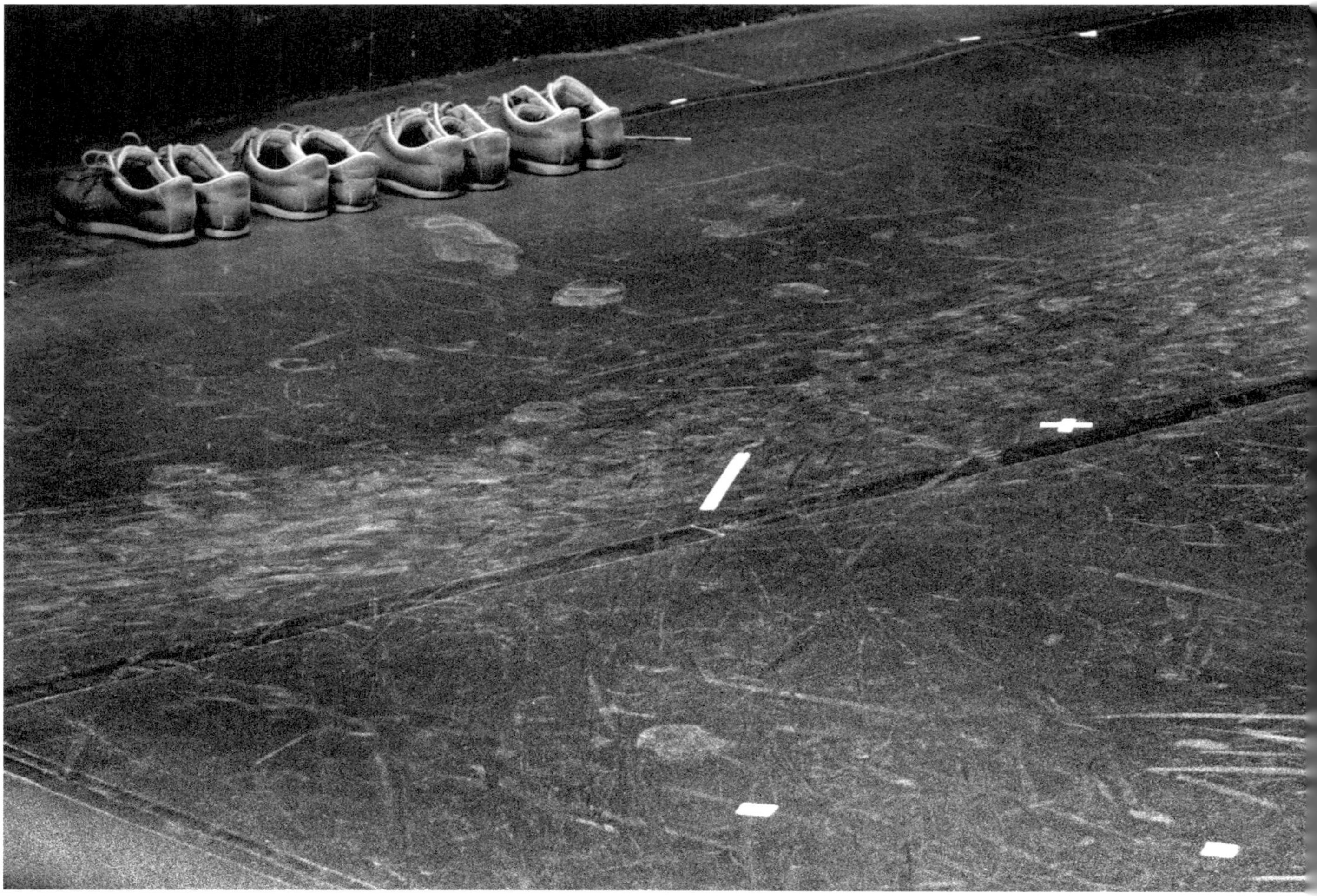

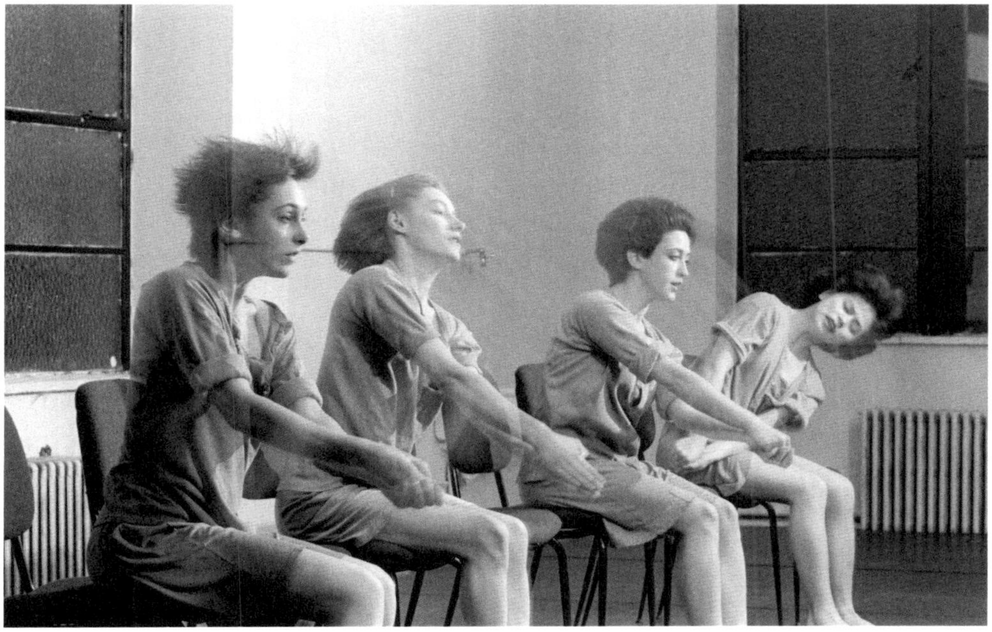

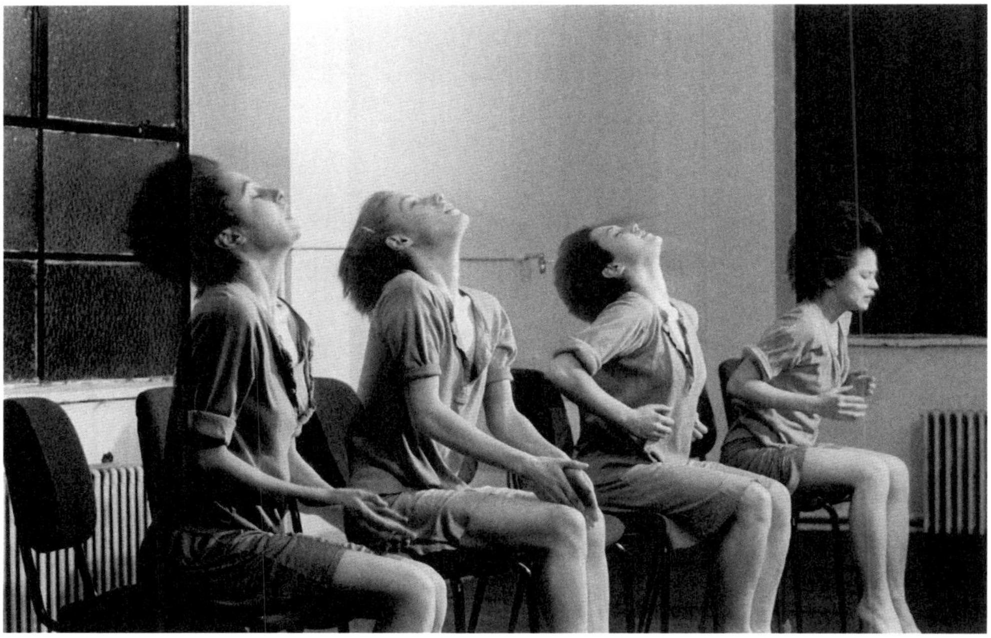

Rosas danst Rosas, 1984
Anne Teresa De Keersmaeker, Michèle Anne De Mey, Adriana Boriello, Fumiyo Ikeda

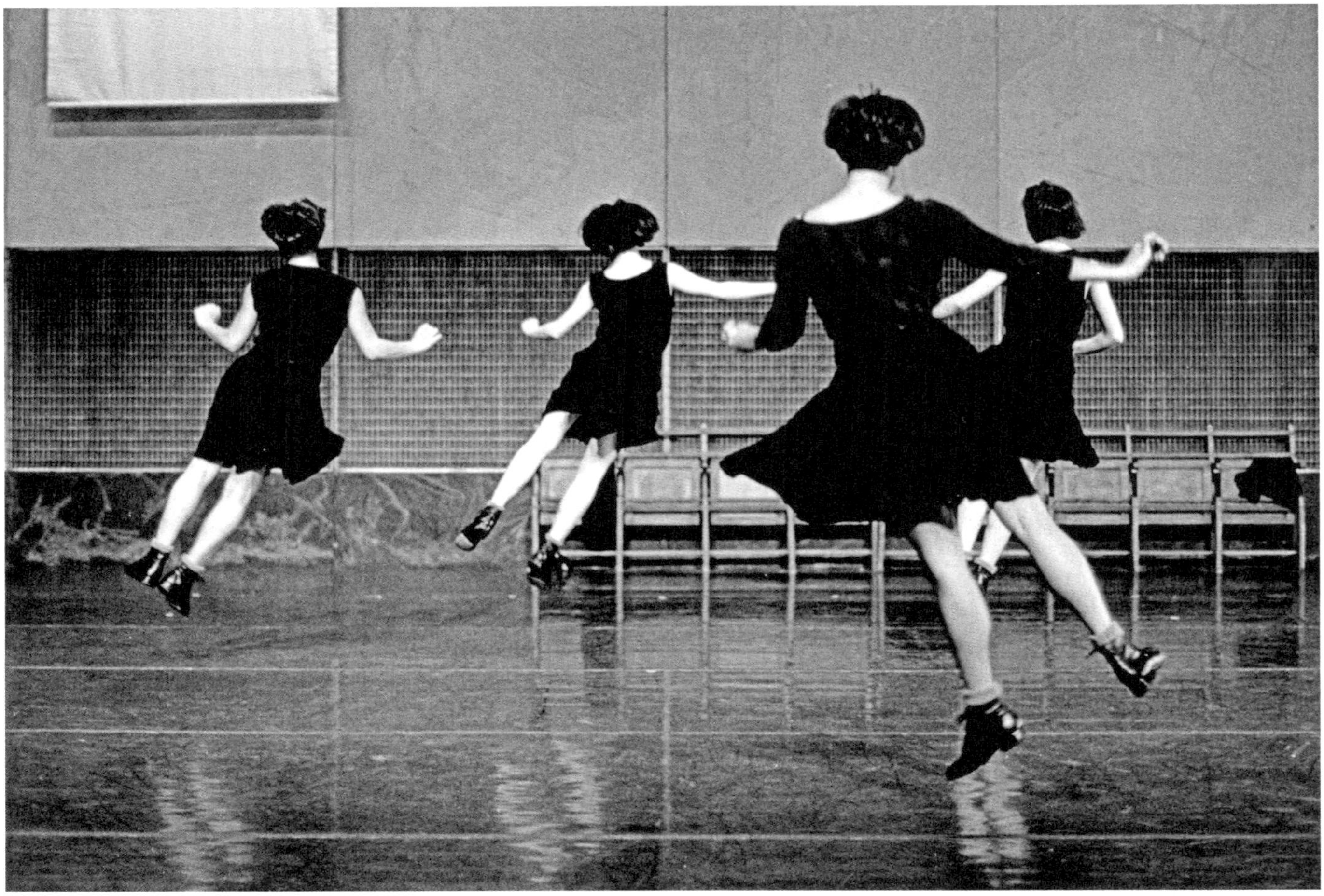

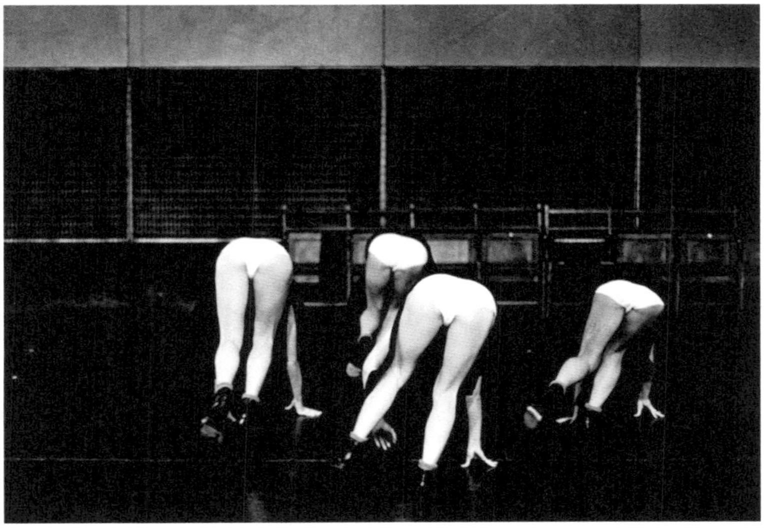

Bartók/aantekeningen, 1986
Johanne Saunier, Fumiyo Ikeda, Nadine Ganase, Anne Teresa De Keersmaeker

EDW: I was thrilled to see the shoes worn in *Fase*, the ones with the heavy soles, in your archives. They weigh quite a lot. Do shoes play a part in defining your score?

ATDK: It's true that in the early performances we always wore shoes when we danced. I had recently begun choreographing when I made *Violin Phase*. In classical dance, you practise a lot in front of a mirror, which you don't do as much in contemporary dance. That frontality of following yourself in the mirror is prevalent in classical dance, but at some point, when I began to choreograph, I came to detest the mirror. I decided to allow myself to be vulnerable, and trust how a movement felt rather than how it looked. Quite simply, the music of *Violin Phase* invited a turning motion, a little similar to folk dance. The dresses guided me towards a spinning movement, like that of the Sufis, but after three days of spinning barefoot, the soles of my foot were severely blistered. It was a disaster. I was in New York at the time and went to St Mark's Place, where I bought a pair of Roots shoes. What's unusual about Roots is that they are negative-heel shoes. I took my shoes to a cobbler and had the heel raised. I loved the weight of the shoes, which, combined with thick socks that gave extra support to the ankle, provided a certain sturdiness that contrasted with the slenderness of the leg. On top of that, Roots shoes are very stiff, and one day we discovered that we could stand on the tips of our toes. 'Look what I can do!' Before long, we decided: 'Okay, let's make a dance out of it.' That became *Clapping Music*.

EDW: And the Roots also created an acoustic effect.

ATDK: Yes, that too. *Rosas danst Rosas* was also choreographed to be performed wearing Roots, this time the brown version. The performance was a continuation of the vocabulary of *Fase* with a feminine touch. The rehearsal costumes for *Rosas danst Rosas* ended up being the performance costumes. Barely two days before the premiere we decided to wear our rehearsal shirts and dye them. And that was that. Hairstyles were also important, so we cut our hair very short for the performance.

EDW: You often base costumes on second-hand clothing. But I'm sure that the search to create an exact replica of an original isn't always easy?

ATDK: These days, it is almost impossible given that fabrics have declined in quality. Occasionally, we also have copies of shoes made. I discovered the boots for *Bartók/aantekeningen* in a shoe shop in Barcelona and had them recreated by a shoemaker who specialised in orthopaedic footwear.

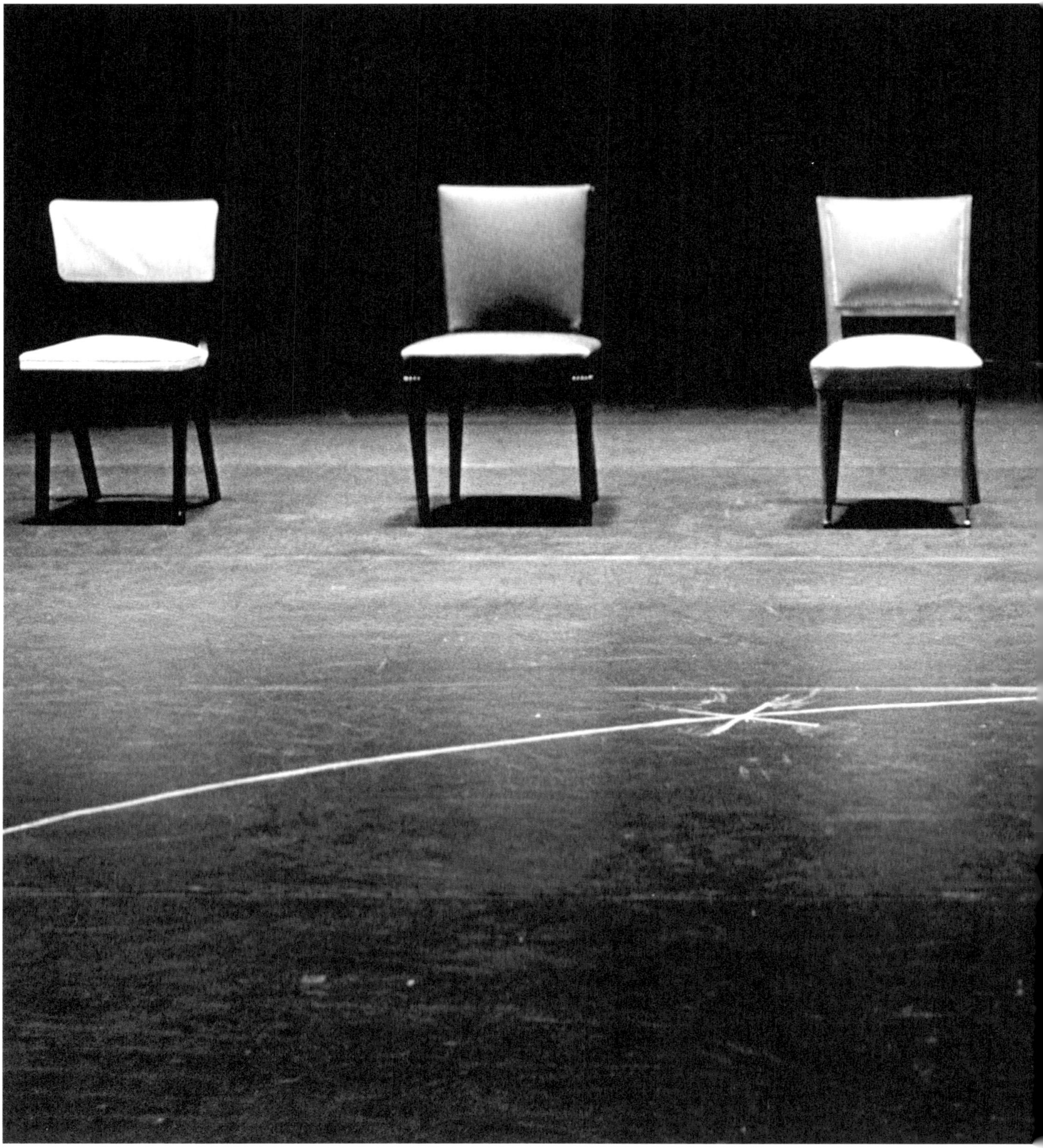

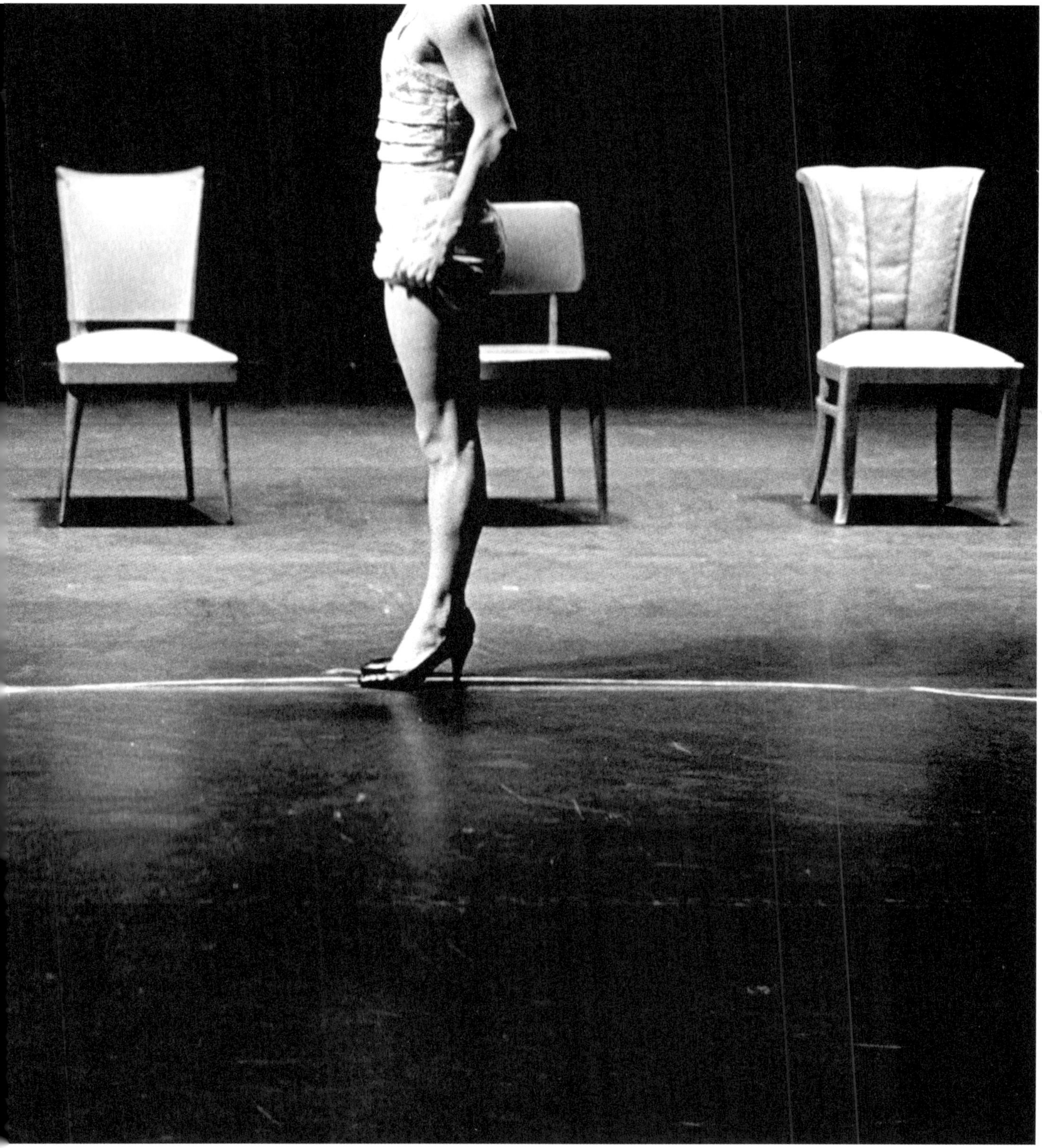

Elena's Aria, 1984
Michèle Anne De Mey

EDW: The shoes and costumes in *Mozart* are exquisite. They were inspired by an eighteenth-century dress. What was that process like?

ATDK: *Mozart/Concert Arias, un moto di gioia* (1992) was a wonderful collaboration with Rudy Sabounghi. We drew on historical garments. That performance stemmed from a period of intensive collaboration with opera house De Munt/La Monnaie, which had culminated earlier in *Ottone Ottone* (1988). At the time, we had recourse to the opera's inventory and impressive archive of historical costumes. Whether it was embroidery, tailoring, wigs or anything else, the opera's workshops had an incredible *savoir faire*. We had access to a degree of craftsmanship that had already become prohibitively expensive and which, by that point, was found only in theatres and opera houses. The expertise and pride of the people who worked on the production were exceptional. You could feel their passion and skill in the costumes.

EDW: Has your approach to costumes changed over the years?

ATDK: In the first performances, in which I danced myself, I always had a clear vision of the costumes from day one. That all changed when I took on the role of choreographer and no longer danced myself. At times, Rosas had such a vast clothing inventory that the design process started there. Using that inventory, we tried out things in terms of structure and colour, in relation to movement and in relation to a certain narrative. The costume designer drew inspiration from the garments we had selected. Sometimes, like for *Achterland* (1990), I bought up dead stock myself. For instance, I came across ten suits in beautiful fabrics somewhere. Some of them have been used; others are still stored in the inventory. The approach was often a synthesis of designing clothes, buying them and reusing them. There were various strategies.

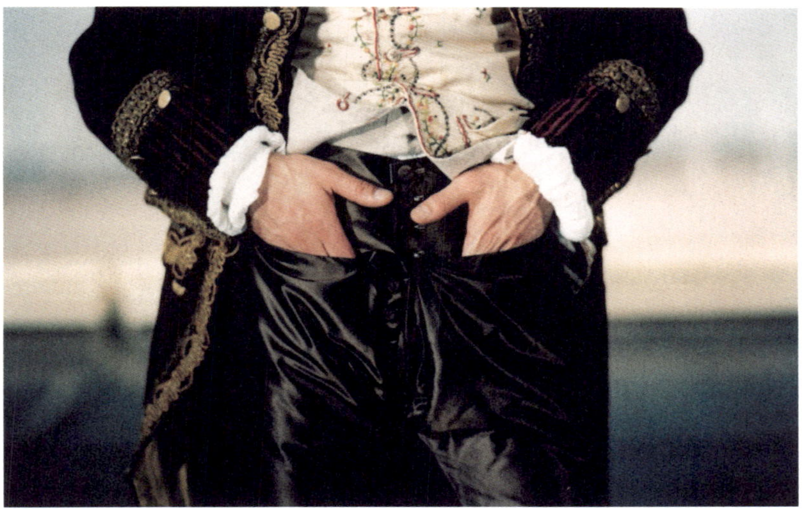

Mozart/Concert Arias, un moto di gioia, 1992
Eduardo Torroja

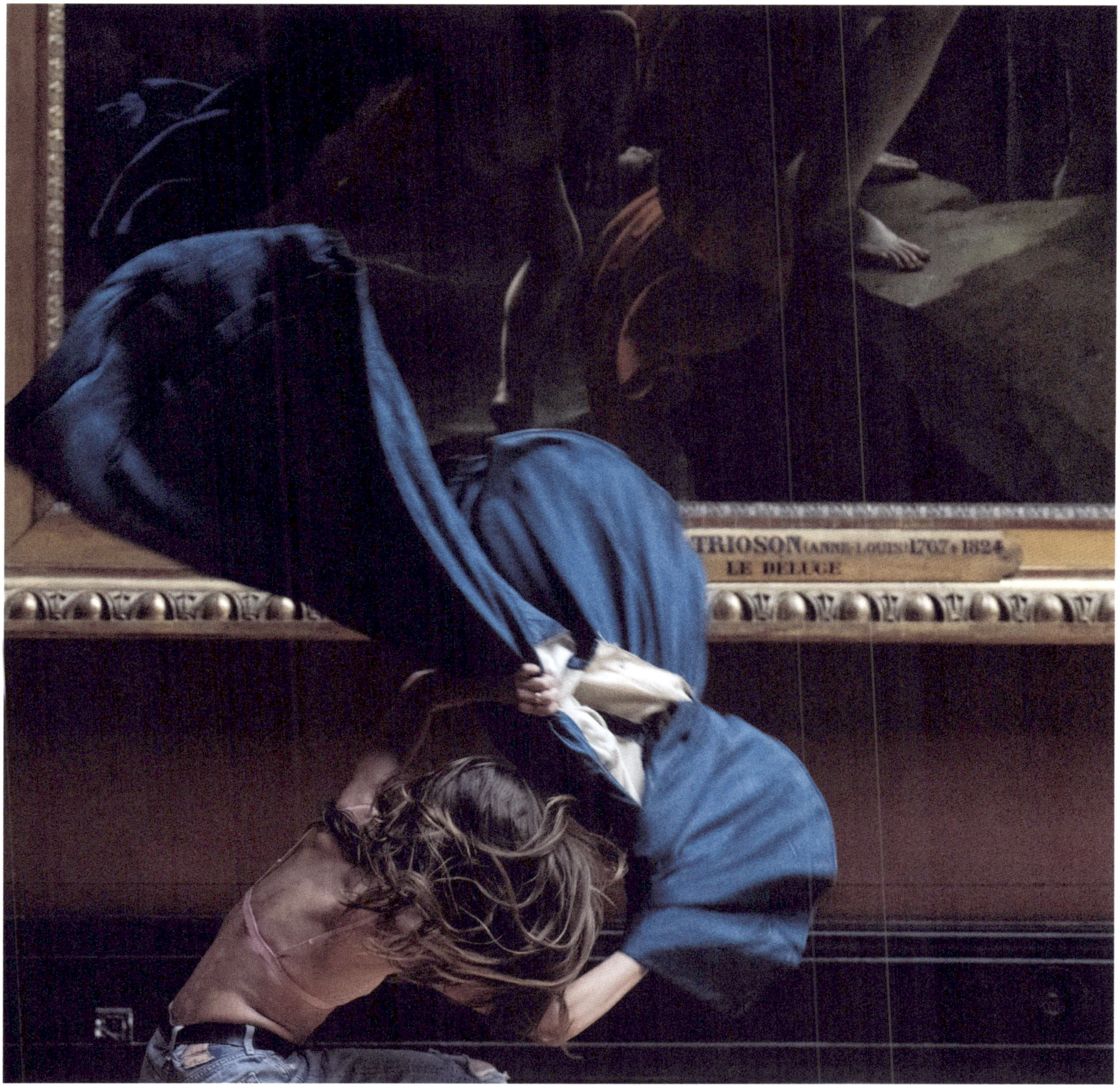

Fôret, 2022
Solène Wachter

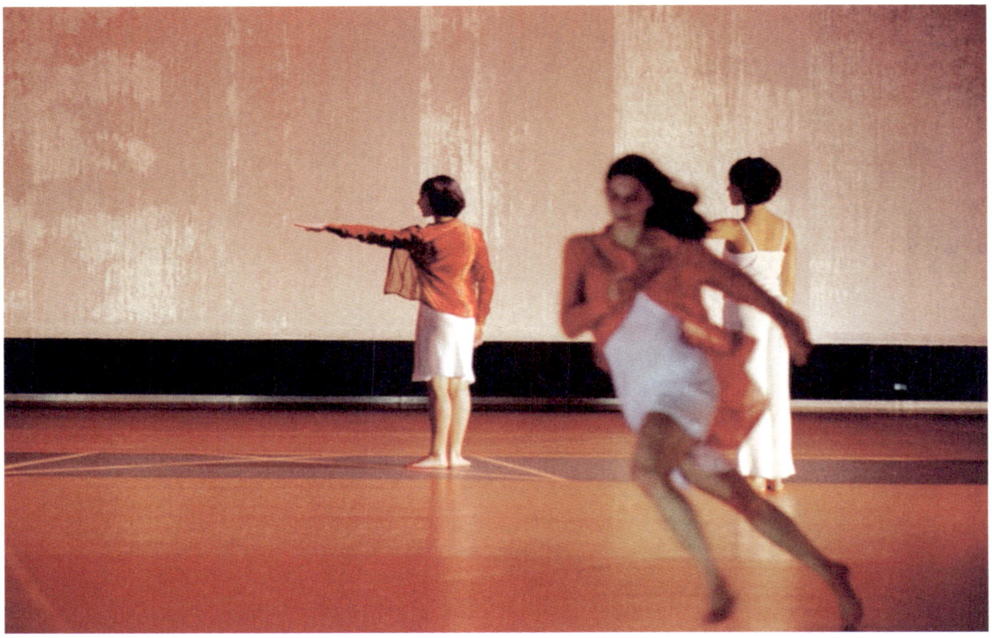

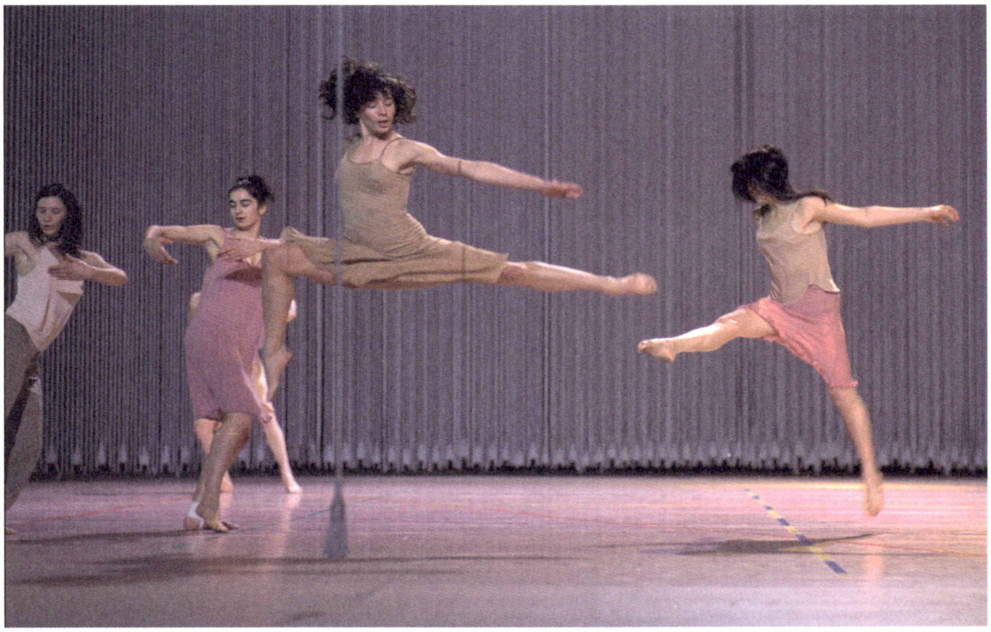

Drumming, 1988
Marta Coronado, Cynthia Loemij, Alix Eynaud

Rain, 2001
Cynthia Loemij, Rosalba Torres, Alix Eynaudi, Fumiyo Ikeda

EDW: How do you know if someone is a good partner for the costumes?

ATDK: To be honest, I have always slightly regretted never having encountered someone like Marion Cito, Pina Bausch's long-standing costume designer. I believe they did almost everything together. Cito's designs were instrumental in helping to shape Pina's oeuvre. I've worked with many wonderful people, but never with such continuity. It's quite complicated because, to me, clothing is extremely important. Collaborating with a designer only works if you can guide the process while simultaneously allowing a lot of freedom. It's about negotiation. It's a different journey each time. It's about intuition and making the right decisions. I have certain systems that guide my choices and... you can't, and you don't always want to, start explaining everything from the beginning.

EDW: Is it about a shared sensitivity and aesthetic?

ATDK: In opera or in certain productions, the set, lighting and costumes are usually decided six months in advance. That's not how I work. When I start a new creation, the ideas for the choreography, music, text, light, sound, set and costumes develop in parallel. These factors are all interconnected and influence one another, which means that you're exploring all of those elements at the same time. I work with people. I don't want to impose anything because I believe it's critical that dancers feel good and beautiful. You want to foster unity, while simultaneously allowing space for their individuality. The big question is how to lead that process. It often starts by asking what a dancer's preferences are, and then the negotiation begins. Finding a partner who can steer that process and with whom I can simultaneously exchange views on readability and so forth is not always easy.

EDW: In other words, the costume designer must gain the trust of the dancers and give them sufficient comfort?

ATDK: That, too.

EDW: Is it important that that person can also attend rehearsals?

ATDK: There isn't a set formula. Some designers need a lot of time; others don't. It's best if the costume designer can be there full-time, but today that's a luxury and isn't always realistic.

EDW: That certainly applies to designers with their own fashion houses or who work as creative directors such as Dries Van Noten, Olivier Theyskens and Ester Manas. Simone Rocha told me that you and she once talked about working together. I can see your worlds converging.

ATDK: These kinds of collaborations are always very intensive processes. Simone Rocha's fashion house is in London and the production we wanted to collaborate on was in Paris. Unfortunately, at that stage, it was not logistically feasible. But at the time I was lucky enough to visit her studio, which was very inspiring.

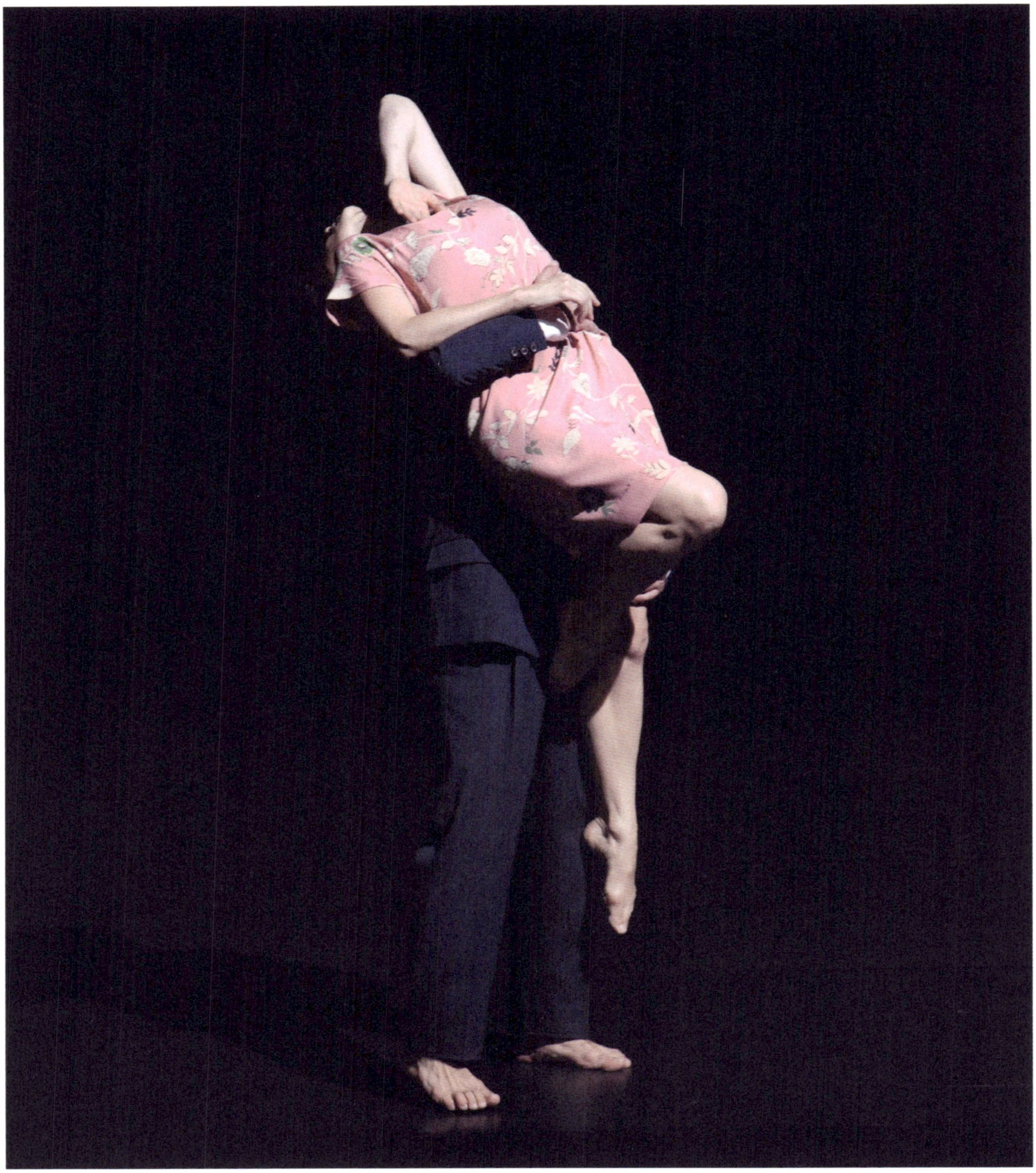

Verklärte Nacht, 2014
Samantha Van Wissen, Nordine Benchorf

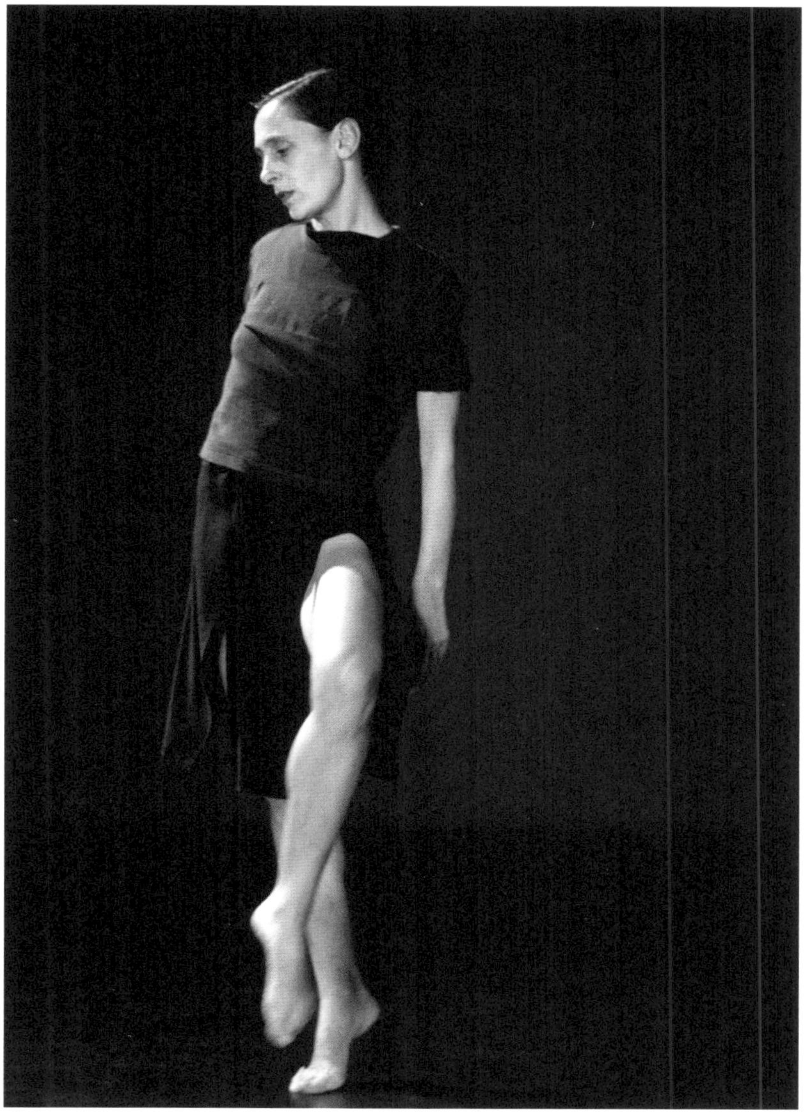

Once, 2002
Anne Teresa De Keersmaeker

EDW: Forty years after your first solo, you danced solo onstage again in *The Goldberg Variations, BWV 988* (2020). You were turning 60 then, and when you danced your first solo you'd just turned 20. You started dancing 50 years ago. I'm curious to know if your approach to the costumes you wear yourself has changed?

ATDK: In *Violin Phase*, I wore a dress that had been made from a pattern based on a floral dress later worn in *Verklärte Nacht* (2014). It really is a lovely dress that flows beautifully. In *Fase*, of course, there were also the trousers and a blouse with rolled-up sleeves. In 2002 I made *Once* in collaboration with Anke Loh. I gave Anke some of my own clothes that she cut up and altered. The open-back dress I wore already had movement cut into it; I was delighted with that collaboration.

EDW: Do you often create a costume around an item from your own wardrobe?

ATDK: I often use my own clothes as a basis. Mostly, but not always, I get them back later. Now and then we clear out the stock and some of the Rosas inventory goes to the dance school P.A.R.T.S. I might occasionally see a student at the school wearing a piece of clothing that once belonged to me, and think, 'That dress looks familiar' or, 'I know that blouse'. [*laughs*]

EDW: Recycling seems to be a theme. Are some of your new performances subtle echoes of previous productions?

ATDK: For my last solo, *The Goldberg Variations, BWV 988*, I wore a dress that Marie Goudot wore previously in *The Six Brandenburg Concertos* (2018). One of my frequent collaborators, An D'Huys, designed the costumes for the performance. I had given her the dress because I thought it would be perfect for Marie. Later on, we made more versions of it, in other colours. Afterwards, I wore the dress in *The Goldberg Variations* and the following year it was also worn in *Mystery Sonatas/for Rosa* (2022).

EDW: What makes the dress so special?

ATDK: The cut, the vertically stitched seams and the sublime transparency. The bodice looks both sensual and fragile. It is black but not heavy, and the sleeves, which I roll up, are the perfect length. The dress falls beautifully and turns in just the right way.

EDW: I saw two versions in your archives: the original and the replica. The original is in a more fluid fabric, and although that may seem like a minor detail, I imagine that it's important to you?

ATDK: Unfortunately, you can never find fabric of exactly the same quality. I had asked Anke Loh to make a copy, but she was in Chicago at the time, and, because of lockdowns, I ended up having a replica of the dress made myself.

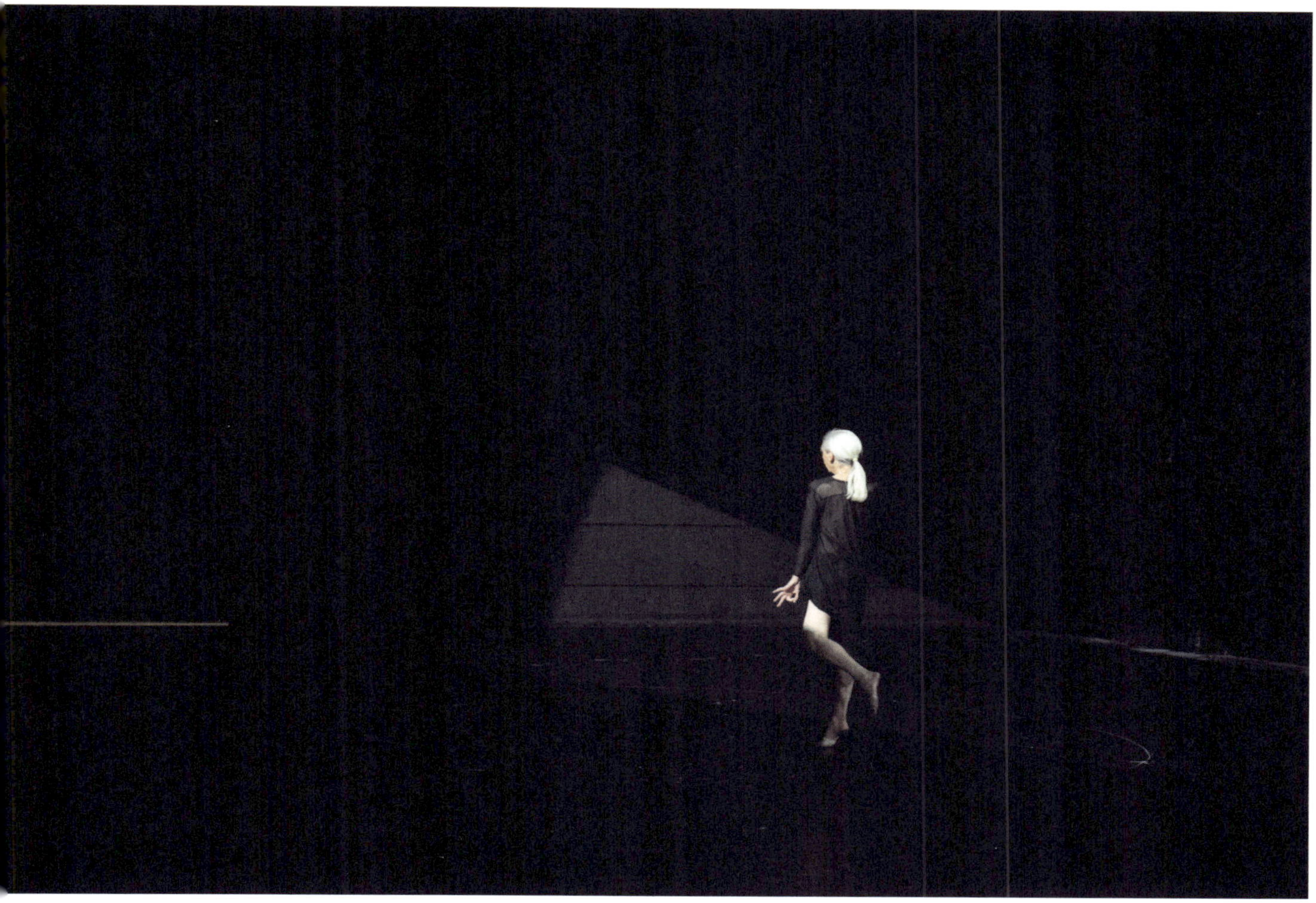

The Goldberg Variations, BWV 988, 2020
Anne Teresa De Keersmaeker

Keeping Still —— *Part 1*, 2007
Anne Teresa De Keersmaeker

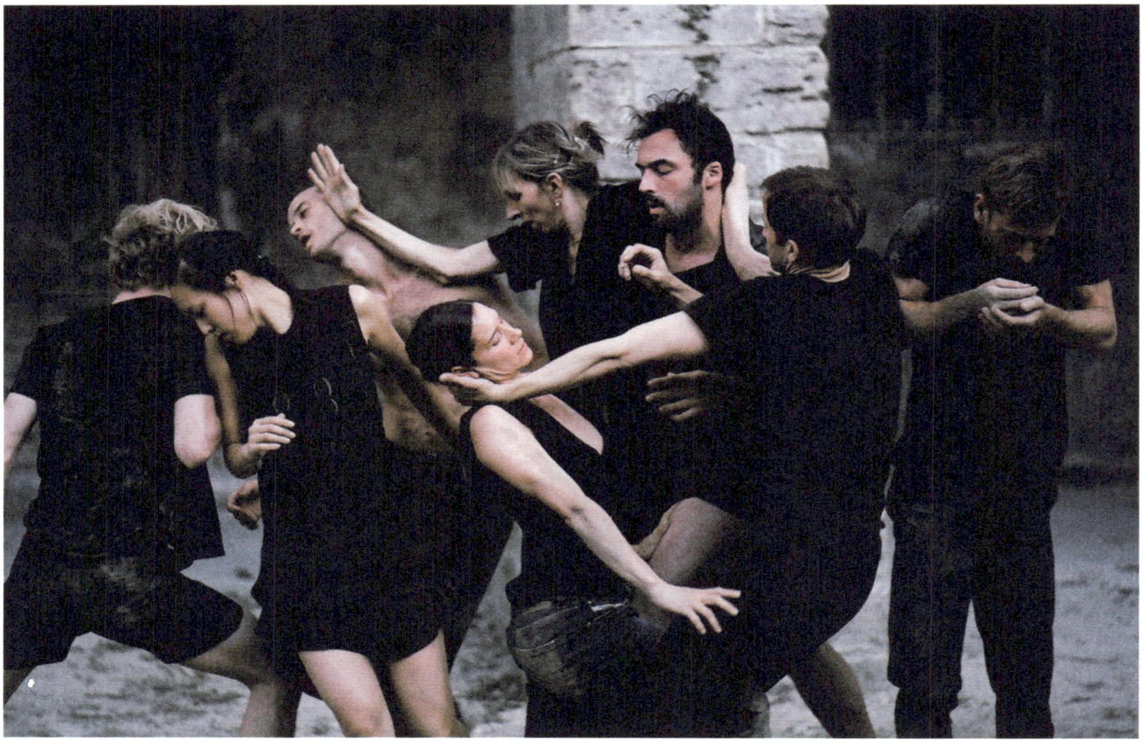

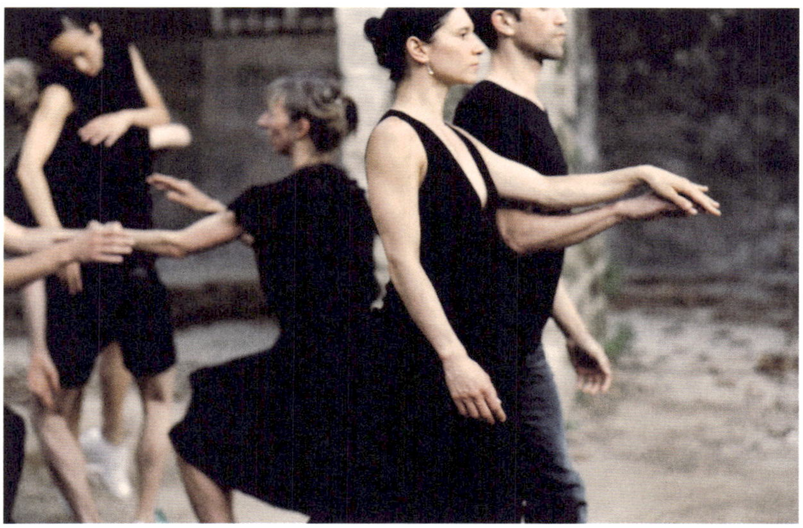

En Atendant, 2010
Mikael Marklund, Sue-Yeon Youn, Carlos Garbin, Cynthia Loemij, Chrysa Parkinson, Boštjan Antončič, Mark Lorimer, Sandy Williams

EDW: Was there another solo?

ATDK: In 2007 I danced *Keeping Still —— Part 1.* That was a special collaboration with Ann Veronica Janssens. Her set and lighting design sculpted the space with light and movement. In that performance, I wore a pair of simple jeans with a white T-shirt.

EDW: In that performance, jeans felt like a departure, a new chapter for the costumes of Rosas. Was it a new shift towards streetwear?

ATDK: That was the beginning of a series of productions in which, all of a sudden, costume was no longer meant to be an issue. We were looking for something 'everyday'. It was the first time I wore jeans.

EDW: In your productions after 2008 it almost feels to me as though they are about the clothes of the performers themselves: a type of realism, with something mundane about it. More recently, in the restaging of *En Atendant*, I noticed how jeans were put on and taken off and exchanged between the dancers.

ATDK: There was a narrative at the core of that production. *Ars subtilior* is a musical form dating back to the fourteenth century at a time when the Black Death devastated two-thirds of Europe's population, including in Avignon, where *En Atendant* (2010) premièred. No one knew where the plague came from. The disease was often spread by fleas or rats, but was also carried by human parasites in clothing.

EDW: In that production, clothes underpin the narrative. I hadn't made that link myself.

ATDK: You don't have to know everything.

EDW: Does the love of clothes run in your family? Is it a legacy from your childhood?

ATDK: There were five of us, all born very close together: January 1958, April 1959, June 1960, 1963 and 1967. For a Catholic family that meant First Communion celebrations every year. These were always major occasions, and I remember my mother having a new party dress made for herself every year. So, once a year, a man dropped by with a large suitcase full of material. The fabrics were spread out in the living room so my mother could take her pick. This usually happened in winter, and the next step was a visit to the seamstresses, 'the ones at Vangerven', to choose a pattern.

EDW: And the children watched this ritual with fascination?

ATDK: Seeing all those lengths of fabric draped about our living room left an impression, but I also thought it was boring. We had to go along to the seamstresses too, and watch how my mother stood there, and how everything was measured and drawn up.

EDW: What do you remember of your own clothing?

ATDK: There were three of us girls and we wore each other's clothes. We were often in uniform. For years I went to school in an apron that we wore over our own clothes. In primary school it was white with blue checks, then at boarding school in Heverlee it was blue with a green trim. What I still like are the name labels we had then, 'De Keersmaeker'. My mother sewed them into all our clothes, from blouses to underwear. My family members weren't particularly interested in clothing. My father was a farmer and my mother was a teacher. My grandmother —— my father's mother —— was born in 1875, and my grandfather in 1865. My father was born when my grandmother was 48. I remember my grandmother dressed in black, in a long black skirt, with her long silver hair in plaits; she was truly the materfamilias. Powerful.

EDW: It's incredible to witness your profound respect for clothes, fabrics, the craftsmanship behind them... and for objects in general.

ATDK: You should see my car! [*laughs*]

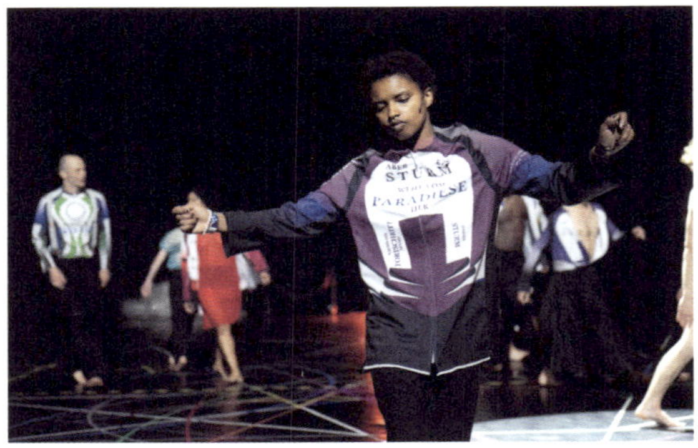

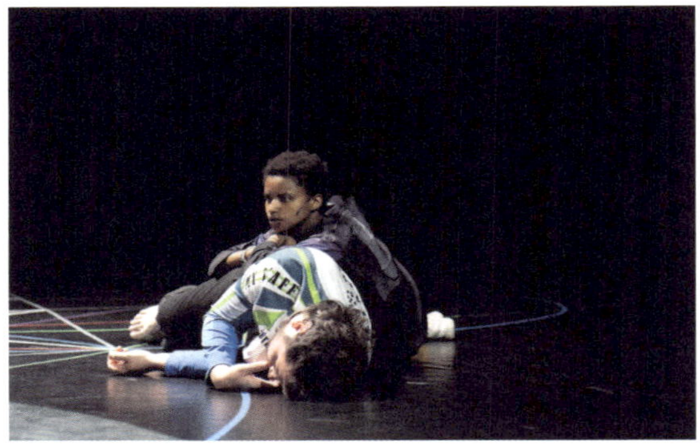

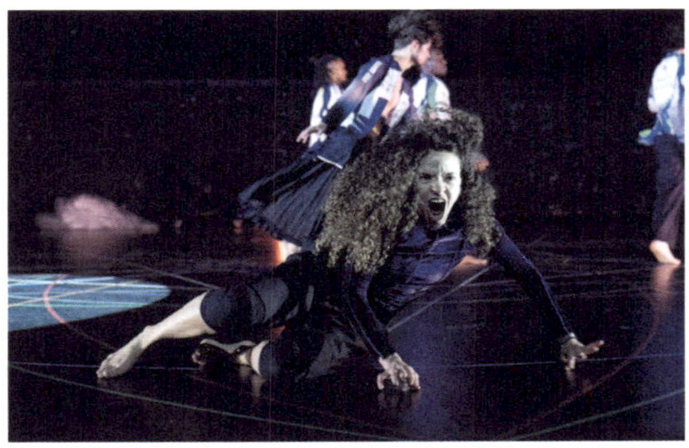

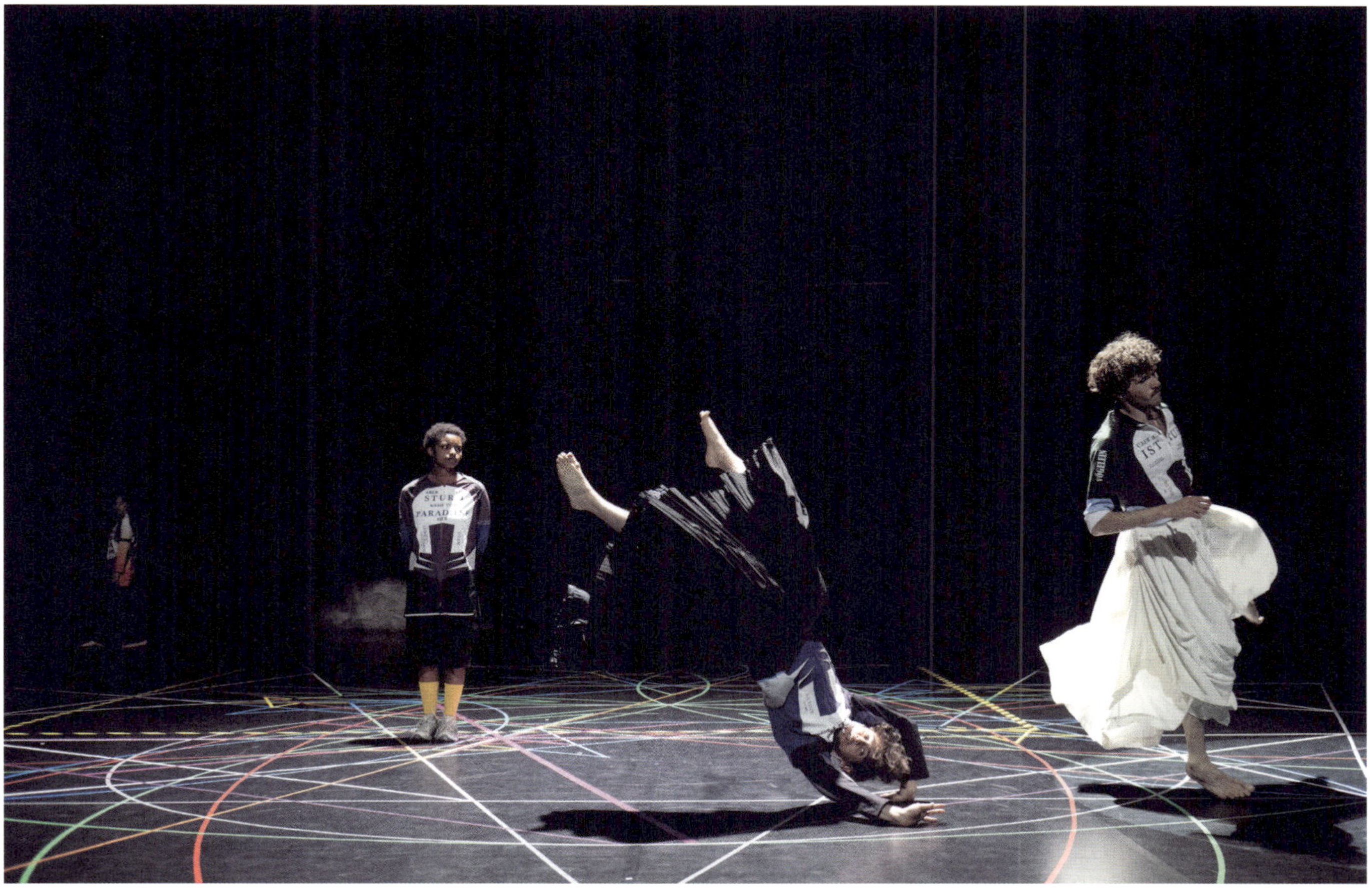

Exit Above — *after the tempest/d'après la tempête/naar de storm*, 2023
Meskerem Mees, Lav Crnčević, Carlos Garbin, Abigail Aleksander, Ariadna Navarrete Valverde, José Paulo dos Santos, Jean Pierre Buré, Mariana Miranda, Rafa Galdino

Costume Designers

MARTINE ANDRÉ & ANNE TERESA DE KEERSMAEKER
Fase, Four Movements to the Music of Steve Reich, 1982

AOUATIF BOULAICH
Exit Above —— after the tempest/d'après la tempête/naar de storm, 2023

INGE BÜSCHER
(but if a look should) April me, 2002

AN D'HUYS
Forêt, 2022; *Dark Red —— Neue Nationalgalerie*, 2022; *The Six Brandenburg Concertos*, 2018;
Mitten wir im Leben Sind/Bach6CelloSuiten, 2017; *Così fan tutte*, 2017;
Kassandra —— speaking in twelve voices, 2004; *Bitches Brew/Tacoma Narrows*, 2003; *Quartett*, 1999

NATHALIE DOUXFILS
With/For/By, 1999; *Woud, three movements to the music of Berg, Schönberg & Wagner*, 1996; *Kinok*, 1994

ELIZABETH JENYON
3 Solos for Vincent Dunoyer, 1997

LILA JOHN
Dark Red —— Beyeler, 2021; *Dark Red —— Kolumba*, 2020; *3IRD5 @ W9RK*, 2020; *Brancusi*, 2019; *Somnia*, 2019

ANNE-CATHERINE KUNZ
Zeitigung, 2017; *A Love Supreme*, 2017; *Die Weise von Liebe und Tod des Cornets Christoph Rilke*, 2015;
Work/Travail/Arbeid, 2015; *Golden Hours (As you like it)*, 2015; *Vortex Temporum*, 2013; *Partita 2*, 2013;
Cesena, 2011; *En Atendant*, 2010; *The Song*, 2009; *Zeitung*, 2008; *Small hands (out of the lie of no)*, 2011

CARINE LAUWERS
Toccata, 1993

ANKE LOH
Desh, 2005; *Once*, 2002; *In real time*, 2000

ESTER MANAS
Dark Red —— Louvre-Lens, 2021

FAUVE RYCKEBUSCH
Mystery Sonatas/for Rosa, 2022

RUDY SABOUNGHI
Verklärte Nacht, 2014; *Duke Bluebeard's Castle*, 1998; *Woud, three movements to the music of Berg, Schönberg & Wagner*, 1996;
Erwartung/Verklärte Nacht, 1995; *Amor constante/más allá de la muerte*, 1994;
Mozart/Concert Arias, un moto di gioia, 1992

DRIES VAN NOTEN
Raga for the Rainy Season/A Love Supreme, 2005; *Rain*, 2001; *I Said I*, 1999; *Drumming*, 1998; *Just Before*, 1997

TIM VAN STEENBERGEN
D'un soir un jour, 2006; *Hanjo*, 2004

ANN WECKX
Erts, 1992; *Achterland*, 1990

ROSAS/ANNE TERESA DE KEERSMAEKER
The Goldberg Variations, BWV 988, 2020; 3Abschied, 2010; *Keeping Still —— Part 1*, 2007; *Stella*, 1990; *Ottone Ottone*, 1988;
Bartók/Mikrokosmos, 1987; *Verkommenes Ufer/Medeamaterial/Landschaft mit Argonauten*, 1987; *Bartók/aantekeningen*, 1986;
Elena's Aria, 1984 (Anne Teresa De Keersmaeker & Annette De Wilde); *Rosas danst Rosas*, 1982; *Asch*, 1980

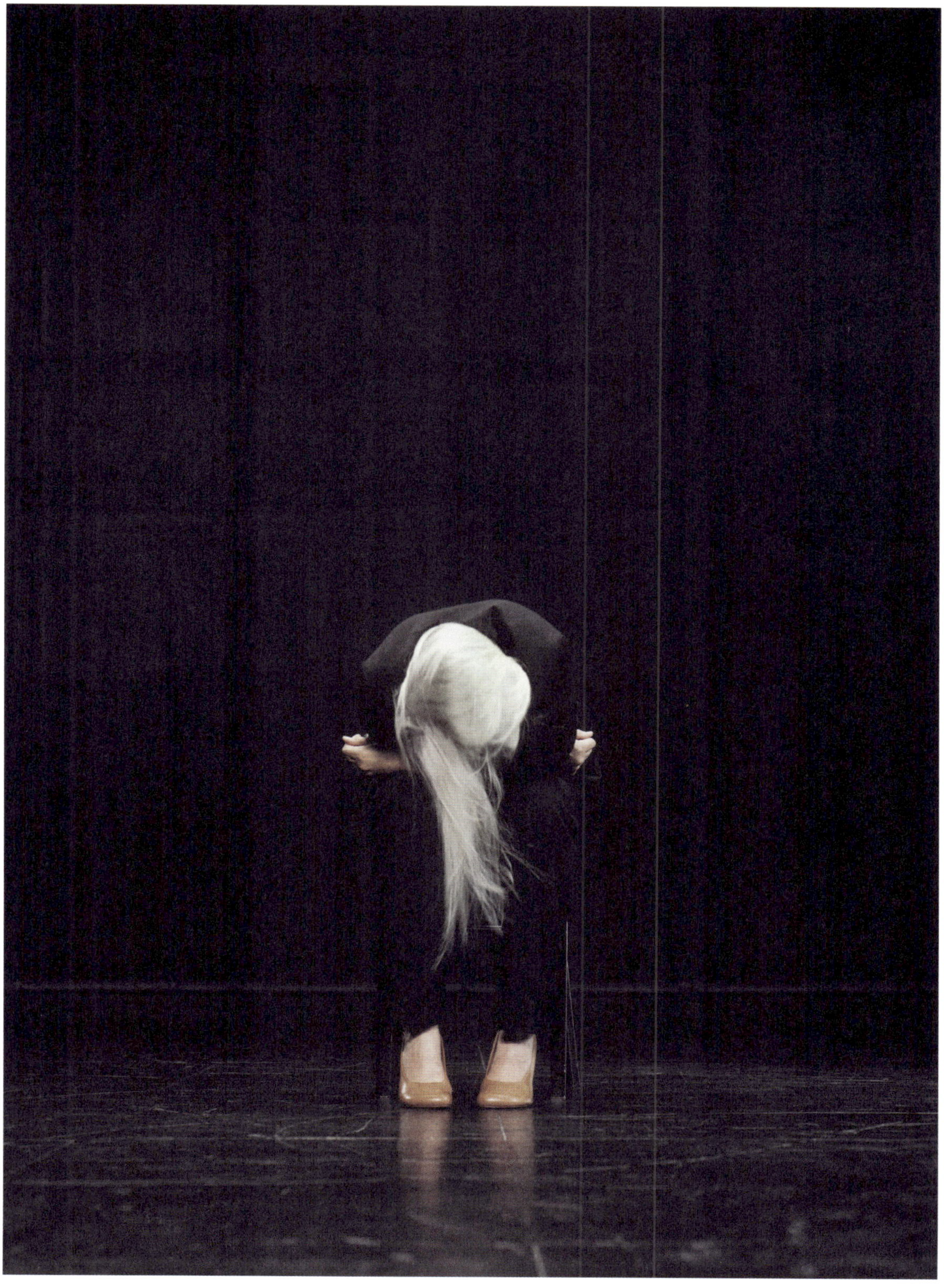

Dries Van Noten's Autumn-Winter 2021-22 collection film,
choreographed by Anne Teresa De Keersmaeker

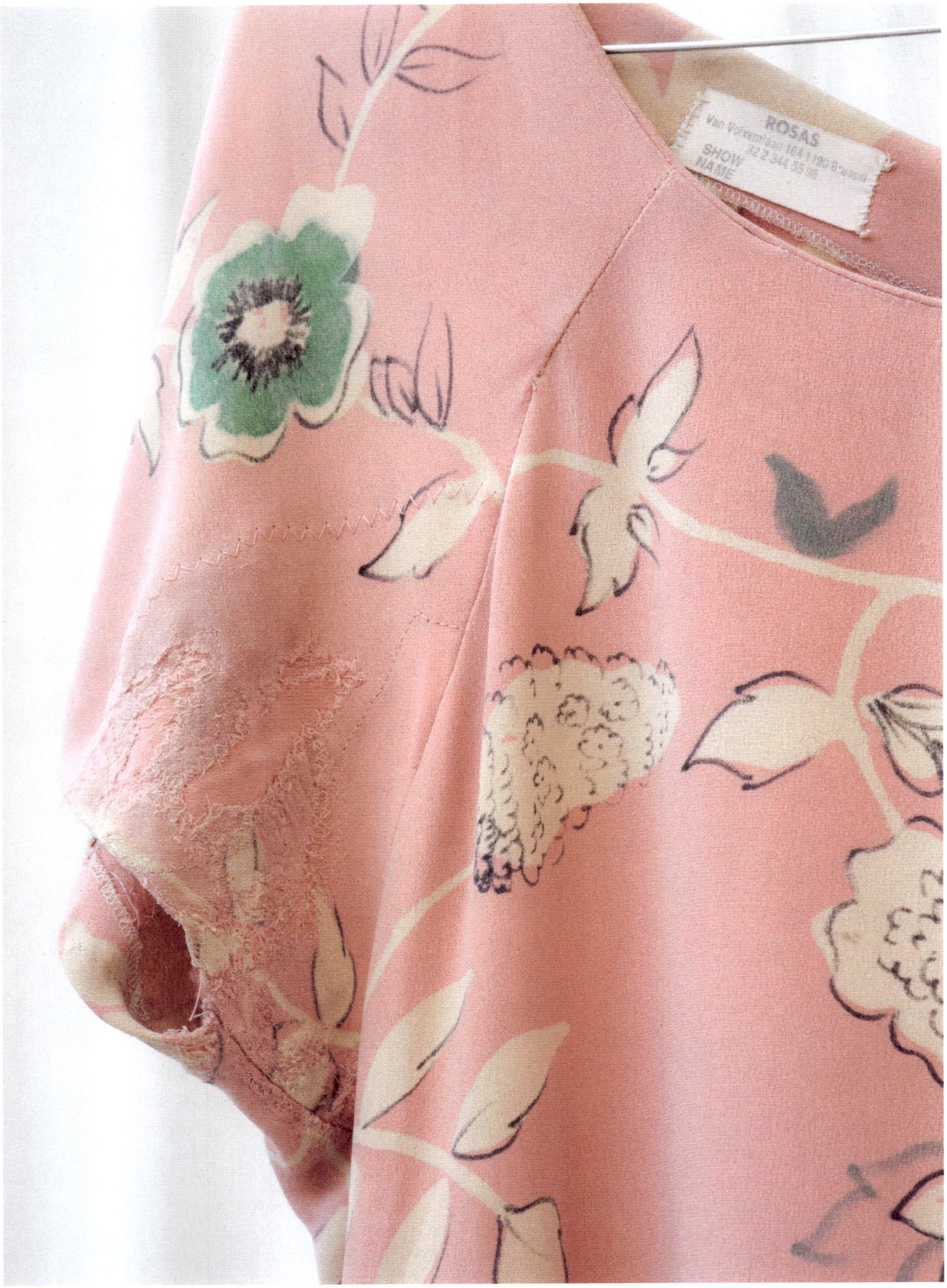

Verklärte Nacht, 2014

The Costume Department

Wear and Repair at Rosas

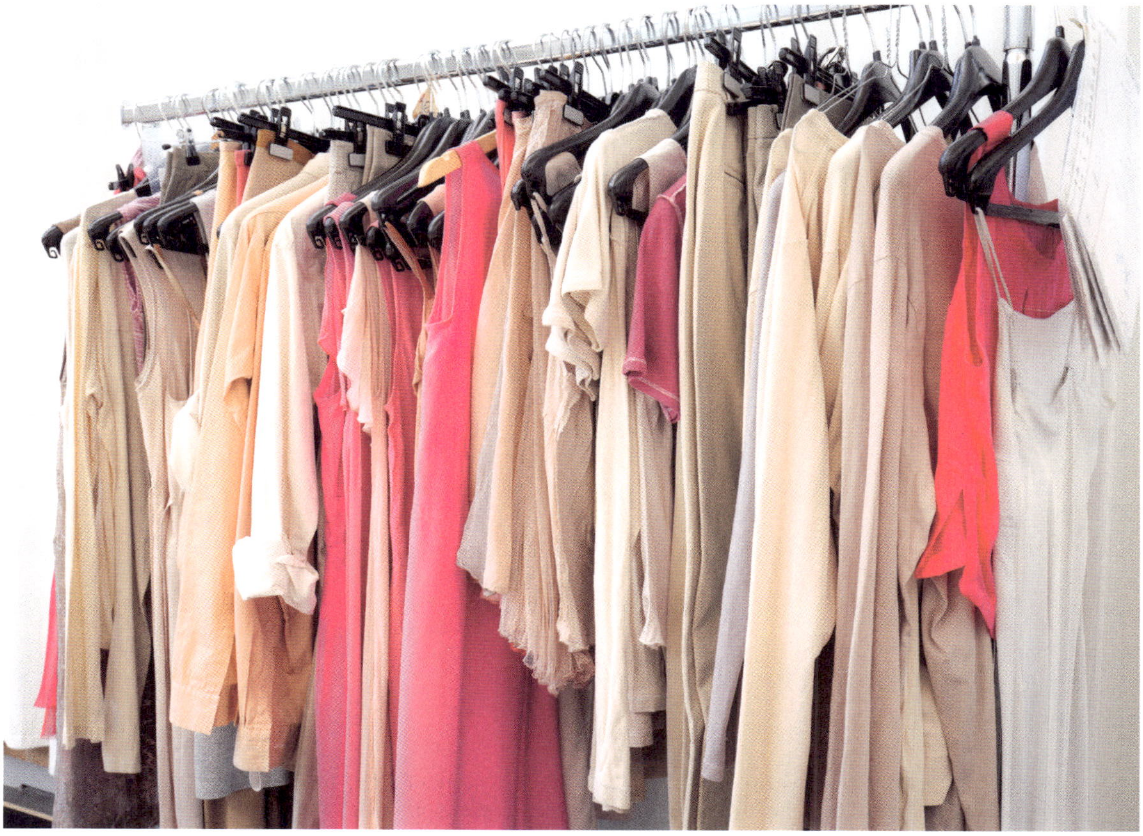

Rain, 2001

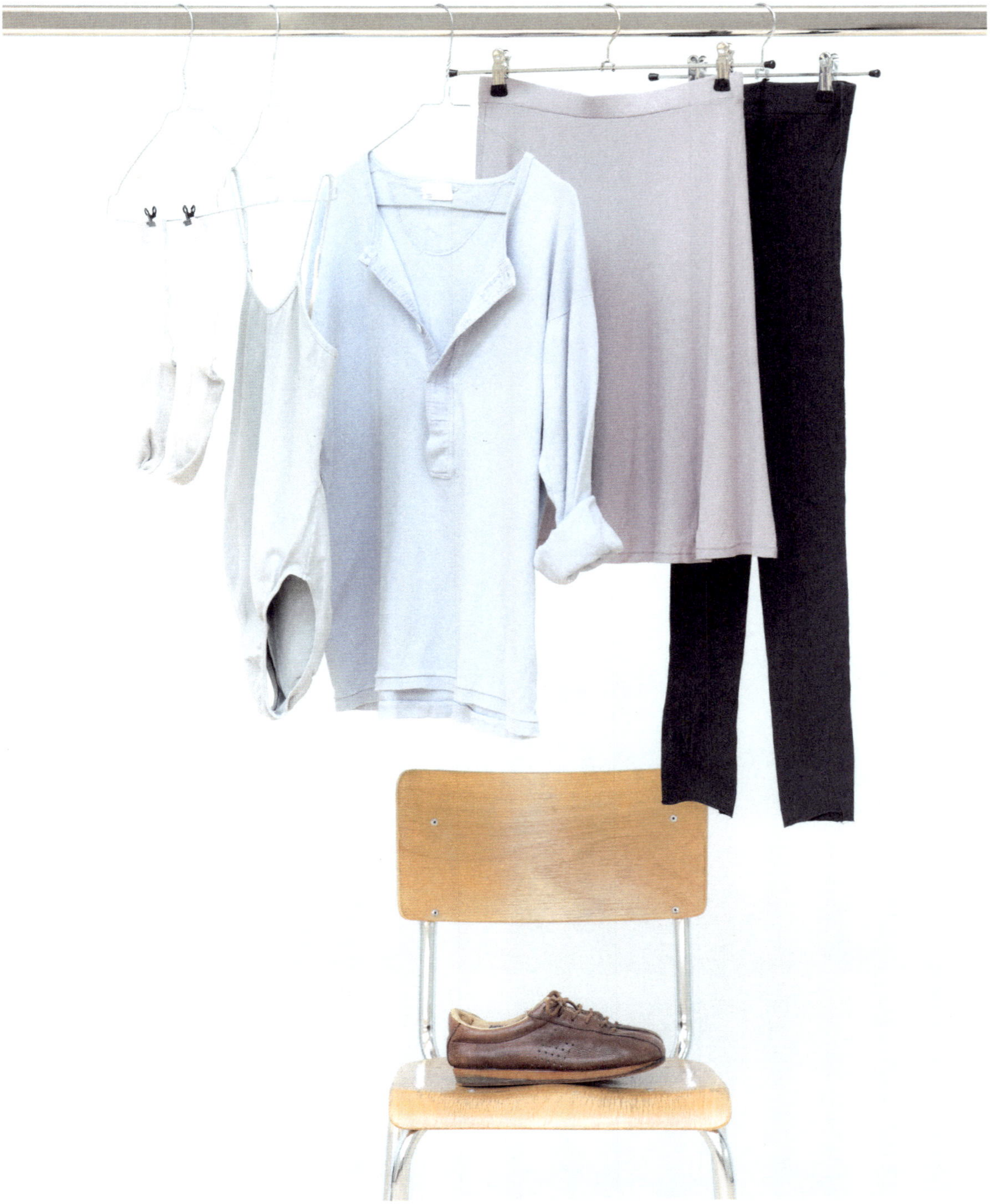

Rosas danst Rosas, 1983

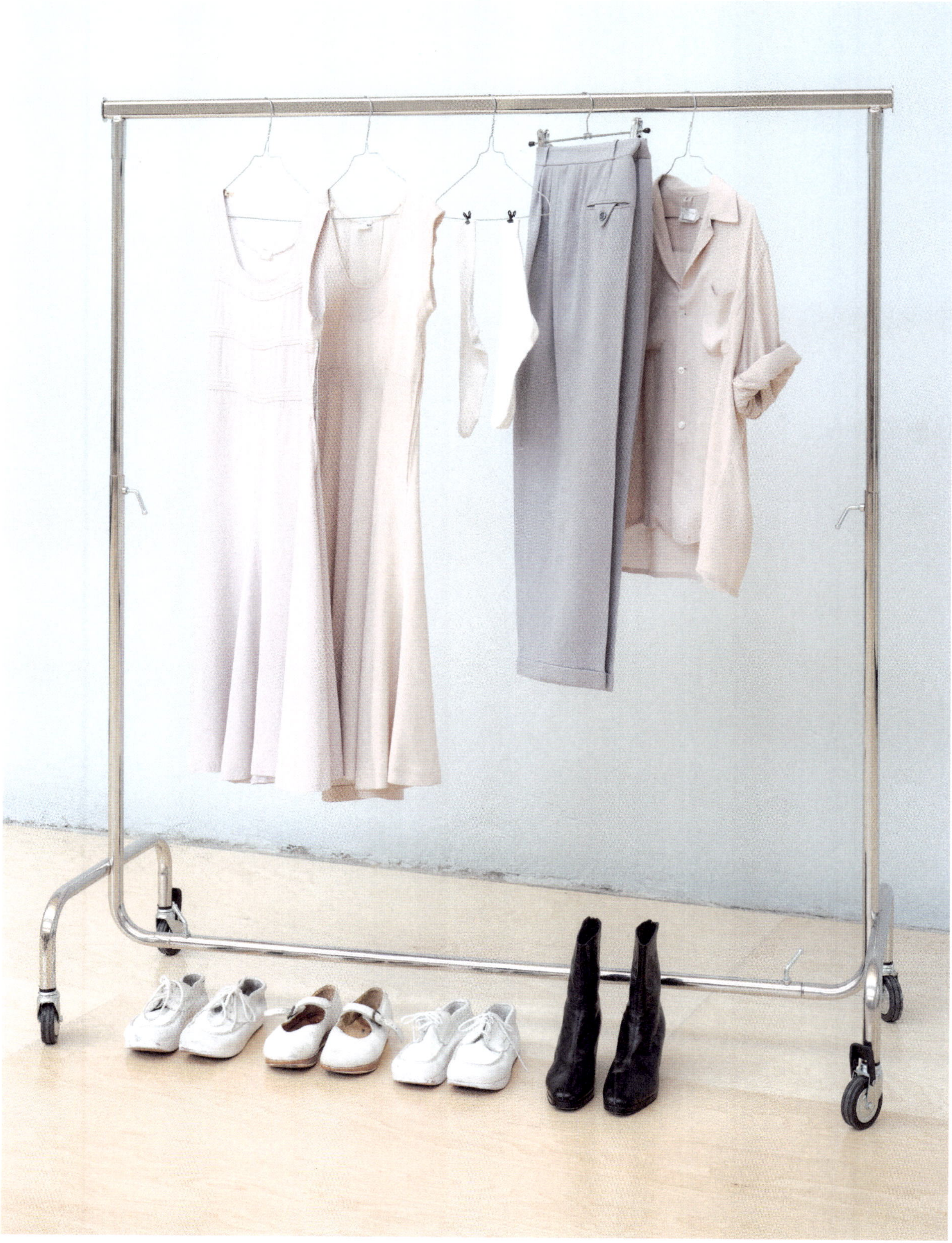

Fase, Four Movements to the Music of Steve Reich, 1982

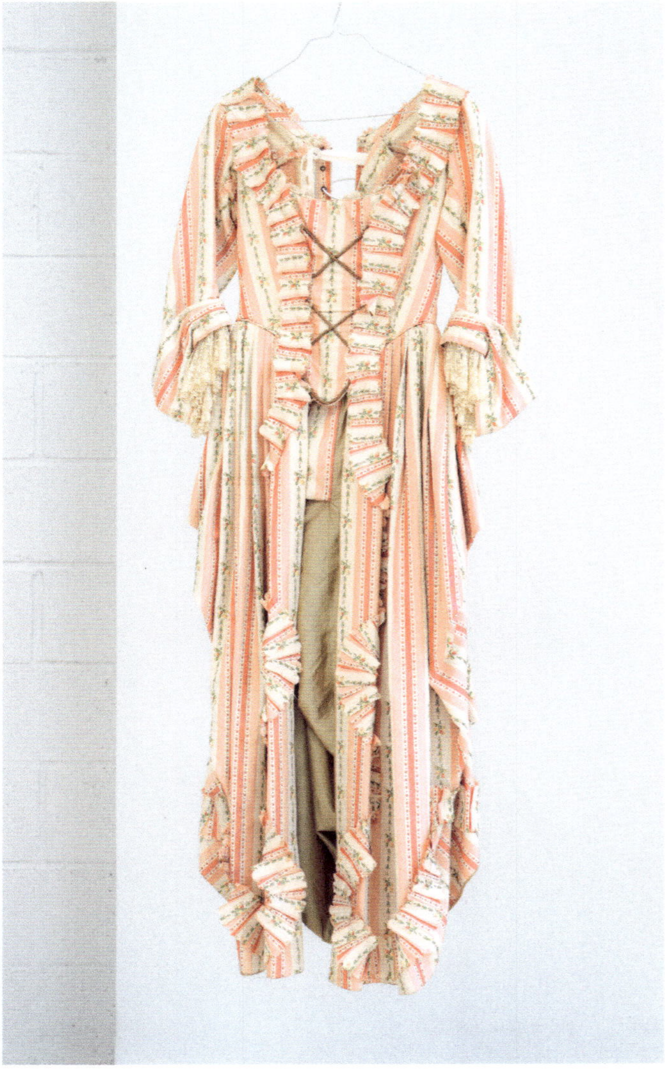

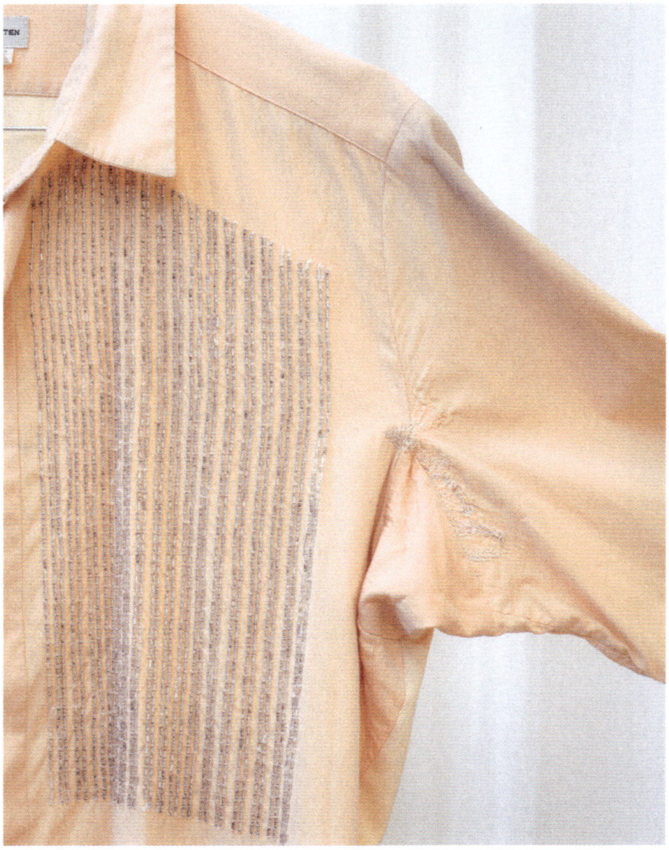

Mozart/Concert Arias, un moto di gioia, 1992

Rain, 2001

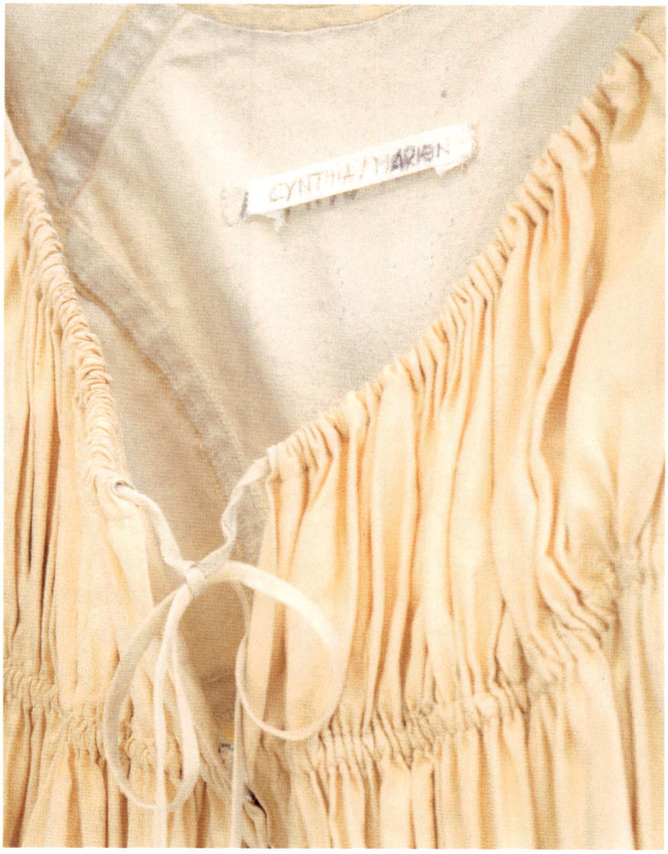

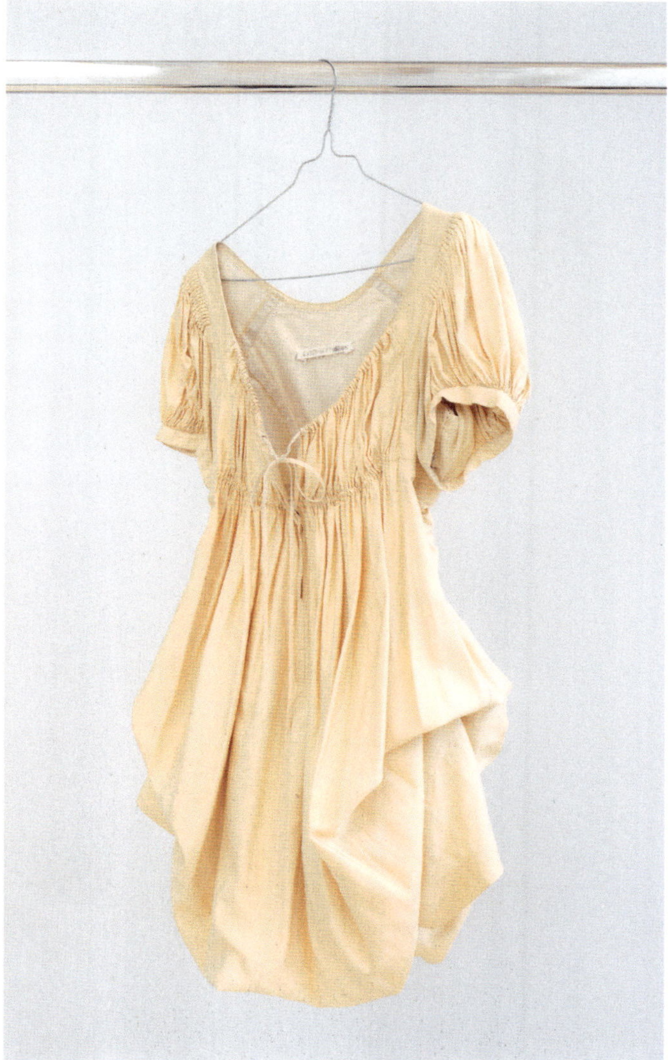

Mozart/Concert Arias, un moto di gioia, 1992

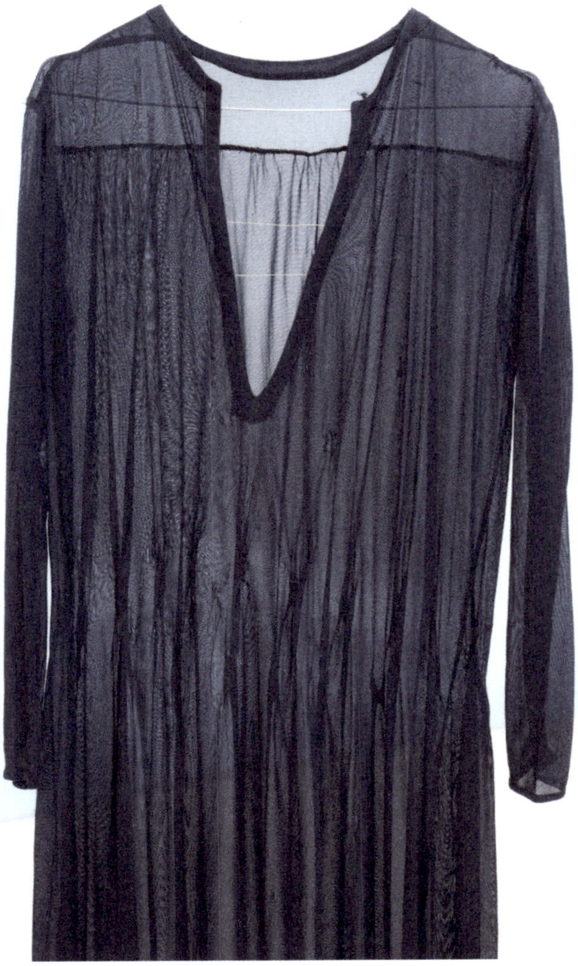

The Goldberg Variations, BWV 988, 2020

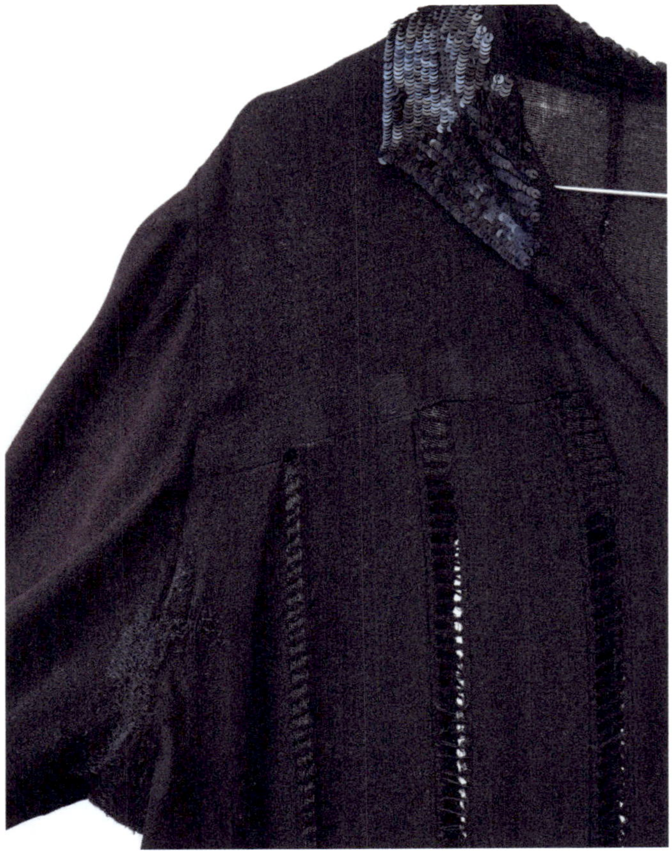

En Atendant, 2010

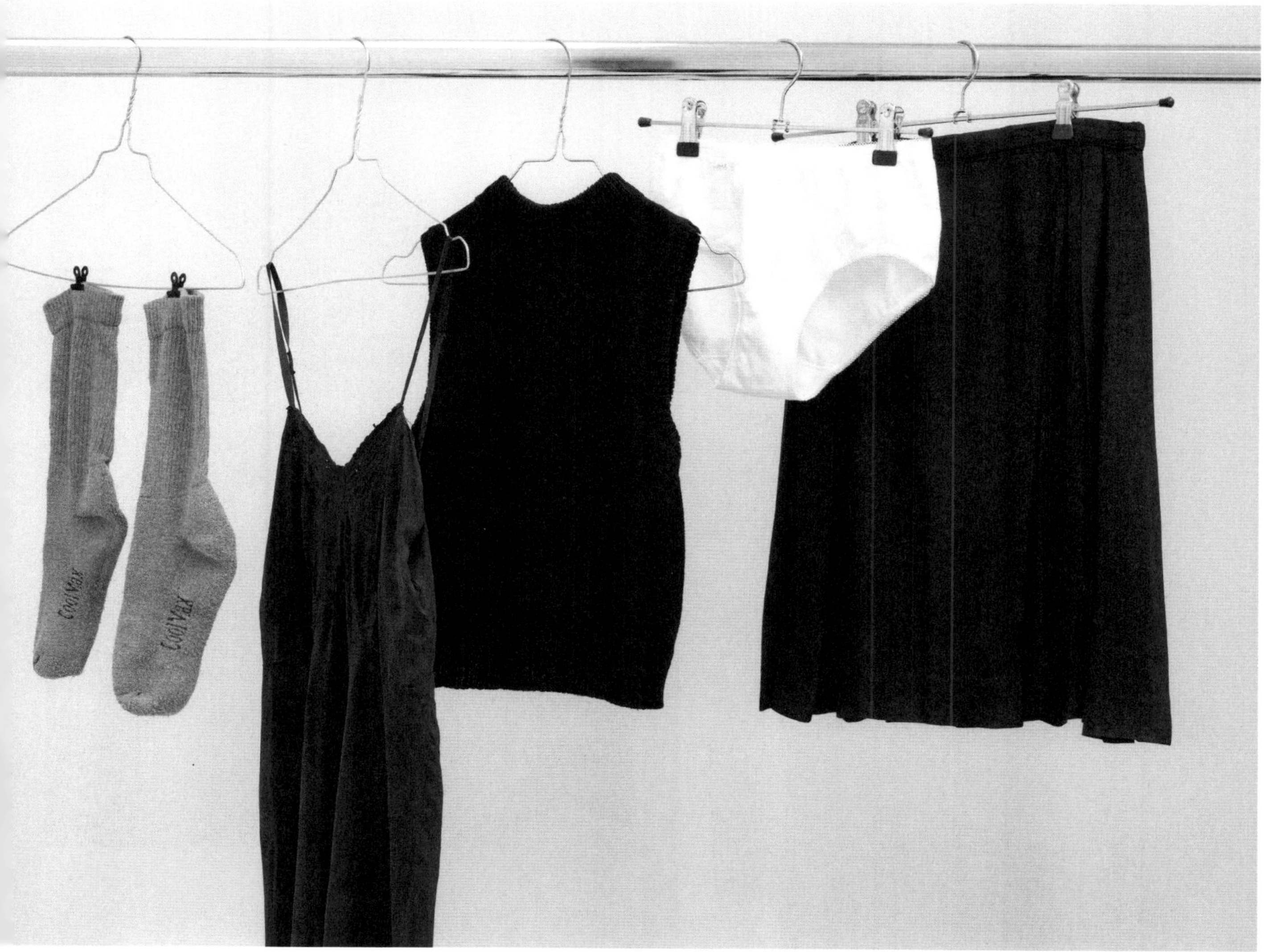

Bartók/aantekeningen, 1986

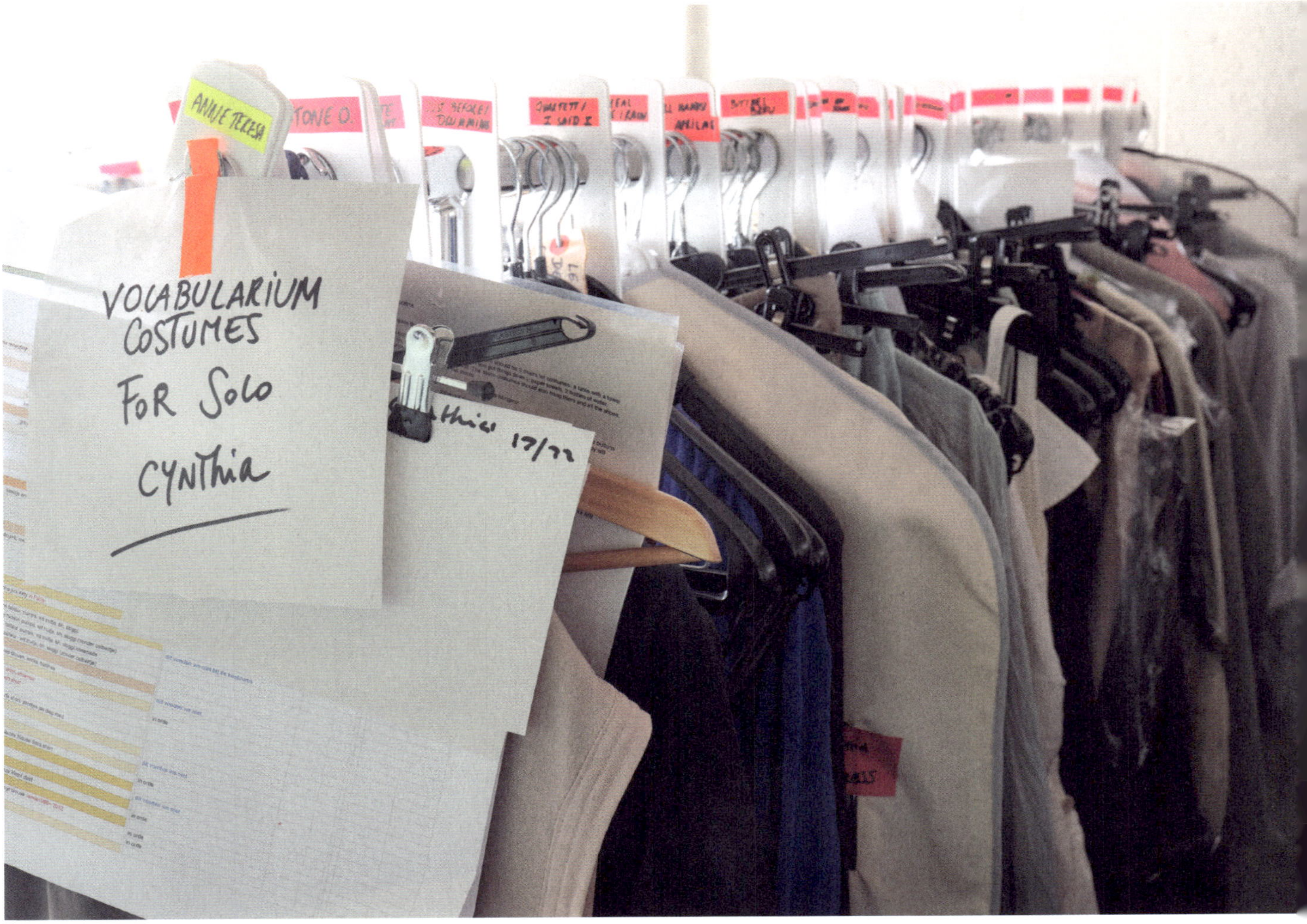

Vocabularium, 2023

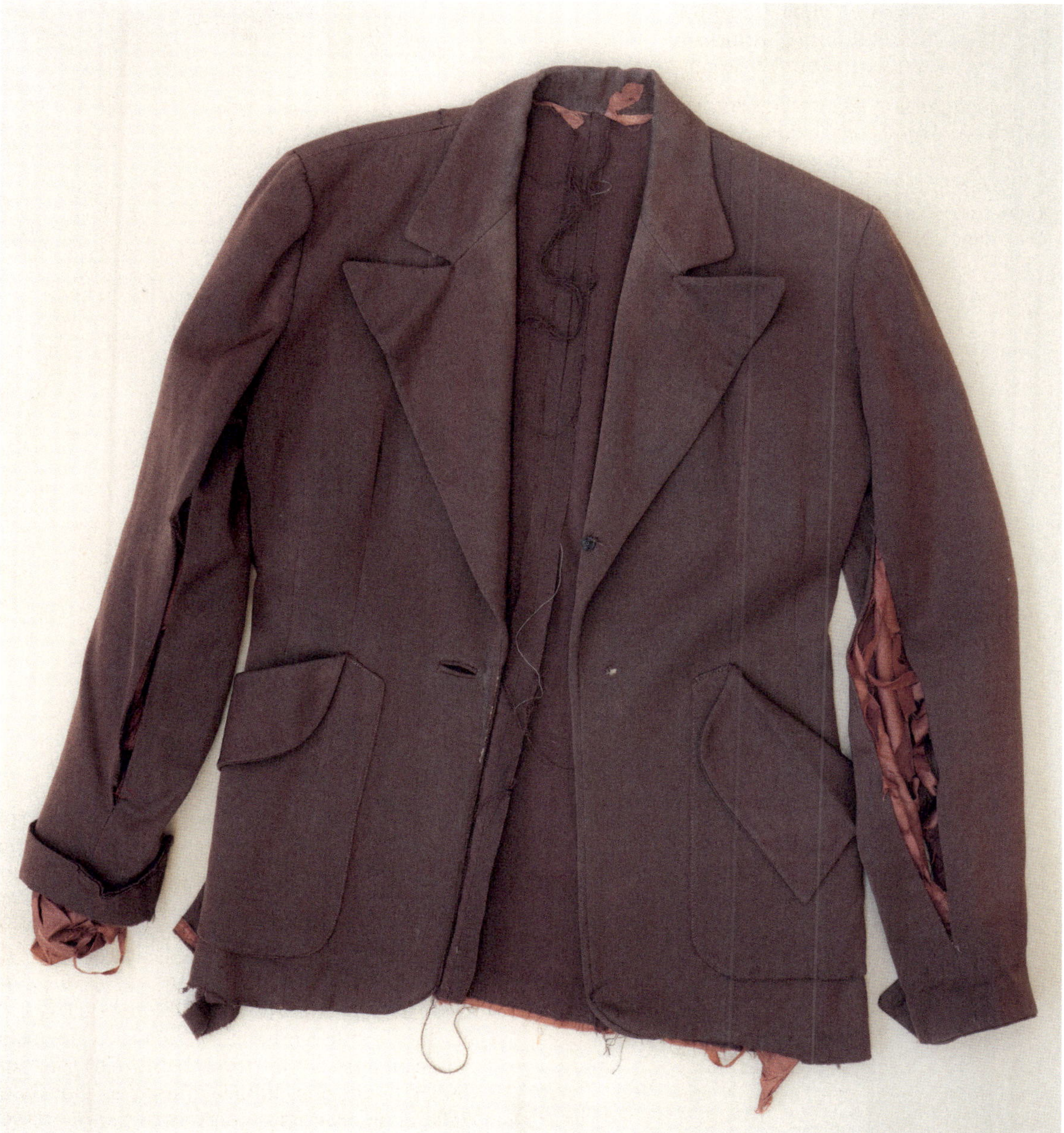

Achterland, 1990

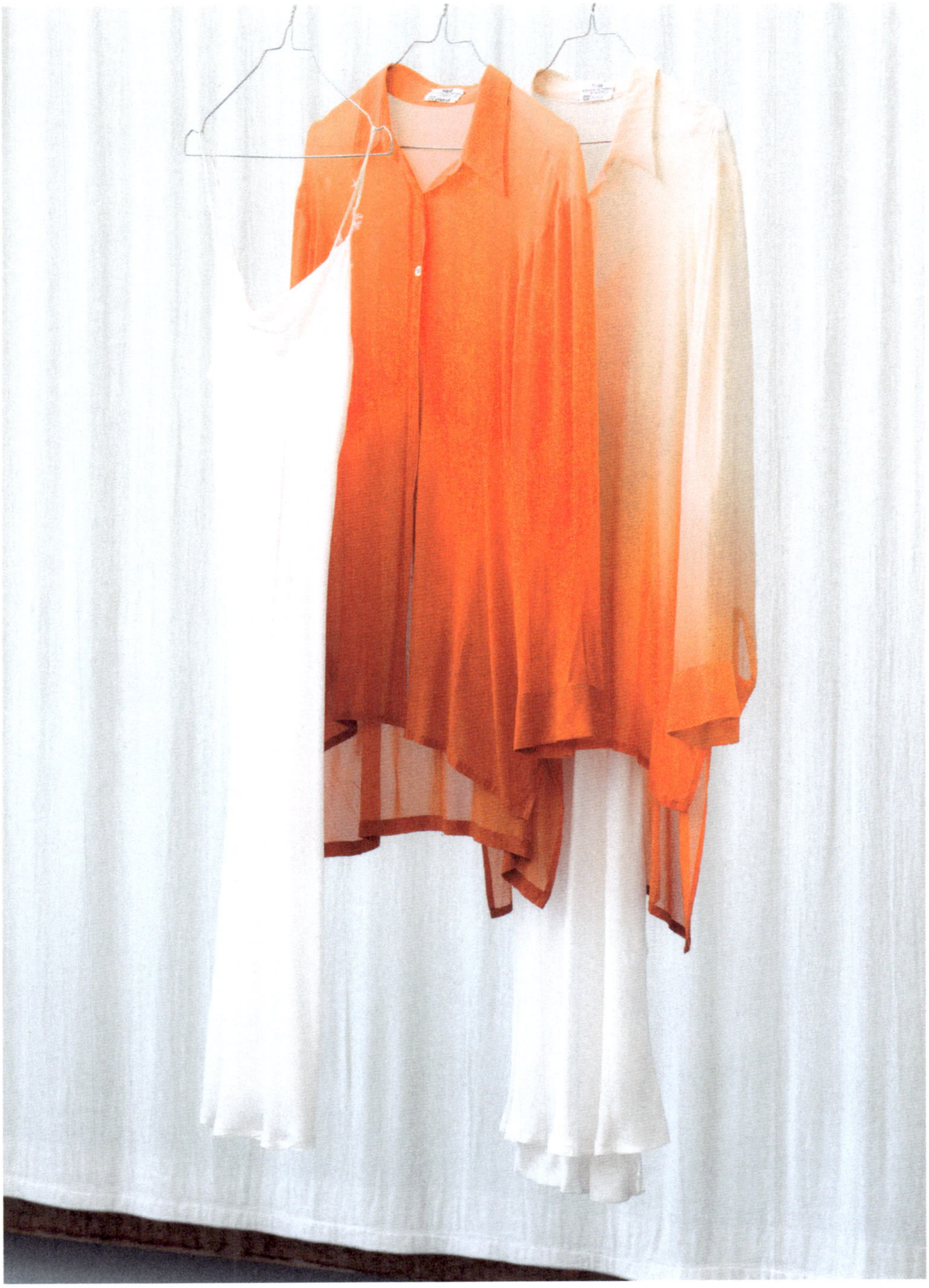

Drumming, 1998

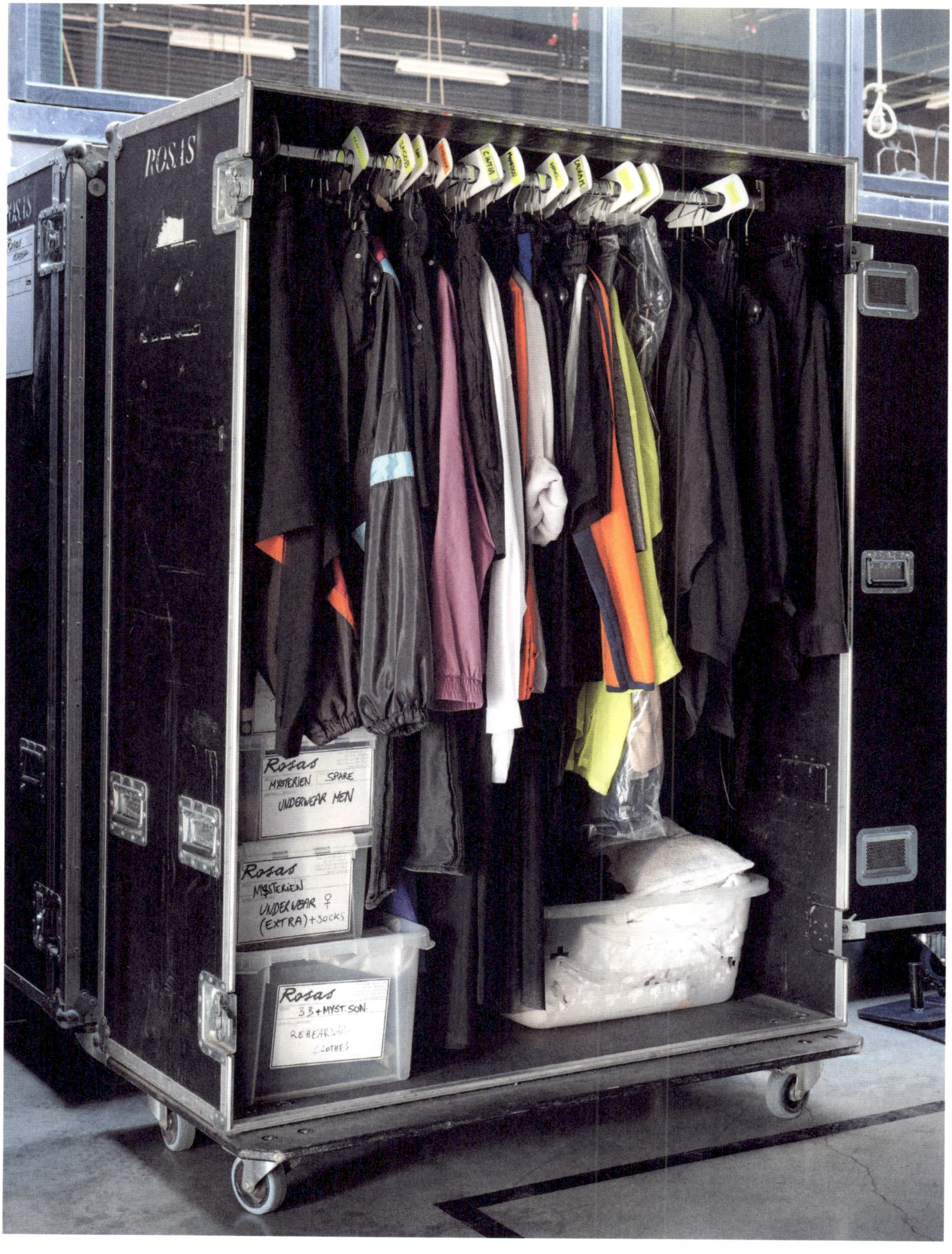

Mystery Sonatas/for Rosa, 2022

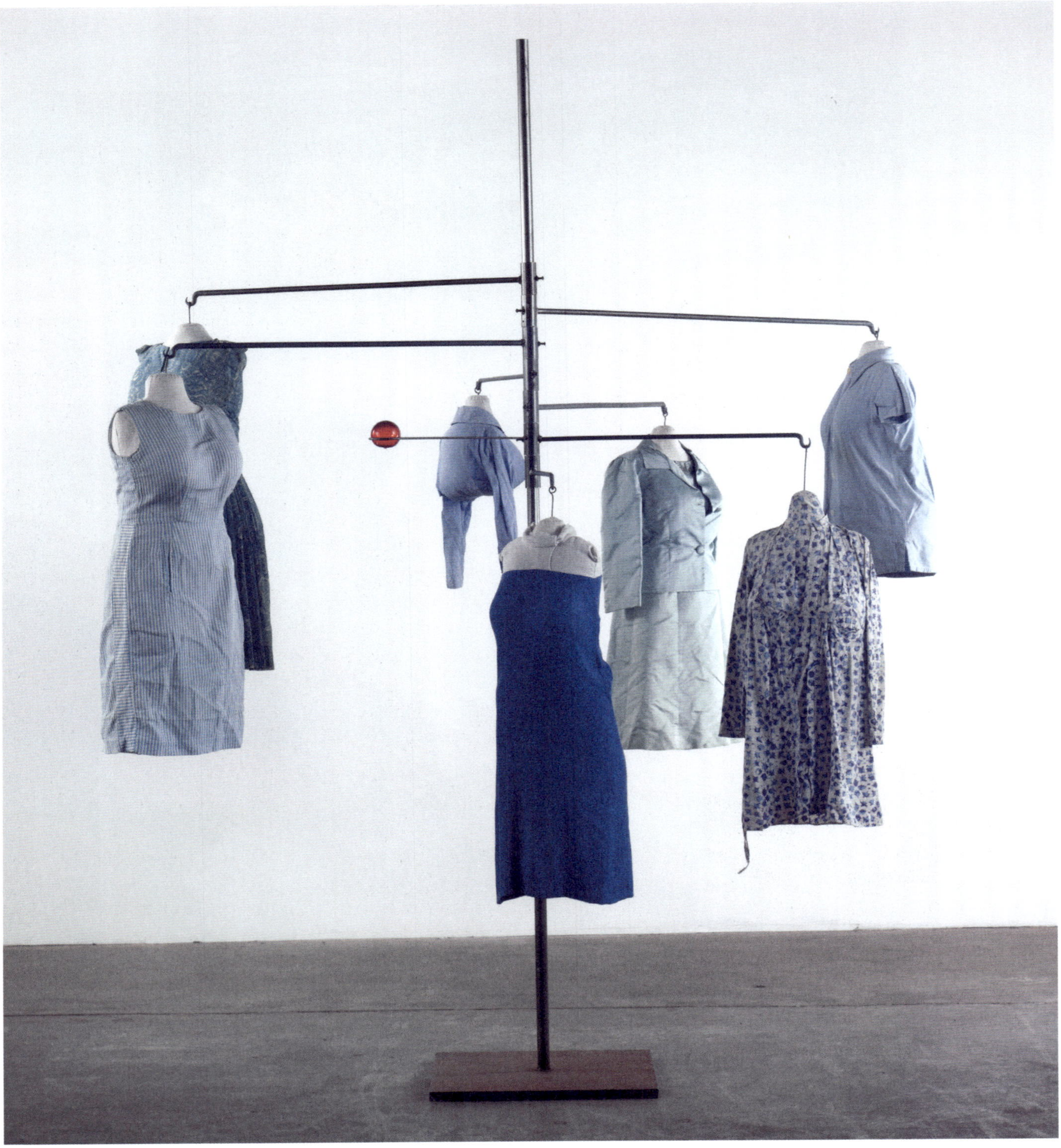

Louise Bourgeois
Blue Days, 1996

CHAPTER V

The Spider / The Restorer / The Conservator

ELISA DE WYNGAERT

ECHO. Wrapped in Memory closes with the sculptural installation *Blue Days* (1996) by Louise Bourgeois. The work belongs to a series of pole pieces, in which she suspended garments on extensions emanating from a vertical axis. In these, she conjured her past selves, her childhood and family members, invoking them by the clothes she had once worn, ensuring that her memories would not be lost. While arranging the loan of *Blue Days*, our team was given clear instructions to conserve the creases and to treat these as evidence of life. They are also evidence of the fact that the garments had been stored in closets for many years because Bourgeois could not let them go.

In technical clothing jargon, the wrinkles in the elbow of a jacket are called 'memories', suggesting the way memory seems to lodge in clothing. As museum workers, we store memories, too. We display, archive and preserve objects. The MoMu Collection grows every year through purchases, long-term loans and numerous donations, and now holds more than 38,000 pieces. The external storage facilities are filled with clothing, accessories, shoes, documents and artefacts that are closely connected to people's lives. Some garments have mysterious stains or smell intimately of their previous wearer. All objects are neatly labelled, protected by tissue paper, supported by cotton padding, hung in Tyvek® covers or stored in acid-free archive boxes. The real enemies of every textile collection —— the most common agents of degradation —— are light, oxygen, VOCs, high temperature, fluctuating humidity and insects. A museum conservator will do anything to protect these textiles and to enhance the object's longevity.

In 1947, Bourgeois made her first small ink and charcoal drawing of a spider. Decades later, beginning in the 1990s, she produced her monumental steel and bronze spider sculptures. The spider became a symbol of her mother, who repaired the tears and holes in tapestries in the family atelier. Bourgeois later took this activity as a model for the restorative possibilities of art.

> "When I was growing up, all the women in my house were using needles. I've always had a fascination with the needle, the magic power of the needle. The needle is used to repair the damage. It's a claim to forgiveness. It is never aggressive, it's not a pin."[1]

In the closing chapter of *ECHO. Wrapped in Memory*, surrounding *Blue Days*, a rather unknown side of the MoMu Collection is displayed to evoke the work and expert care of MoMu's own spiders: the textile conservators. In the coming pages, you will see how these objects symbolise the tenderness of decay and the intimacy of stains and creases. Most of these will, due to their fragile condition, remain sleeping in their boxes and will never again be mounted. These are stories of a life lived, of scars, sweat, tears and joy —— stories about nurturing your garments, about being sustainable and allowing things to be imperfect.

> When I finally am going to get dressed
> What dress will I wear, closets full of
> dresses meet my eyes dozens of dresses
> on hangers, some are old others dusty
> others out of season others are dirty with
> stains in the front, unwearable, I start
> to panic. What has happened, how could those dozens
> of dresses have been neglected to this extent ——
> but I still like them and I have no intention
> to throw them away, nothing will make me throw them
> away, they are my past, it is about my present that I don't care,
> not about my past that I want to understand.[2]

1 Louise Bourgeois, 'Self Expression Is Sacred and Fatal: Statements', in Christine Meyer-Thoss, *Louise Bourgeois: Designing for Free Fall* (Zurich: Ammann Verlag, 1992), p. 178.
2 As quoted in Rachel Cusk, "The Fabricated Woman" in Lynne Cook, Rachel Cusk, Julienne Lorz and Ralph Rugoff, *Louise Bourgeois: The Woven Child* (London: Hayward Gallery Publishing and Berlin: Hatje Cantz Verlag, 2021), p. 27: Louise Bourgeois, loose sheet of writing, 1967; LB-0106 (Louise Bourgeois Archive/The Easton Foundation).

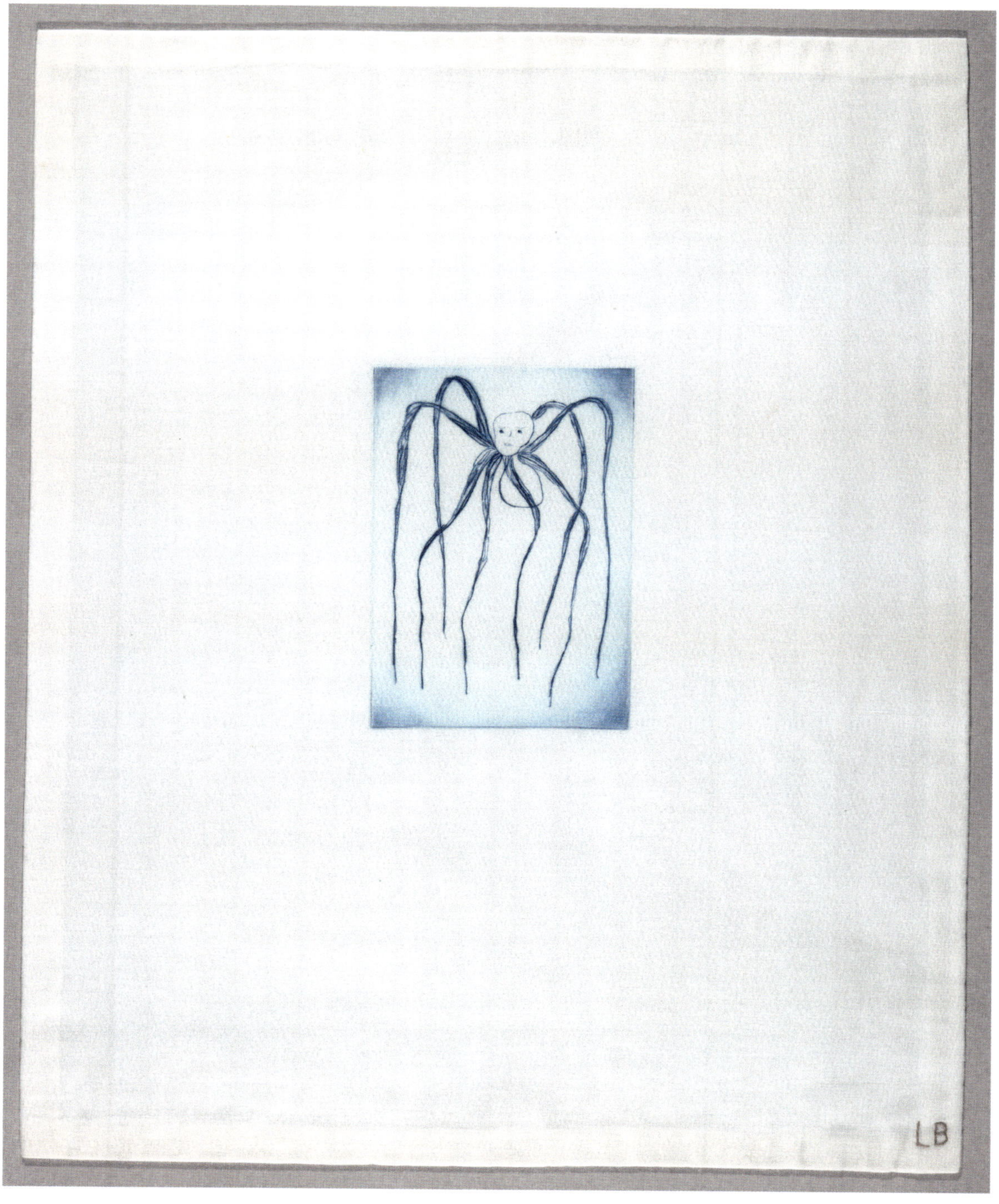

Louise Bourgeois
Self Portrait (Mother), from the series *Self Portrait*, 2009

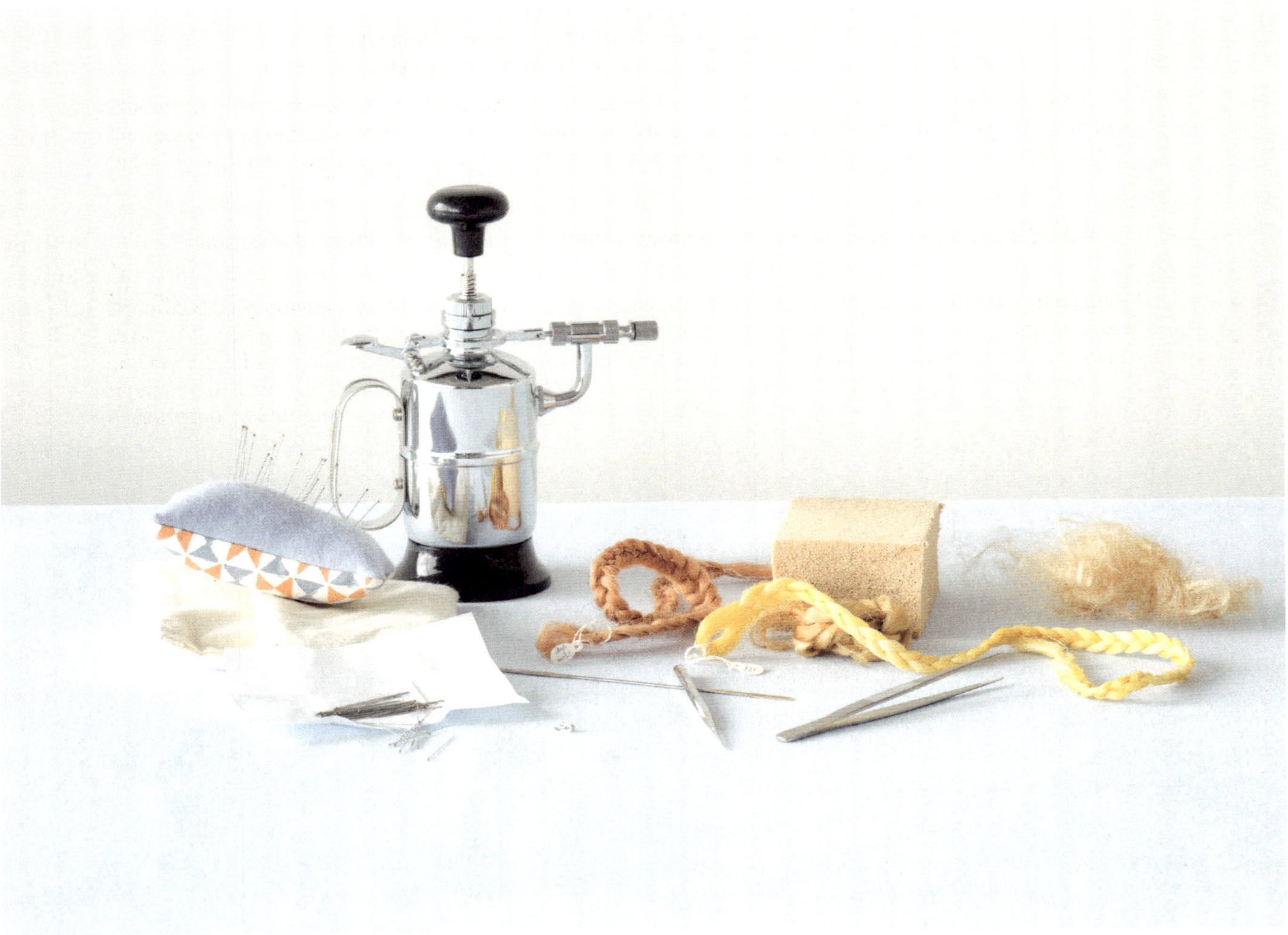

- **Dahlia spray** to spread a very fine mist over an object to be treated for cleaning, to gently moisten an object or to flatten objects.
- **Vulcanised latex sponge, pH-neutral,** to dry-clean textiles and paper.
- **Fine insect pins** to apply a support fabric to a fragile textile. Because they are so fine, they do not cause unnecessary additional damage.
- **Tweezers** for more delicate work. Sometimes to work more precisely when inserting a needle, to apply a support fabric locally, to remove old stitches or older restorations, to take a fibre or a sample for further analysis.
- **Two-ply silk thread** for securing damaged areas of fabric to a support using a long stitch. The conservators dye the silk thread with synthetic dyes that are colour-fast and approved for textile preservation. Colours that match the original as closely as possible are found using formulas. Thanks to this yarn, an almost invisible intervention can be carried out.
- **Archival calico sandbags** serve as weights to level an object.

CHAPTER VI

Worn, Torn, Degraded Restored, Cared for, Preserved

The MoMu Collection and Study Collection

A conservator's fight against time —— imitation leather

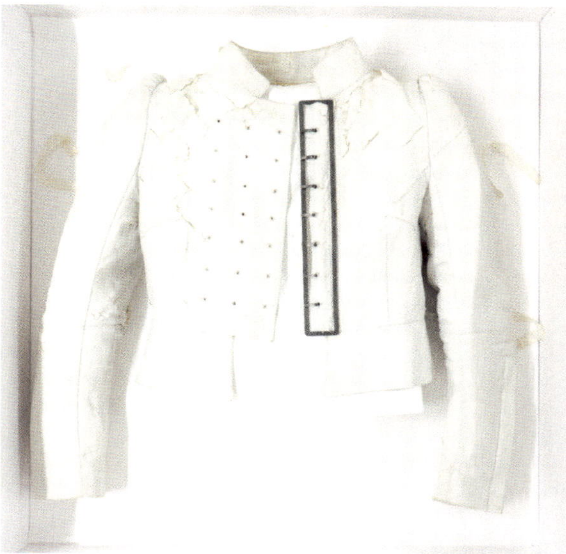

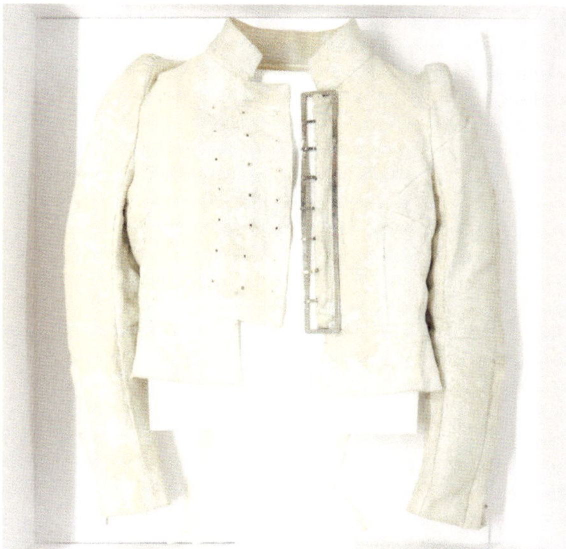

Maison Martin Margiela, jacket: two stages of deterioration, Spring-Summer 1990
Collection MoMu inv. T00/329 and study object

Experimentation with plastics made its debut in the 1950s and was actively used from the 1960s onwards. Coatings were applied to textile substrates on clothes, shoes and accessories to imitate leather or to achieve a glossy surface. Today, it is often difficult to tell the difference between real and synthetic leather.

Over the years, manufacturing processes of coatings changed by banning some materials because of health issues. This resulted in a shorter lifespan of coatings in general. Signs of deterioration include peeling, where the coating comes off, yellowing, stickiness and blooming (white deposits). Shiny coated surfaces are mostly produced by using TPU (thermoplastic polyurethane), a group of polyurethane plastics that pose the biggest challenge for conservators. Conservators at fashion museums worldwide, including MoMu, are researching the best way to preserve and care for these objects.

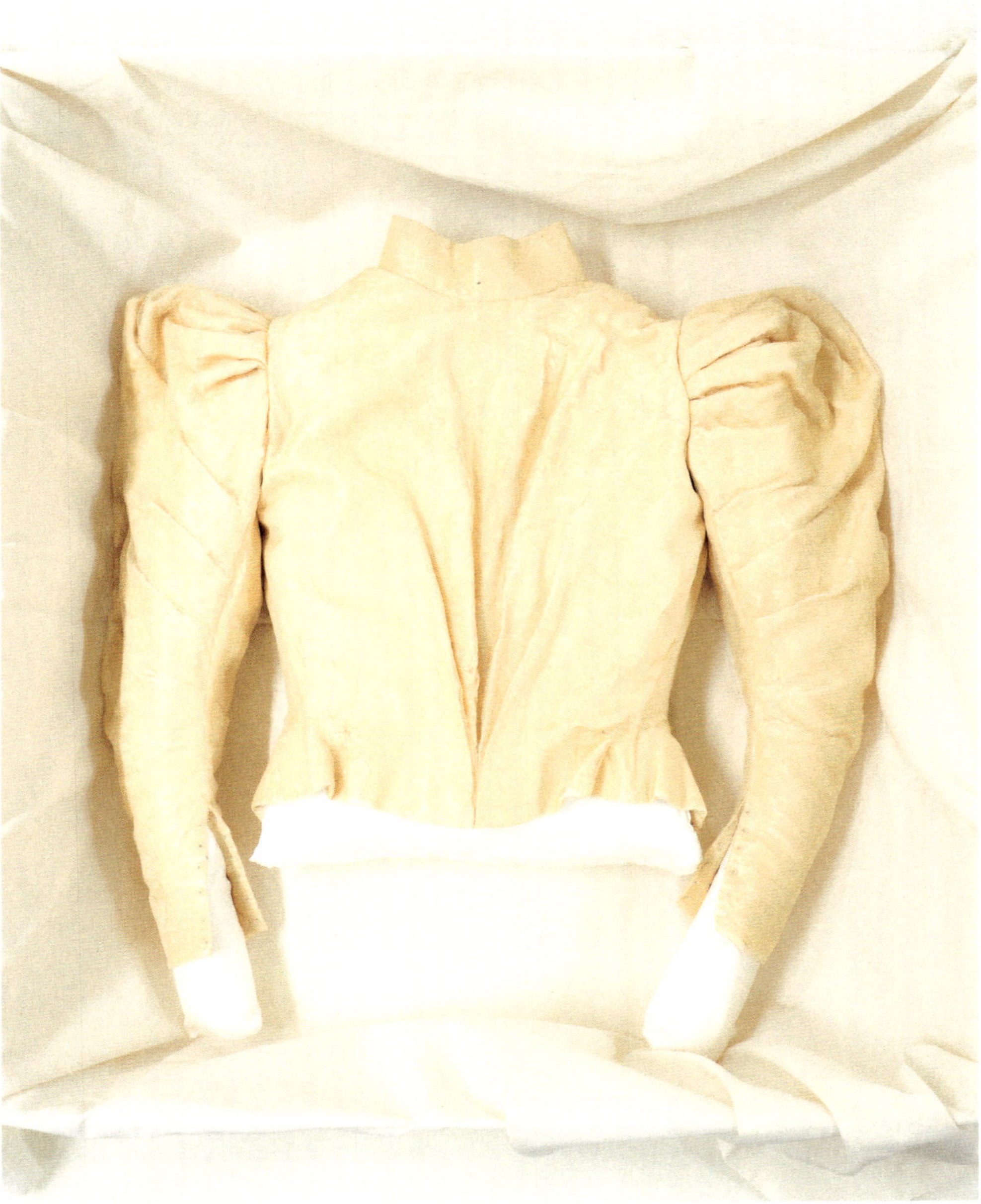

Bodice by Hirsch & Cie, Brussels, c.1890–1900
Collection MoMu inv. T82/126

This weighted silk satin bodice has been restored. As treatment began, the silk started to shatter. Backing fabric was applied in places to strengthen the largest sections. The most effective way to keep the original silk in place was to encase the bodice entirely in silk crepeline. The silk will continue to decay, but this barely visible layer offers support and prevents the loss of the original material.

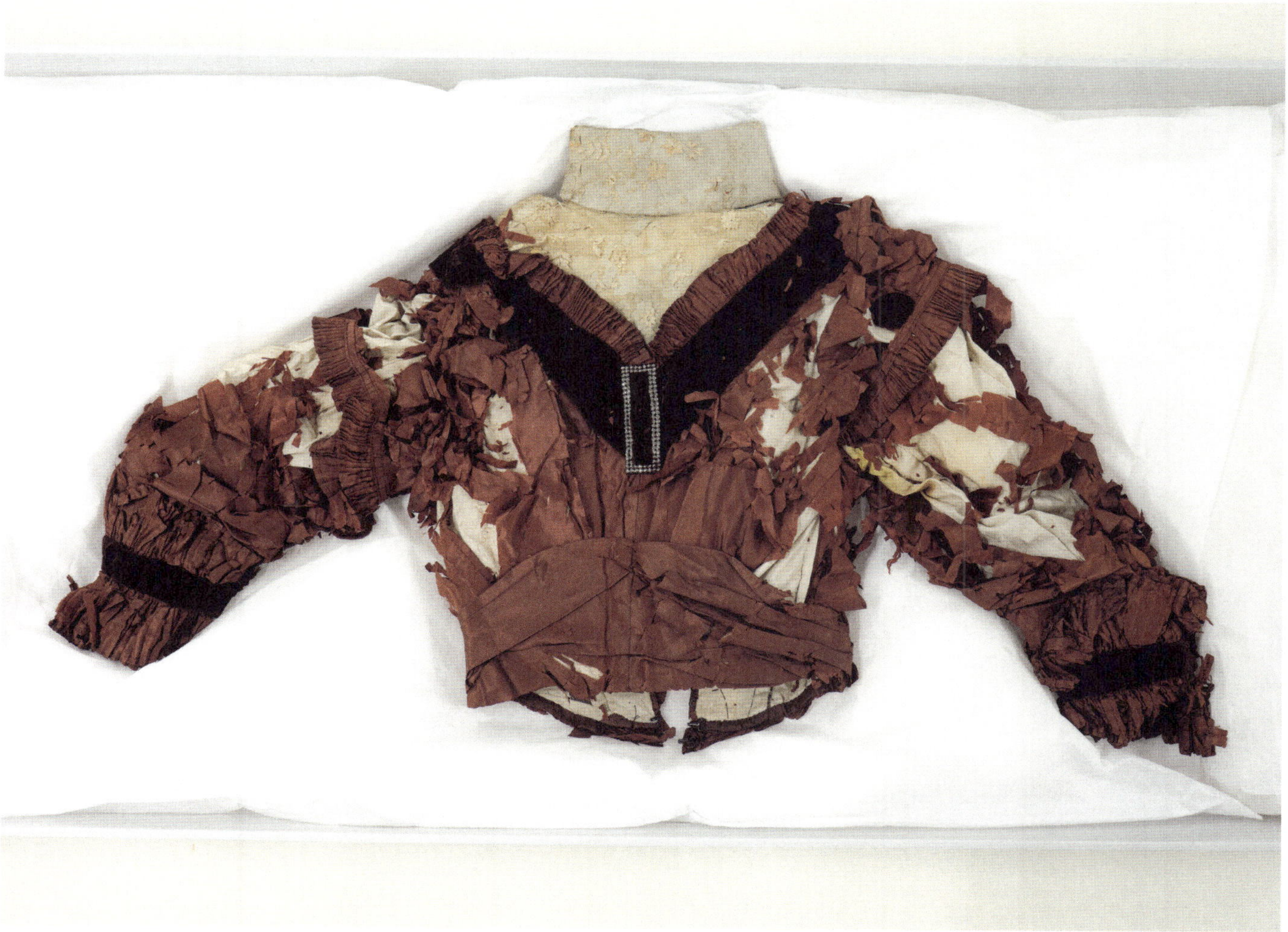

Bodice, *c.*1880–1900
Study Collection inv. ST81124A

From the late nineteenth century to around 1950, silk was often weighted using chemical solutions based on salts of iron, tin and lead to enhance its value, lustre and weight. Silk was sold by weight, and the greater the weight of the fabric, the higher the selling price. Weighting also improved certain processes such as dyeing. Conserving weighted silk presents complex challenges. Numerous studies have attempted to identify conservation treatments. Given their frailty, weighted silk garments shatter and gradually disintegrate; there is an almost poetic fragility in this process. Depending on the fabric treatment and use, weighted silks were known to start shattering after several years. In 1930, new legislation obliged manufacturers to label silks that had been weighted. Delicate objects of this kind are rarely exhibited.

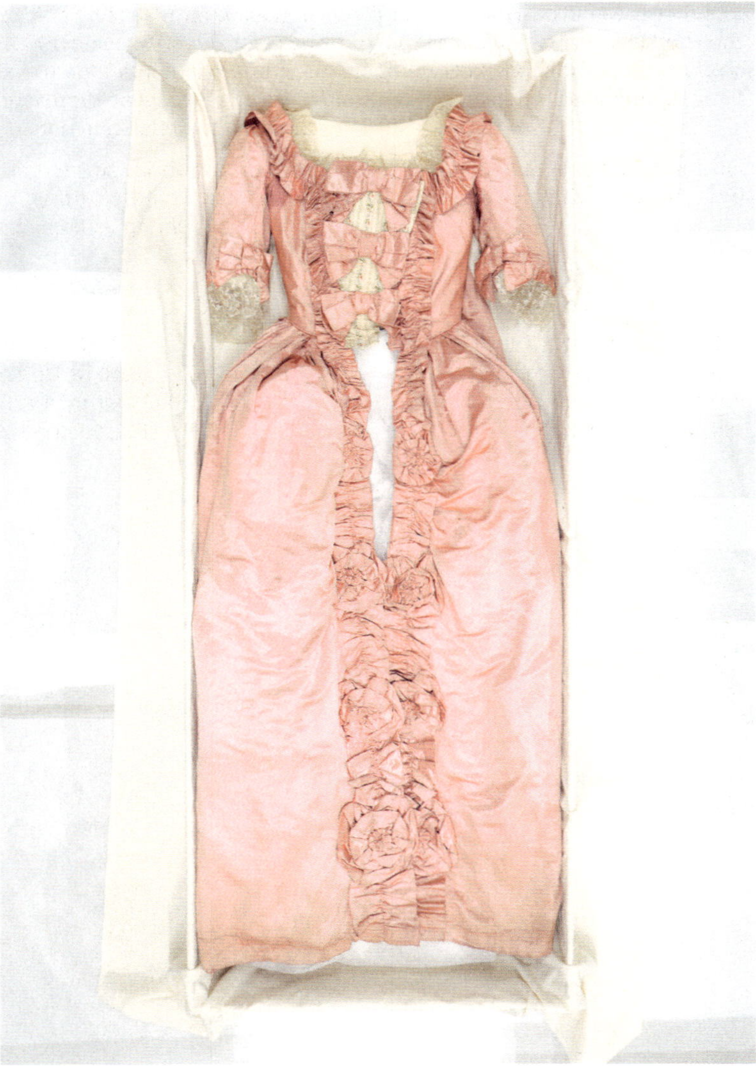

Gown made by C. Palm, The Hague, *c.*1900–1905
Collection MoMu inv. T12/1309/J236

This fancy dress gown made of silk, cotton and machine lace dates from 1900 and is inspired by an eighteenth-century *robe à la française* with a Watteau pleat. Historical dresses also fascinated previous generations, a reminder that we, too, are living in a brief moment in world history. In the 1900s, costume balls were popular. Those who could, wore vintage attire that had ended up in dressing-up boxes. Others had fancy dress outfits specially made, often dressing up as historical figures, such as the French queen Marie Antoinette and the royal mistress Madame de Pompadour. Vintage garments and new costumes were altered regularly and worn time after time. This gown is in remarkably good condition. Perspiration stains around the armpits have weakened the silk significantly, causing the fabric to decay. This type of damage is common in historical garments, and the site of the damage made it difficult, if not impossible, to mount the objects for display.

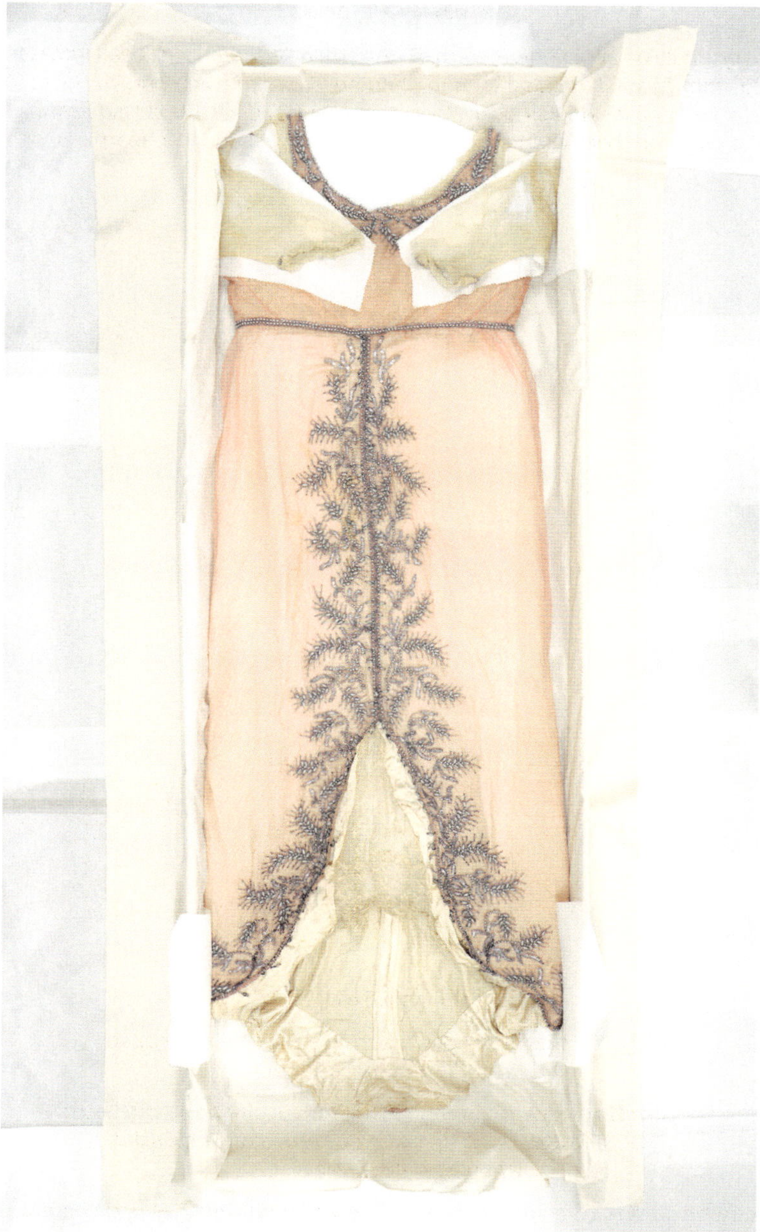

Evening gown by Maison Vandenbemden, Brussels, *c.*1910–1913
Collection MoMu inv. T04/49

The heavy wooden aluminium-coloured beaded embroidery on the pink silk voile makes the fabric very fragile and turns this dress into a sleeping beauty: it must lie flat and can no longer be displayed on a mannequin. Made of crepeline silk, the sleeves are torn in several places and are so delicate that the garment is almost too fragile to move.

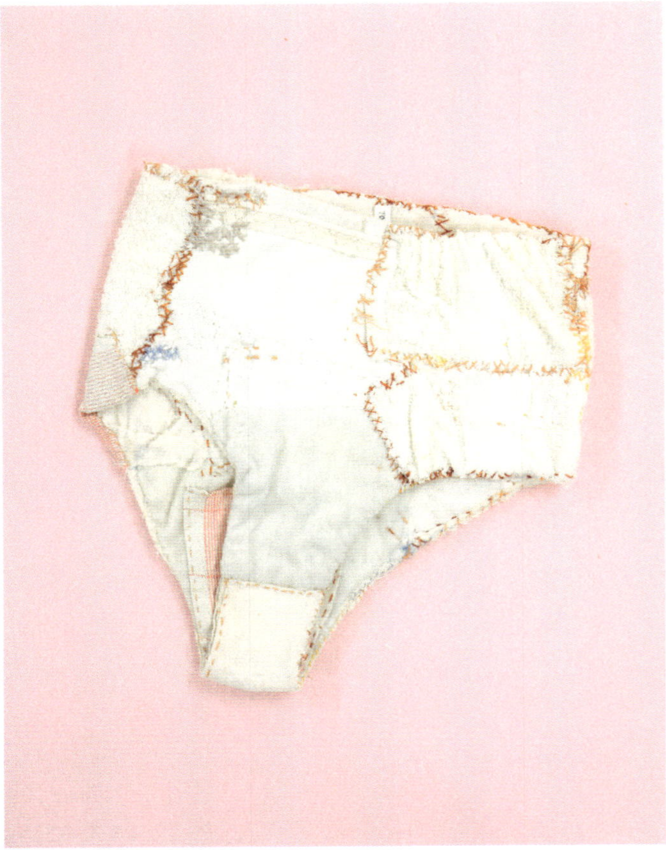

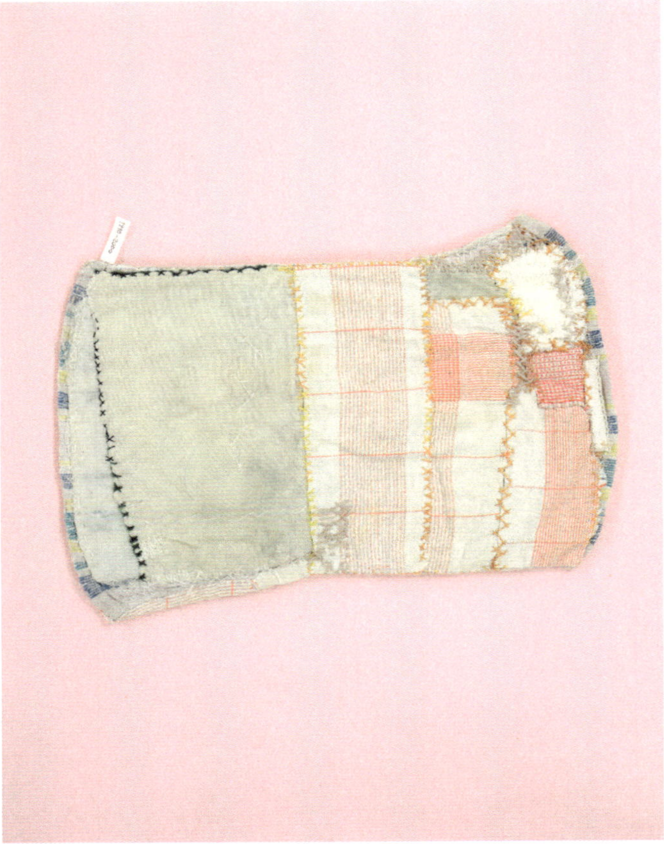

Underwear and cleaning cloth, Antwerp, *c.*1990–2000
Collection MoMu inv. T05/232-233

These objects were made by a lady with dementia. She also kept notebooks, jotting down her thoughts in a language no one else could understand. The meticulous, almost obsessive, textile repairs by someone experiencing memory loss is heartrending. It reveals a longing for sensory stimulus, a return to familiar activities of the past, such as craft techniques. Her fondness of and care for the objects are also evident. The underwear and cleaning cloth were made with patches of fabric, such as tea towels and hand towels, sewn together using herringbone stitches in rust brown, yellow, white and blue.

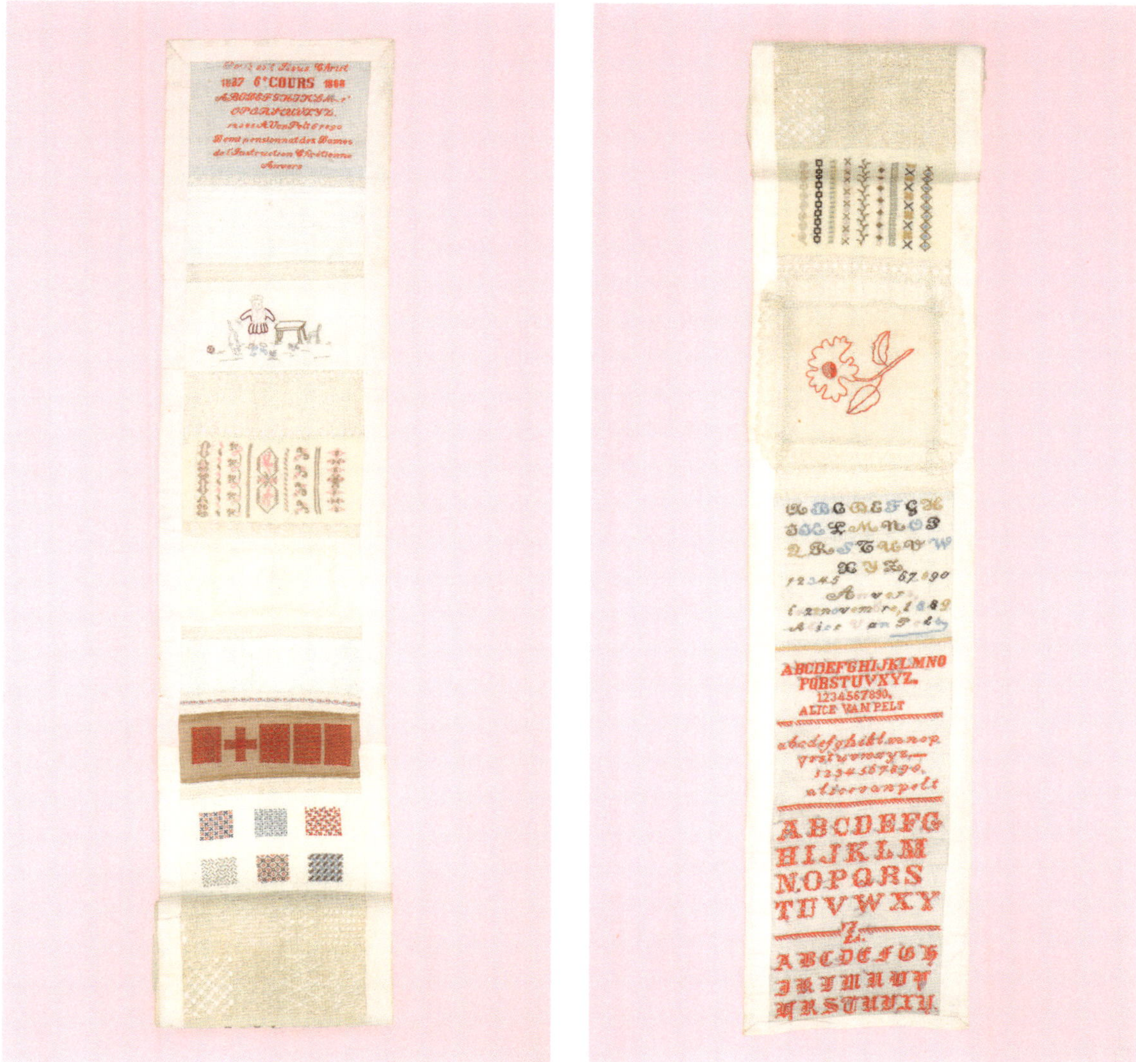

Alice Van Pelt, needlework sampler with embroidery, crochet, knitting and darning, and various sewing exercises, *c*.1887-1888
Collection MoMu inv. T3411

From the late nineteenth century, girls educated at boarding school produced needlework samplers, known as *pronklappen*. In the 1900s, the main purpose of girls' education was to prepare them to become good wives and mothers. Produced in convent boarding schools, these samplers, sometimes several metres in length, consisted of various crochet, knitting, sewing, darning and embroidery exercises produced over several years, and sewn together. As well as embroidery and other decorative techniques, darning was an important skill, because clothing was expensive and had to last as long as possible. On completing her education, this sampler served as proof of a young lady's needlework skills —— hence the Dutch name *pronklap*, or 'showpiece'. Sometimes such samplers were also referred to as *souvenir de ma jeunesse*, implying that the pupil would have fond memories of her school days.

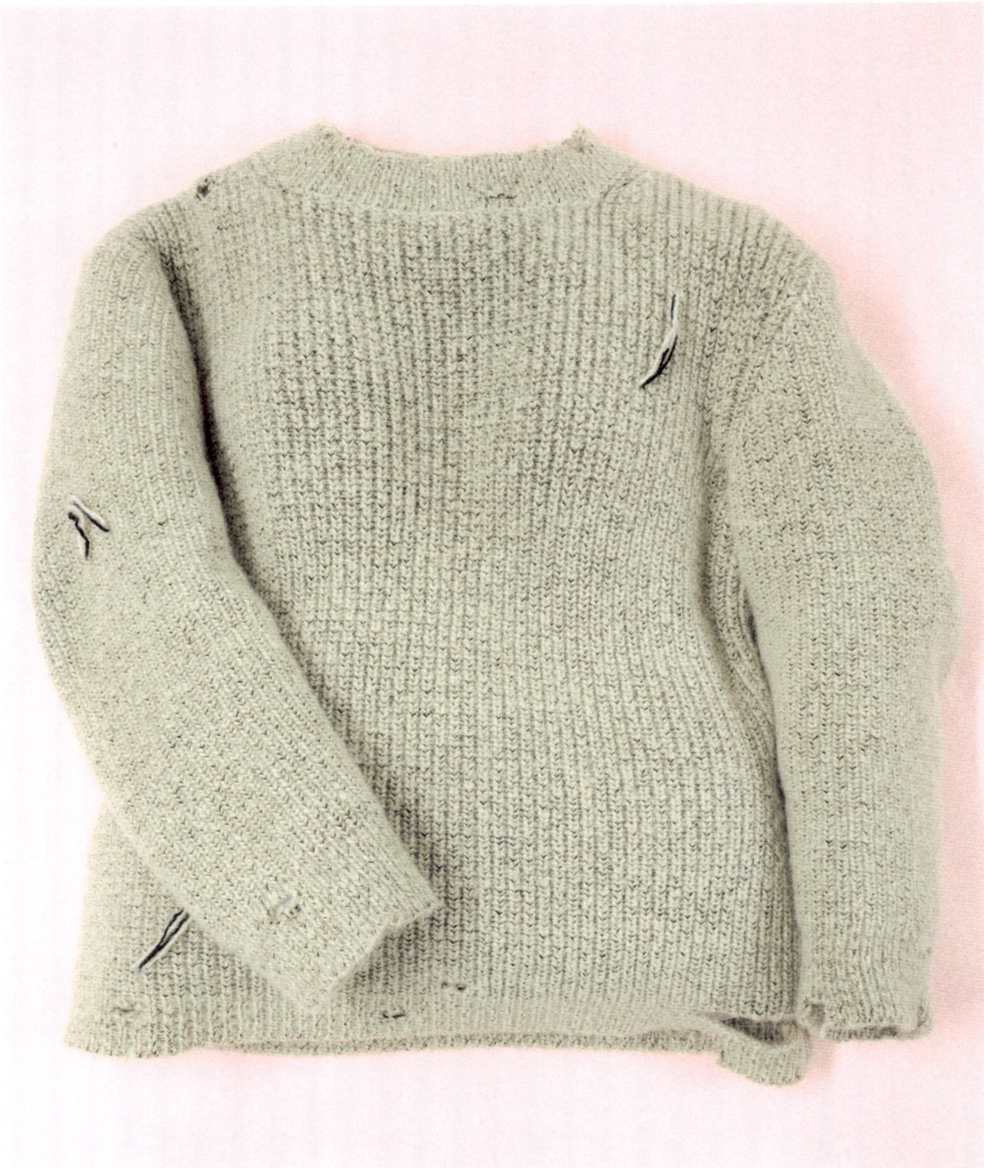

Maison Martin Margiela, Autumn-Winter 2000-01
Collection MoMu inv. T00/124

This woollen jumper was Margiela's first attempt to produce garments that look distressed, faded and worn. The project posed a challenge to his knitwear producer Miss Deanna Ferretti. The sweater was thermoformed on a plus-size mannequin in an oven normally used in the automotive industry. This process highlighted body contours such as elbows and breasts, as if the garment recalls a previous owner. 1,000 such sweaters were produced. When purchased new, the garment looked as though it had been worn by someone else for years.

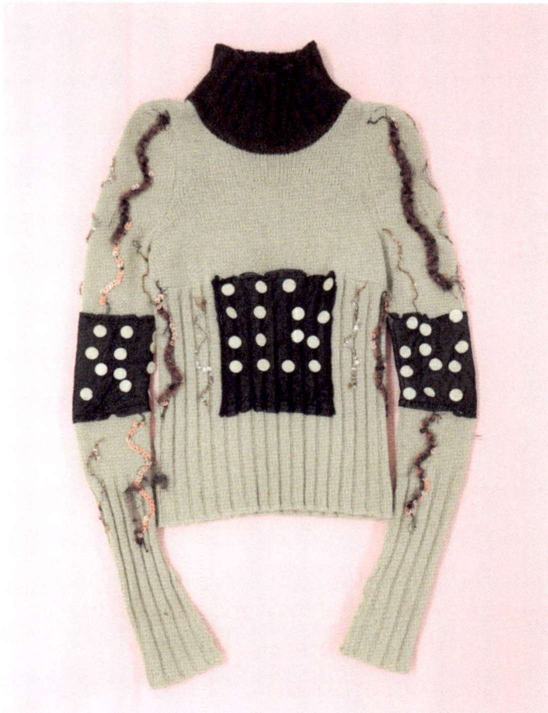

Maison Martin Margiela,
Autumn-Winter 1989-90
Collection MoMu inv. B19/1

This jumper features embroidery and appliquéd patches of black tulle embellished with large beige sequins, and snakes embroidered in brown crepe with smaller metallic sequins. The garment was provided on long-term loan by Inge Grognard, who collaborated as a makeup artist with Margiela and gathered iconic pieces over the years. The sweater is a surreal and decorative symbol of the joy and beauty of restoration.

Jurgi Persoons,
Autumn-Winter 1999-00
Collection MoMu inv. B10/92

When Jurgi Persoons' label was discontinued in 2003, MoMu acquired a large portion of his archives. By adding decorative elements as subversive layers, Persoons transformed traditional silhouettes into 'trash couture'. Missing one sleeve, this white knitted jumper displays deconstructed machine-made lace that contrasts with visible, irregular red embroidery. The sweater reveals Persoons' inclination to add elements in a naive, personal and almost audacious manner. He wanted to disrupt the banality and perfection of items of clothing and does that here by employing erratic, almost nervous, embroidery stitches. The result is both rebellious and tender.

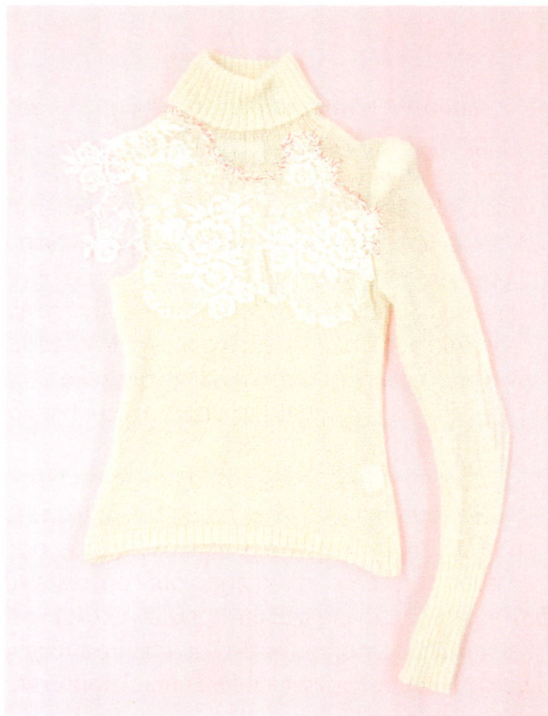

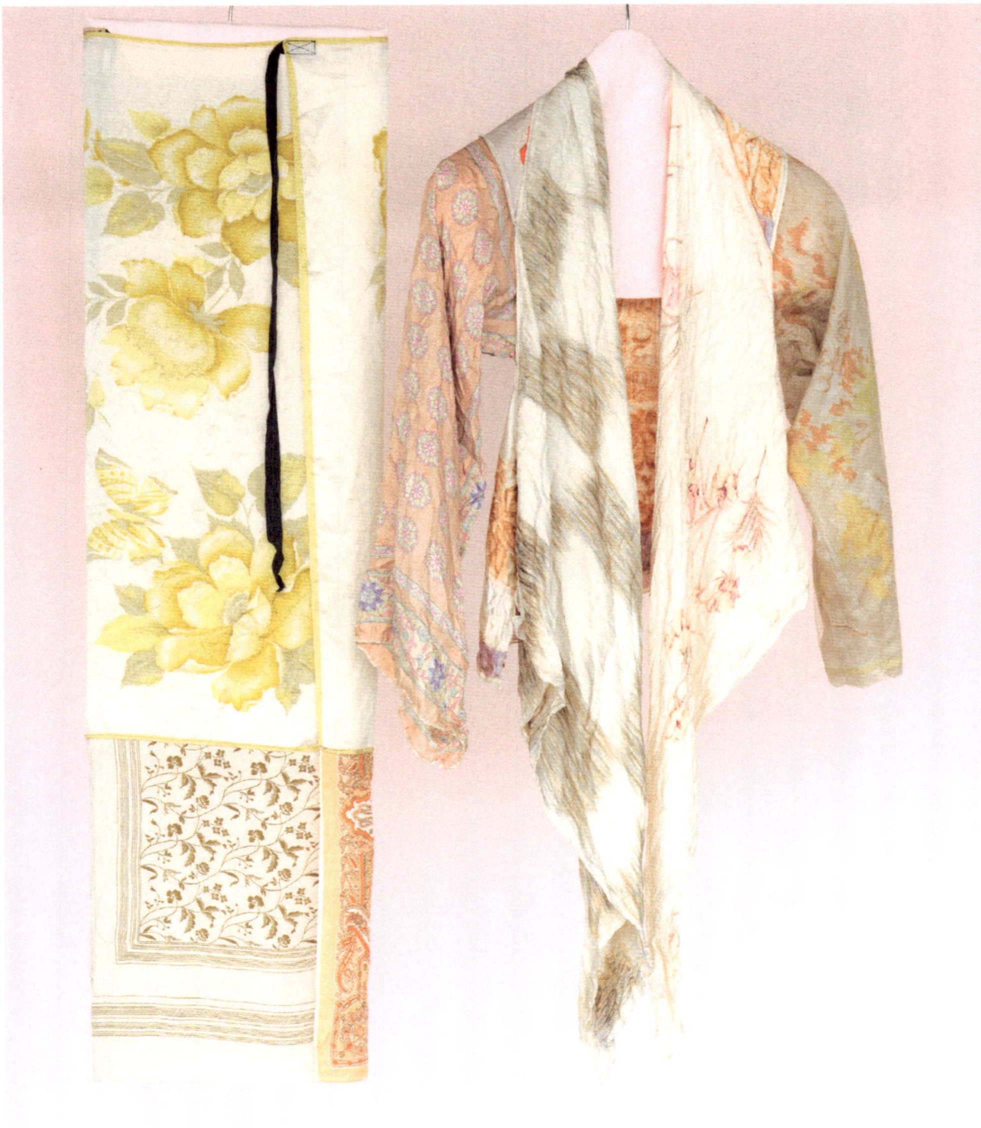

Maison Martin Margiela, skirt worn by Kristina De Coninck and top worn by Inge Grognard, Spring-Summer 1992
Collection MoMu inv. T19/713AB and B19/51

This long wrap skirt and top are made from four sections of fabric of different lengths, repurposed from printed silk vintage foulards and sewn together. The skirt is tied with a black cotton ribbon. As creases are integral to the design, they should be preserved in the collection. The pieces conceptualise the idea that clothes are allowed to live, and imperfections and creases are part of that.

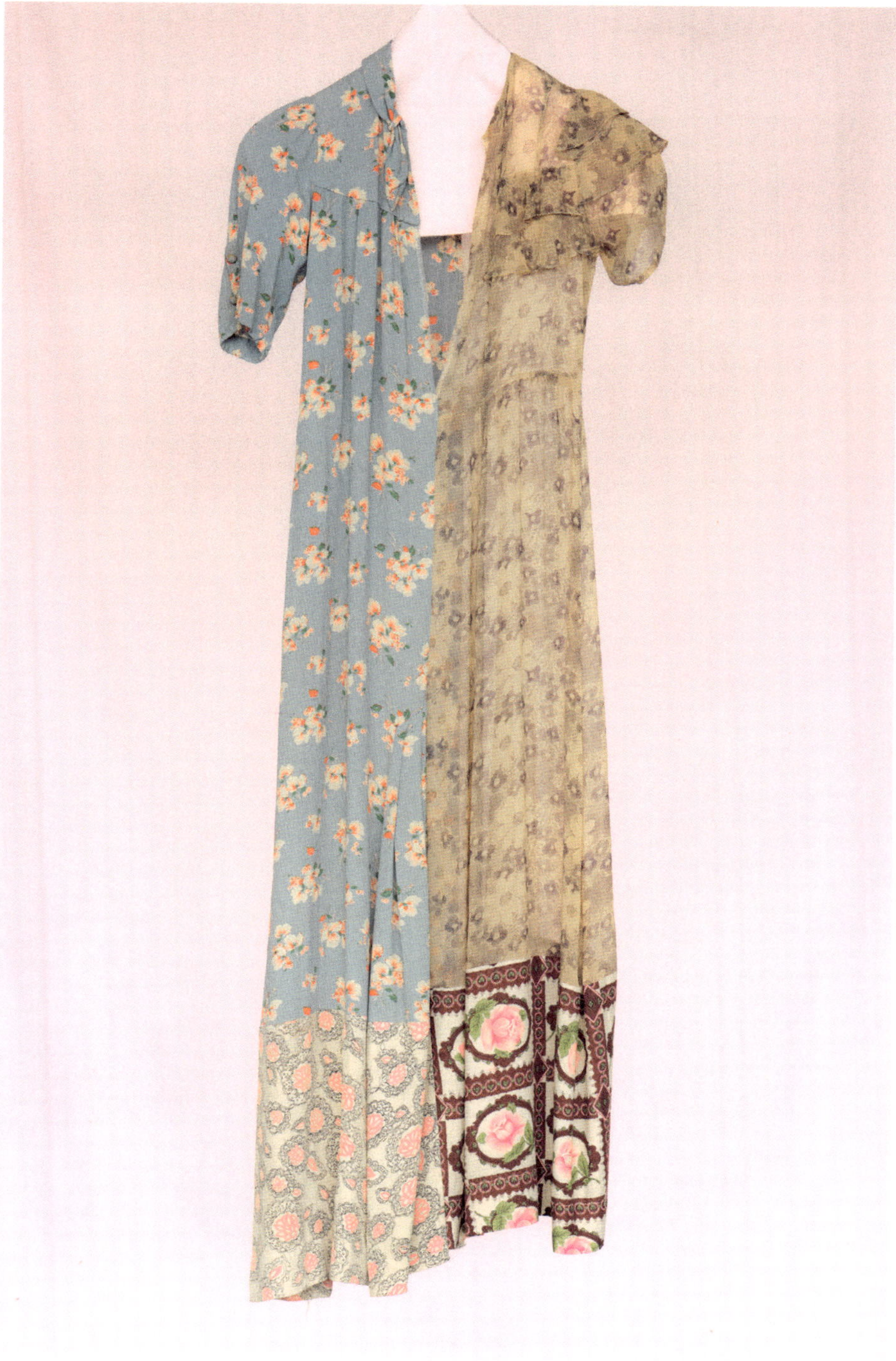

Maison Martin Margiela, Autumn-Winter 1993–94
Collection MoMu inv. T19/710

This garment was made from different 1940s-era dresses Martin Margiela found at flea markets. He made the dress for his close friend Kristina De Coninck. He chose the colours especially for her. The dress is a symbol of friendship and upcycling.

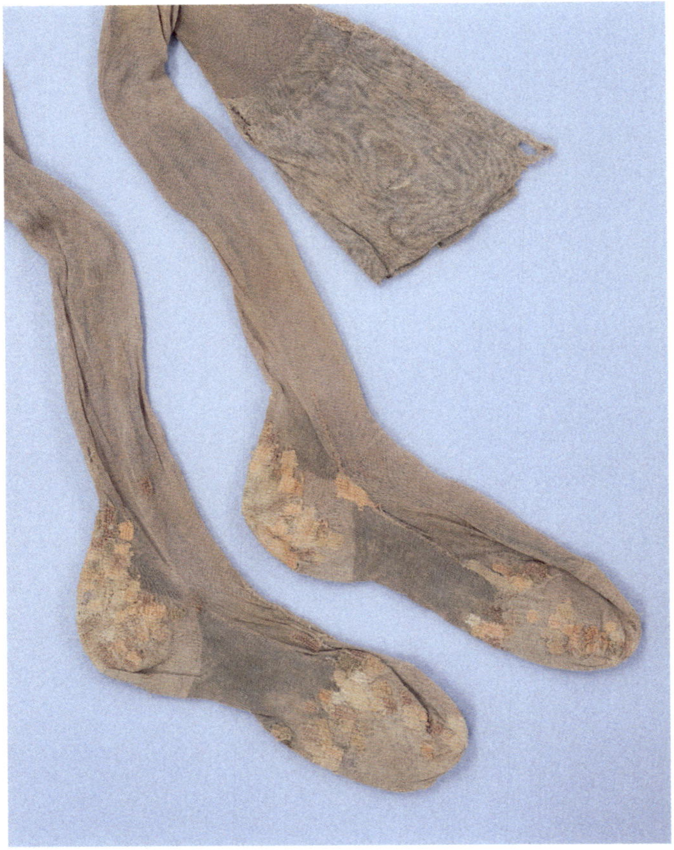

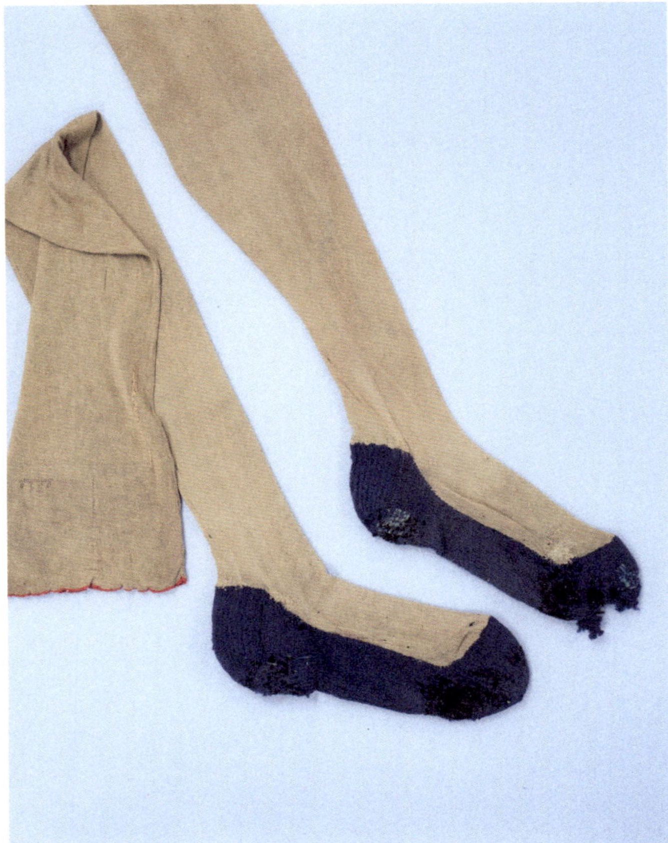

Pair of silk stockings with the feet darned in different shades of cotton thread, c.1910–1930
Collection MoMu inv. T03/423AB

Nowadays, few people darn tights or stockings, but throughout history, stockings, like other garments, were repaired to extend their lifespan as long as possible.

Pair of silk tricot stockings with the feet replaced by soles knitted in a more durable blue wool yarn, c.1910–30
Collection MoMu inv. T03/425AB

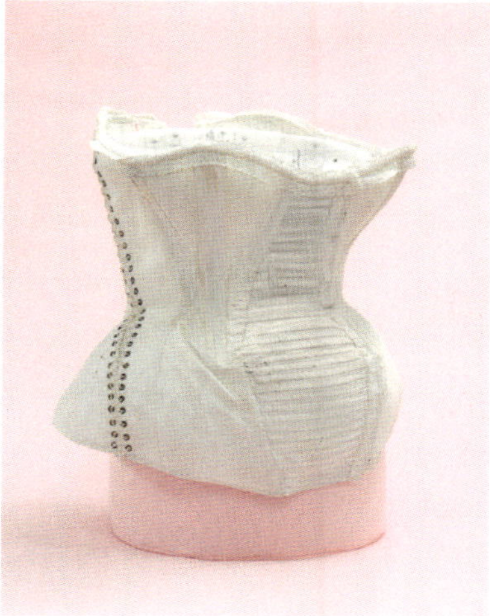

Maternity corset, c.1865
Collection MoMu inv. T12/1062/85

In the nineteenth century, pregnancies were barely mentioned or referred to in books and magazines, and seldom in correspondence. They were certainly not portrayed in fashion plates. References to pregnancy were usually pejorative. 'Une dame souffrante' referred to physical discomfort and the dangers that pregnancy could bring. This corset shows how closely maternity garments followed fashion trends and were adapted to the popular fashion silhouettes of the time. The corset could be worn during pregnancy thanks to the elasticated section stitched into the front, which incorporates small metal springs that expand where needed, and elastic lacing in the side panels.

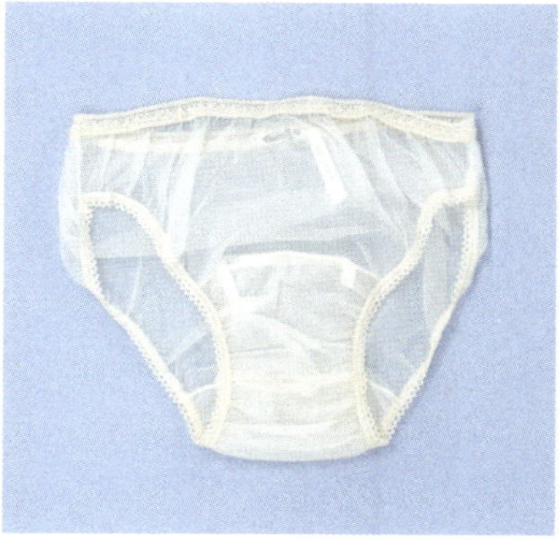

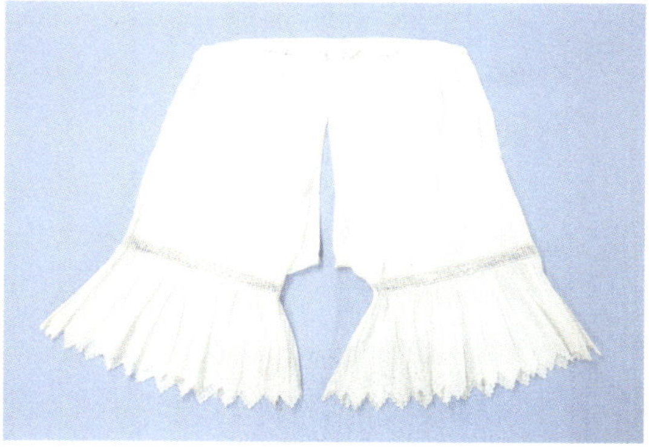

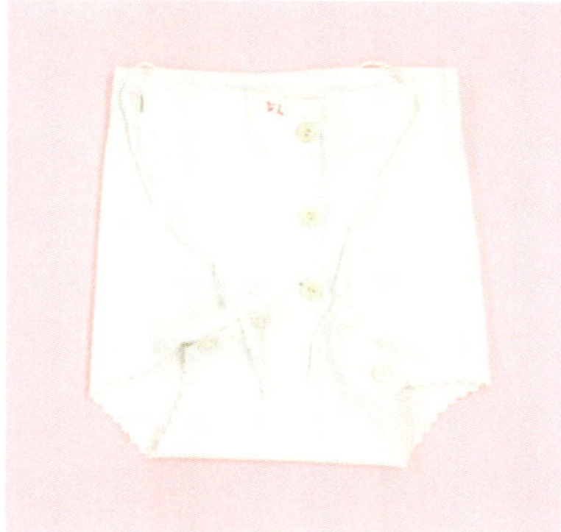

Left to right

Nylon mesh sanitary panties, c.1950–1955
Study Collection inv. ST2048

The gusset has an impermeable plastic lining with a white loop at the front and back.

Open crotch cotton underpants, c.1900
Study Collection inv. ST2068

Nappy made of a triangular piece of cotton, with molton on the inside, four mother-of-pearl and four white glass buttons, and the baby's initials, c.1900–1910
Study Collection inv. ST2021

The word *diaper* derives from the 'diaper weave' used to weave the linen from which nappies were made. The shape, material and closure method were not standardised prior to the Industrial Revolution and mass production. Most families used old clothes or worn sheets. Outside Europe, naturally absorbent materials such as moss were often used. Disposable nappies were first used in the 1890s, although the concept didn't catch on for a long time because of the high production costs. Disposable nappies became popular in the 1960s and are no longer made of cotton but of polyethylene, polypropylene and polyester fibres. Today, sustainable alternatives are becoming increasingly popular.

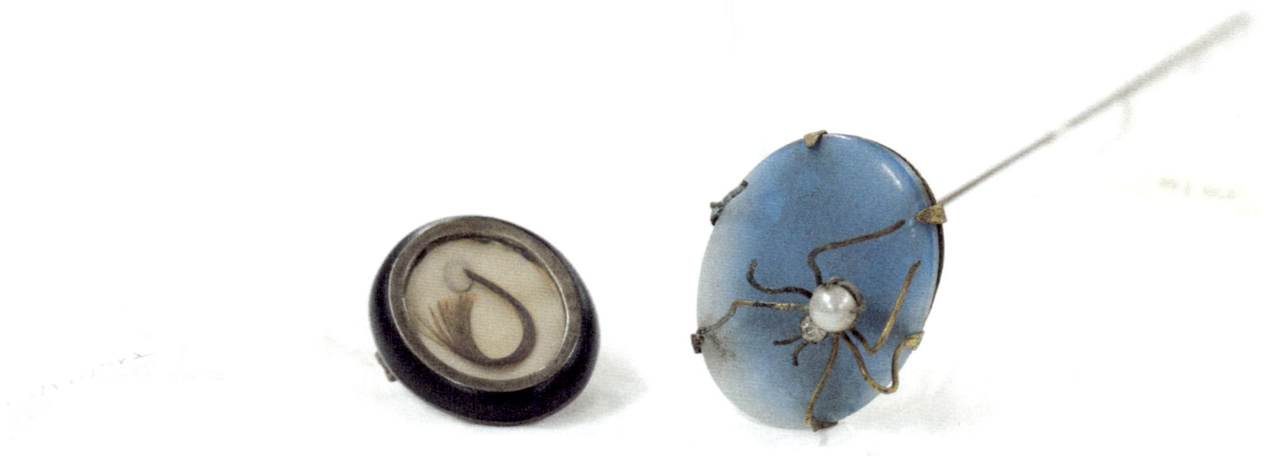

Ornamental brooch, *c.*1850–1900
Collection MoMu inv. T16/111/E217

This ornamental pin is an example of mourning jewellery, which incorporated a lock of hair belonging to a departed loved one. Jewellery of this kind dates back to the seventeenth century but regained popularity in the Victorian period (1837–1901). In 1861, for example, Prince Albert, the husband of the British Queen Victoria, died. His widow, the queen, mourned him by wearing black until her death in 1901.

Hat pin with a rhinestone spider with a pearl as an abdomen and metal legs, *c.*1900–1920
Collection MoMu inv. T89/195

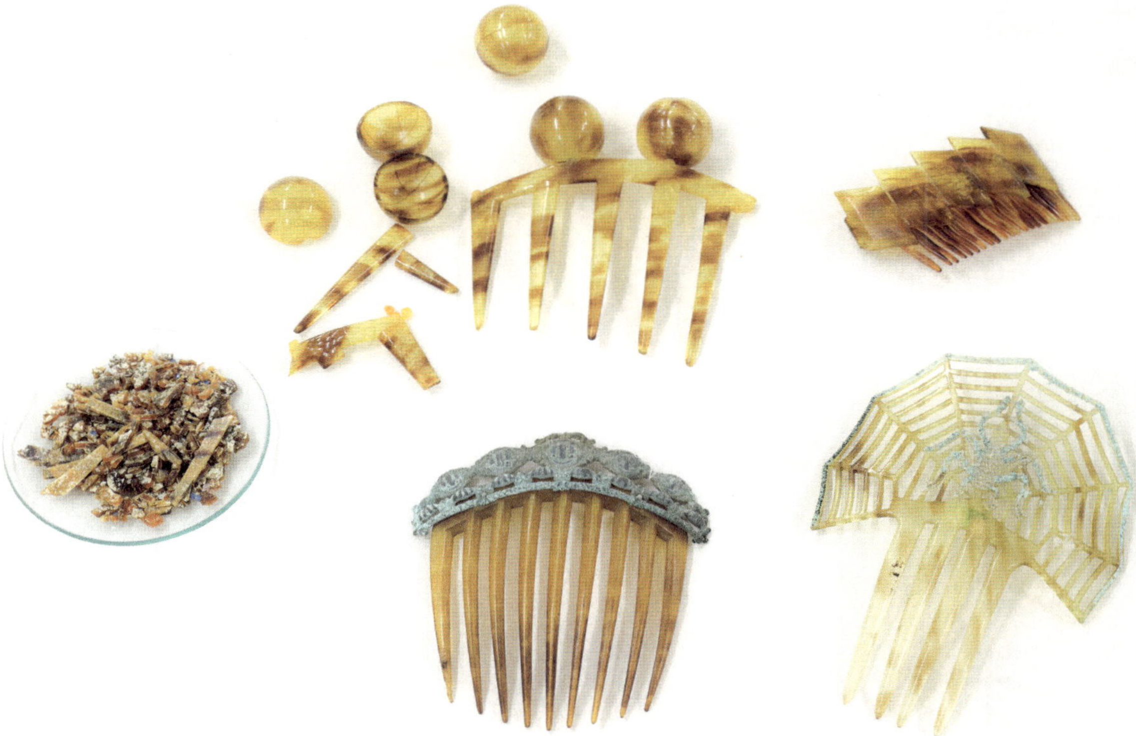

Still life showing the deterioration of imitation tortoiseshell combs, *c.*1900–1930
Collection MoMu inv. T89/89, inv. T4177, inv. T4181, inv. T4193B, inv. T03/407, inv. T21/6731

These hair combs show the various stages of deterioration that may occur with objects made out of cellulose nitrate. These hair combs show the typical characteristic sugar-like pattern of decay and the characteristic odour of camphor that was used as a plasticizer for this material. The camphor comes out of the object and causes the combs to deform, break, fall apart and eventually crumble. Cellulose nitrate gives off a constant stream of acidic vapours that destroy not only themselves but also adjacent materials. A clear example of this can be seen in the combination of cellulose nitrate and metal: they may corrode, turning the metal green. In the watch glass are the remains of a comb with blue stones that sparkle through the crumbs.

Set of baby clothes in taffeta silk, silk rep, silk trim and Mechlin bobbin lace, linen lining, The Netherlands, c.1750

Collection MoMu inv. T23/1135/K500A, inv. T23/1191/K500B, inv. T23/1136/1-2/K500CD

This outfit is from the estate of a Dutch countess and was a cherished family heirloom until the 1960s. The jacket was combined with a linen undershirt and a long gown. The silk bonnet was worn over an inner cap of linen. Babies were usually carried in what was known as a christening blanket or a bearing cloth.

Padded baby carrier in cotton and white embroidery, with a matching jacket, c.1870–1880

Collection MoMu inv. T13/631AB/K79

Decorated baby gowns were worn at christenings or on a special occasion when the baby was presented to family and friends. Infants' clothing largely reflected trends in women's fashion. As such, short sleeves and low necklines were the norm for a long time, but as ideas about children's welfare changed, warmer, roomier garments came into vogue and, from 1880 onwards, high-necked bodices and longer sleeves became more common.

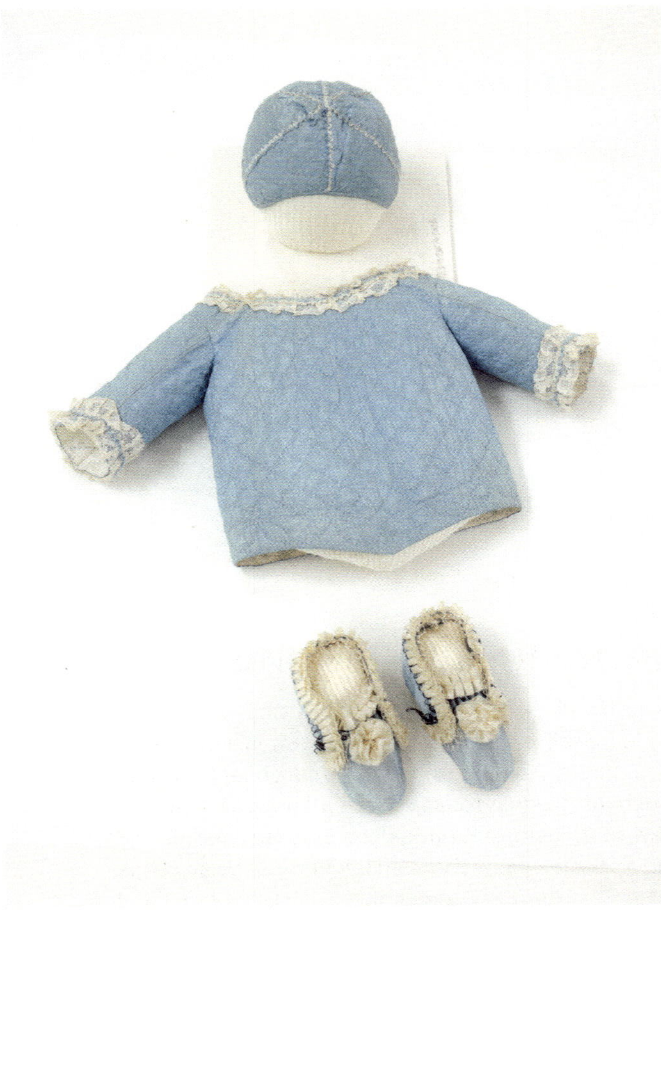

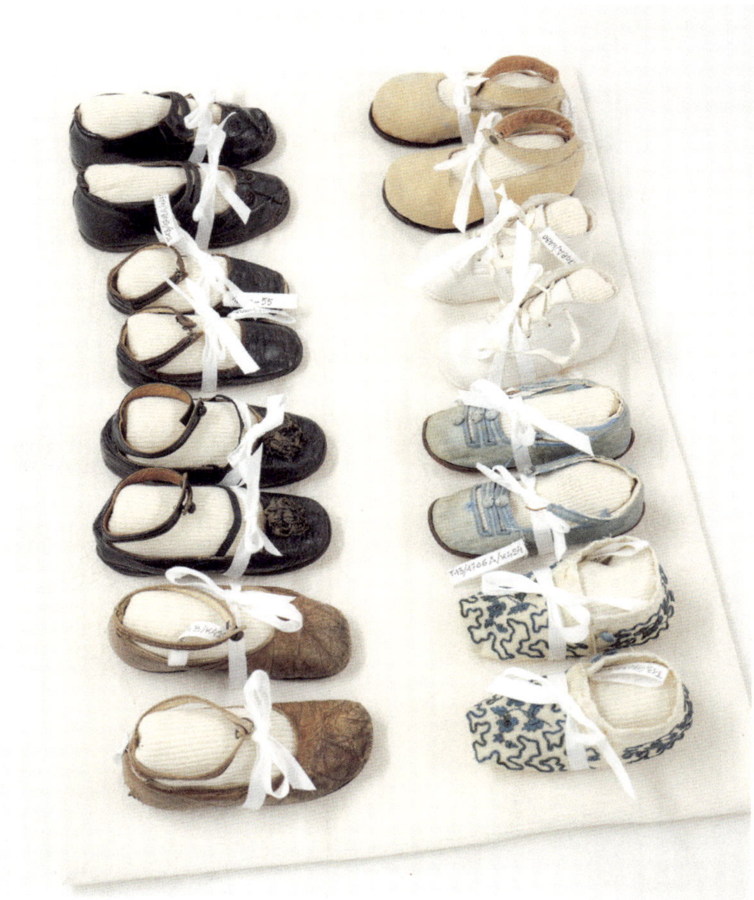

Left to right

Shoes, c.1850–1870
Collection MoMu inv. T13/1702AB/K431
Shoes, c.1920–1940
Collection MoMu inv. T13/1705AB/K432
Shoes, c.1856–1860
Collection MoMu inv. T13/1701AB/K428
Shoes, c.1940–1970
Collection MoMu inv. T13/1708AB/K430

Shoes, c.1850–1870
Collection MoMu inv. T13/1703AB/K423
Shoes, c.1850–1870
Collection MoMu inv. T13/1706AB/K424
Shoes, c.1850–1900
Collection MoMu inv. T13/1705AB/K429
Shoes, c.1850–1880
Collection MoMu inv. T13/1707AB/K422

The modern concept of parenting and childhood emerged in the early nineteenth century, along with clothing designed for children. Gradually, people came to realise that children are different from adults, and need more freedom to move. Garments became less restrictive and, over time, footwear was designed based on the morphology of a child's foot. Around 1900, children's clothing became gender-specific. Styles that today are traditionally associated with girls, such as Mary Janes, heeled mules, and ballerinas, were also worn by boys. After World War I, with the advent of psychoanalysis and the realisation that childhood experiences shape adult well-being, greater emphasis was placed on children's health.

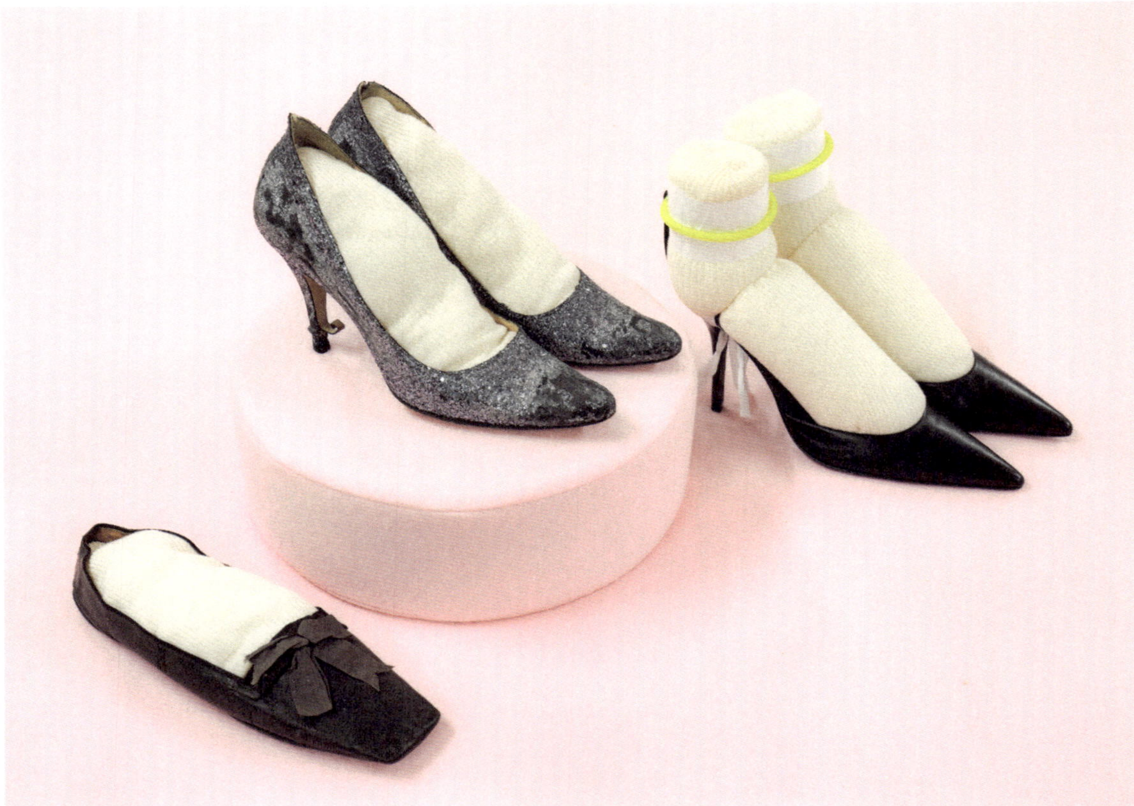

To ensure shoes retain their shape, and for their long-term preservation, they are padded with inert materials. Custom-made pillow inserts are fitted inside the shoe to maintain its shape. The shoes are placed on a sheet of high-quality acid-free cardboard, with Ethafoam support to keep each shoe in position.

Left to right

Leather shoe worn by Henri Myin during his wedding to Adèle Le Gros on 13 June 1833
Collection MoMu inv. T3434

Maison Martin Margiela, Spring-Summer 2005
Collection MoMu inv. T18/556AB
'After Party' heels with fake signs of wear where the leather on the inside of the heels has apparently come loose and curled, and the sequins and glitter appear to have fallen off.

Helmut Lang, Spring-Summer 2003
Collection MoMu inv. T10/440AB
Black leather high heels with a yellow silicone ankle strap. Although silicone is a fairly stable plastic, over time the plasticisers leach out in the form of a sticky liquid, for which reason this plastic is monitored regularly.

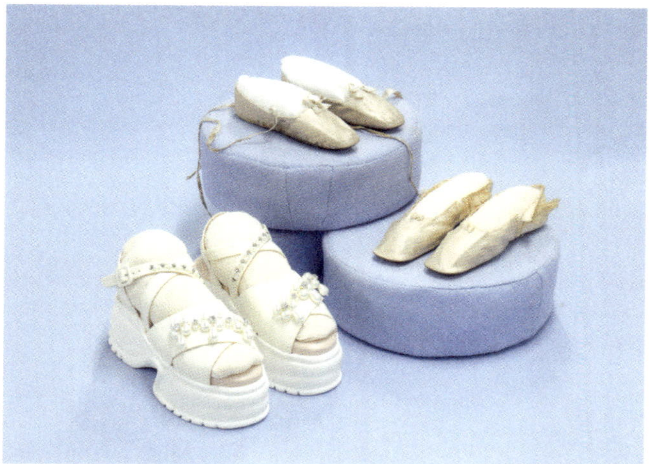

Left to right

Simone Rocha, Spring-Summer 2021
Collection MoMu inv. T22/1922/1-2

Flat square toe shoes in white satin with ribbons, c.1828
Collection MoMu inv. T99/195AB

Flat square toe shoes in white satin worn by Mrs Génard-Beghein, c.1828
Collection MoMu inv. T99/195AB
The silk of these shoes is so brittle and delicate that the material deteriorates each time they are moved. Pillow inserts give the shoe structural support and make sure it doesn't lose its shape.

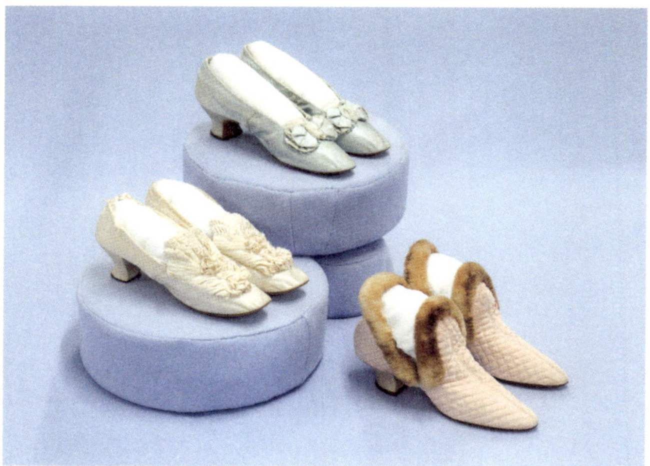

Left to right

Silk satin shoes with bows, gently worn, with slight signs of wear and discolouration, c.1900-1910
Collection MoMu inv. T12/1382AB/S39

Satin shoe with rosettes, with signs of wear, especially at the heels, c.1880-1890
Collection MoMu inv. T12/1371AB/S12

Quilted silk and fur slippers, mint condition, c.1890-1910
Collection MoMu inv. T12/135AB/S63

In addition to the fashion and costume collection and library, MoMu also houses a rich Study Collection that comprises roughly 2,000 objects that visitors can study up close. The Study Collection consists of historical and contemporary garments, regional costume, textile fragments and fabric samples. Researchers also benefit from the opportunity to inspect and examine objects, and study the techniques and materials used in the linings, back panels and details of garments.

During and just after the war, fabric was in short supply. Clothing was expensive and, because of rationing, could only be bought with clothing coupons. Garments were treated with great care, and damaged fabrics were meticulously darned by hand.

World War II chequered cotton dress with the wearer's initials, 'J.B.'
Study Collection inv. ST2253

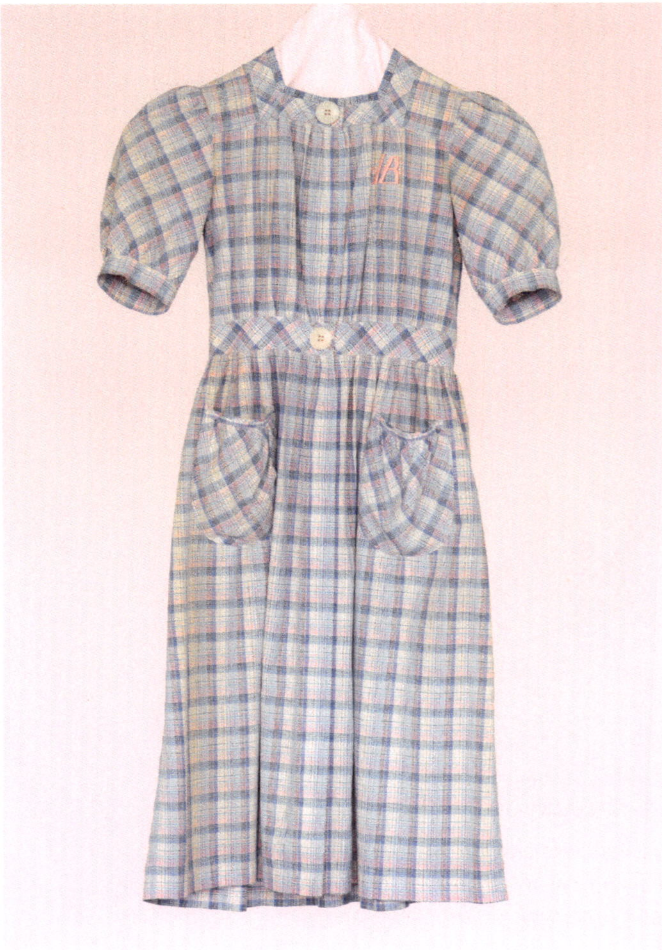

Child's outfit from China in cotton damask with round metal buttons and printed trousers, discoloured in several places, *c.*1900–1940
Study Collection inv. ST917 and ST919

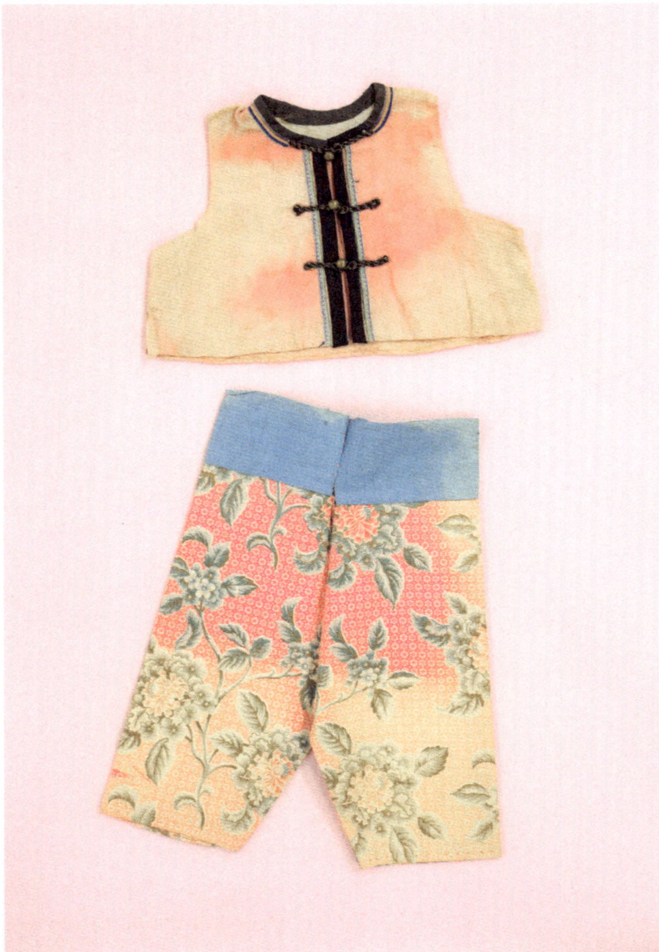

TEXTILE FRAGMENTS

In the past, materials were used sparingly and with care. Textiles are precious, so clothing fragments and fabric samples were carefully preserved with the intention of reusing them later. In some of these samples, the shape of an old pattern part is still visible. These fragments are a valuable resource for research and education. They teach us a great deal about the materials and techniques used throughout history.

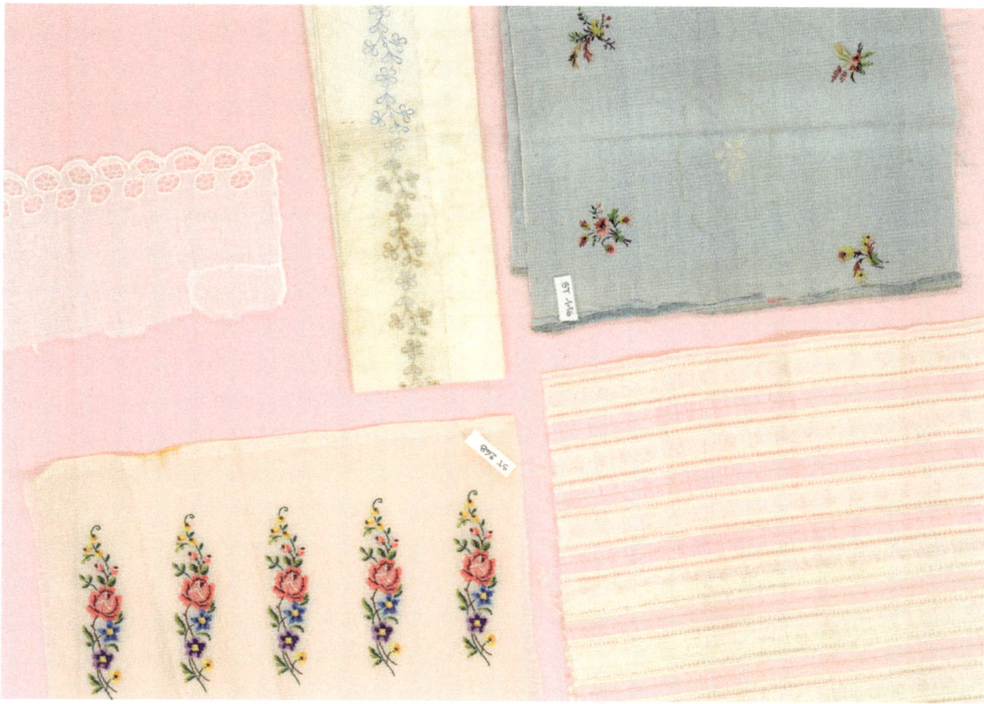

Left to right

Brocaded taffeta with pattern warp motifs, *c.*1770–1790
Study Collection inv. ST116

Striped pink and white fabric in white plain weave alternating with an ajour garland weave pattern, *c.*1870–1890
Study Collection inv. ST200AB

Strip of cotton pre-printed with blue flowers; intended to be hand-embroidered in white; partially completed, *c.*1850–1900
Study Collection inv. ST255

Strip of cream-coloured artificial silk with five floral sprigs with roses embroidered in petit-point; made using a manually operated embroidery machine, *c.*1940–1970
Study Collection inv. ST268

Strip of cotton with reticella and white embroidery, with decorative fillings in buttonhole stitch; a patch was sewn on to repair the edge, *c.*1800–1850
Study Collection inv. ST25AB

Left to right

Dress fabric fragment, c.1740–1760
Study Collection inv. ST821

Dress fabric fragment brocaded with silver filament and frisé, c.1740–1760
Study Collection inv. ST996

Dress fabric fragment in satin with white weft forming floral motifs; pitch stripes with diamond and dot motifs, c.1770–1780
Study Collection inv. ST1061AB
The fabric no longer has its original finish, which makes it very limp.

Dress fabric fragment in off-white taffeta with brocaded multicoloured sprigs of flowers among wavy tendrils, c.1760–1780
Study Collection inv. ST118

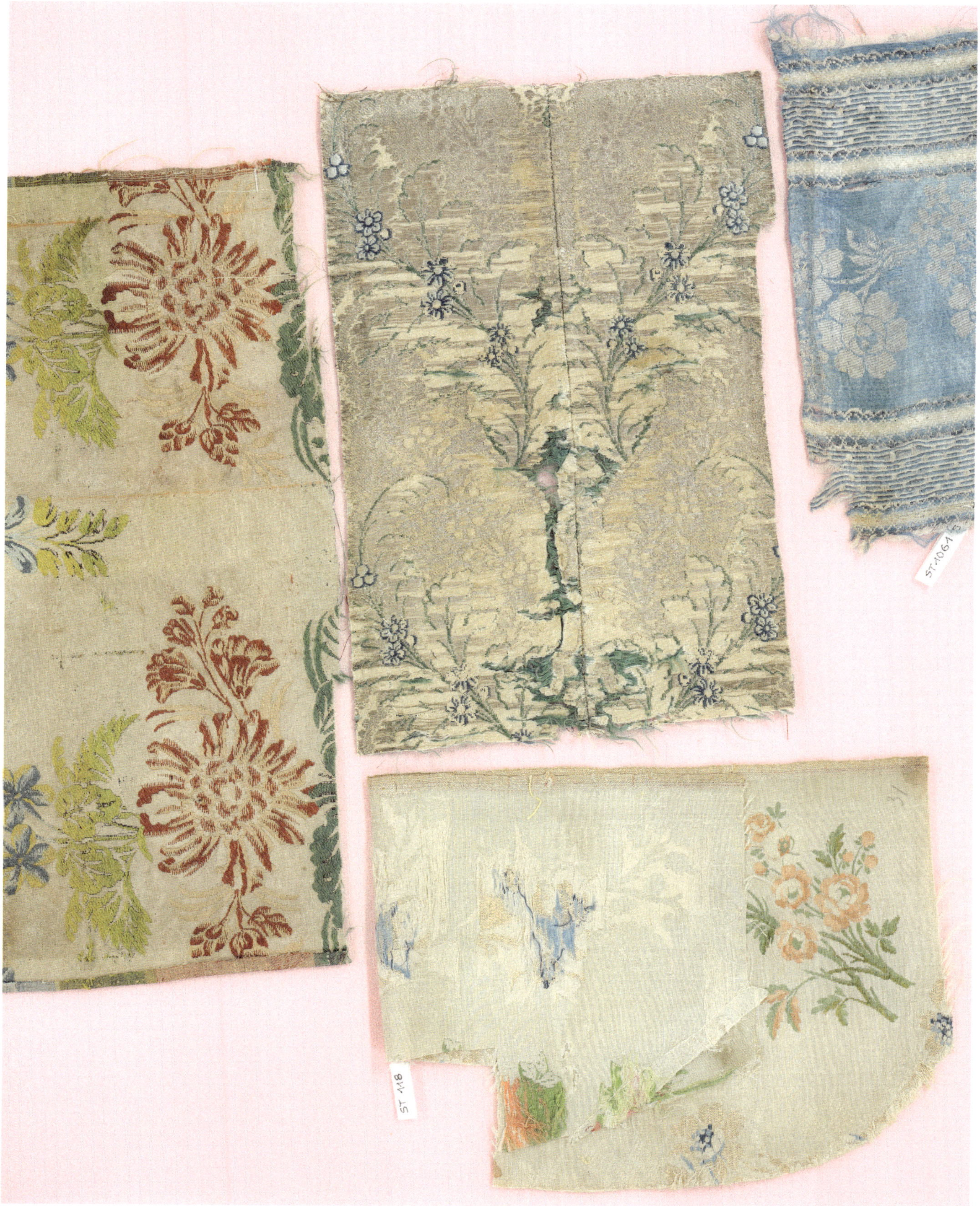
ST 1061
ST 118

Material Time

Wornness, Memory and the Power of Imperfect Garments

ELLEN SAMPSON

"Memory is the seamstress, and a capricious one at that.
Memory runs her needle in and out, up and down, hither and thither.
We know not what comes next, or what follows after. Thus, the most ordinary movement in the world, such as sitting down at a table and pulling the inkstand towards one, may agitate a thousand odd, disconnected fragments, now bright, now dim, hanging and bobbing and dipping and flaunting, like the under-linen of a family of fourteen on a line in a gale of wind."[1]

In the pages of *Orlando*, a poetic and maze-like meditation on love, gender and time, Virginia Woolf calls upon two material metaphors to evoke the workings of memory: a needle darting through cloth and the fluttering of laundry on a washing line. These metaphors evoke the intimate and tactile nature of our relationships with our clothes, the way they become records of the actions performed within them. The objects in this exhibition sit at the peripheries of conventional understandings of fashion; creased and torn, decaying and shattered. What unites these diverse objects is their imperfect materiality: they are records of time's passing, of how bodies, materials and styles change. This short essay considers the multiple ways that garments show the passage of time, altering through entropy and use. In doing so, it asks why such garments matter, and why we should care for, preserve and attend to these damaged and imperfect things.

Clothes are among our most intimate possessions, both bodily and in the sense that they are loaded with meaning. They are simultaneously markers of identity and vessels of experience, so that more than almost any other object, clothing remembers, retaining traces of what has gone before. We measure our lives in textile markers, in dresses and stockings, coats, hats and shoes. From baby shoes and prom dresses to widow's weeds, clothing situates us in a particular place and era, allowing us to look back and identify decades, seasons and days. This mnemonic function is both stylistic — the way a garment's style and construction locate it in a specific time and place — and material — how garments alter and age.

Thus, garments are records of fashion's circuitous forward progression, one style replacing the next, and their inevitable material decay. Though entropy is inherent to all material things, used clothing often ages in particular ways, breaking down where body and garment meet. Thus, imperfect garments are records not only of changing styles and tastes, but also of the bodies that inhabited them, and the gestures performed within them.

Although the majority of our clothes are mass-produced, our intimate and tactile relationships with them render them unique. Over time, garments become records of lived experience, covered with the marks of use. Clothing touches and holds us, containing our bodies and recording our gestures and interactions with the world.[2] These interactions, 'the stuff that makes up the material texture of our daily practices',[3] alter the garment's material form, so that in wearing, clothes become biographical: repositories for both the bodily and tacit histories of our lives. The marks (a run in a stocking, a missing button, stains on the edge of a hem) record lost gestures and missing movements, acts of care and destruction. Our gestures —— fleeting and temporal —— are retained in the material of our clothes: in the folds of skirts and creases at the elbows of a jacket. There is an intimacy to these gestural traces, the ways in which they relate not to bodies in general but to one particular body, so that as Amy de la Haye writes of items in the Messel Family collection, 'each garment bore imprints and possessed its own biography; many were poignant holders of personal memory'.[4]

This entanglement, 'the transposition of thing into person and person into thing which take place through wearing',[5] changes our clothes so that they age along with us, becoming bodily and imbued with trace. Time is materialised across our garments: we see its passage in crumples and creases, in stains and folds. These marks make apparent our clothes as mediators of experience, as companions to our bodies moving through the world. There is a poignancy to these details, these minute traces that stem, I think, from their ability to sit between two times: the time when they were worn and the time we are in now. They both are 'of a time' (the date they were made or worn) and embody the passage of time: the distance between then and now. To borrow from Roland Barthes, used garments possess a 'spatial immediacy and temporal anteriority'; they are both 'there then', in the past, and 'here now'.[6]

1 Virginia Woolf, *Orlando* (London: Penguin Classics, 1928), p. 436.
2 For further exploration of the potency of these traces, see Ellen Sampson, *Worn: Footwear, Attachment and the Affects of Wear* (London: Bloomsbury, 2020).
3 Lucia Ruggerone, 'The Feeling of Being Dressed: Affect Studies and the Clothed Body', *Fashion Theory*, vol. 21, no. 5, 2016, pp. 573–93, p. 8.
4 Amy de la Haye, 'Vogue and the V&A Vitrine', *Fashion Theory*, vol. 10, no. 1, 2006, p. 132.
5 Ellen Sampson, 'Affect and Sensation', *Fashion Studies*, vol. 3, no. 1, 2020, pp. 1–19, https://www.fashionstudies.ca/affect-and-sensation, accessed 5 June 2023.
6 Roland Barthes, 'Rhetoric of the Image', in *Image Music Text*, trans. Stephen Heath (London: Fontana Press, 1977), p. 44.
7 Anja Aronowsky Cronberg, (2019) 'Paris Saudade: An Echo of the Past in the Future', *Extra, Extra*, no. 12, 2019, https://extraextra magazine.com/talk/saudade-an-echo-of-the-past-in-the-future-by-anja-aronowsky-cronberg/, accessed 5 June 2023.
8 Peter Stallybrass, 'Worn Worlds: Clothes, Mourning, and the Life of Things', *The Yale Review*, vol. 81, no. 2, 1993, pp. 35–50, p. 2.

Aronowsky Cronberg writes, 'Our old clothes, after all, reflect our history, becoming tangible material memories of times past, love lost or found, disappointments endured, or victories won. These often-forgotten objects of desire could be read as a map to our past, resurrected and brought back to life once more.'[7] As such, imperfect garments both evoke and invoke, allowing us to recall the specific —— friends, relatives, lovers —— and the general —— behaviours, traditions and styles. Their imperfections —— the curled fingers of gloves, the holes in stockings danced through, the fraying edge where a hand has entered a pocket many times before —— are gestures made material. In his essay on the death of his friend, Peter Stallybrass writes of how Allon's jacket —— its texture, weight and smell —— brings his lost friend back for him:

> "I was inhabited by his presence, taken over. If I wore the Jacket then Allon wore me. He was there in the wrinkles of the elbows, the wrinkles which in the technical jargon of sewing are called 'memory': He was there in the stains at the very bottom of the Jacket, he was there in the smell of the armpits."[8]

These traces are evocative because they are personal; in their wearing, both fashion items and everyday dress become bodily and intimate. Imperfect garments offer us an alternate temporality to fashion's cycles, not only typifying an era but also materialising lived experience and the passage of time. In the complex patterns of wear and decay we see the tangible evidence of lives lived and our impacts on the material world.

Thus, imperfect garments are important because they present a counterpoint to fashion's often exclusionary fixation on the perfect and the new. The garment as thing, rather than image, idea or fantasy. These garments make visible the embodied experience of wearing, and the constellations of relationships that are manifest in our clothes: the hands through which they have passed, the bodies with which they have interacted and the webs of connections and affordances that created them. It is the traces of these practices, our entanglements with the world, that afford damaged garments their value. These evocative objects, laden with trace, return us to the material nature of our relationship with clothes.

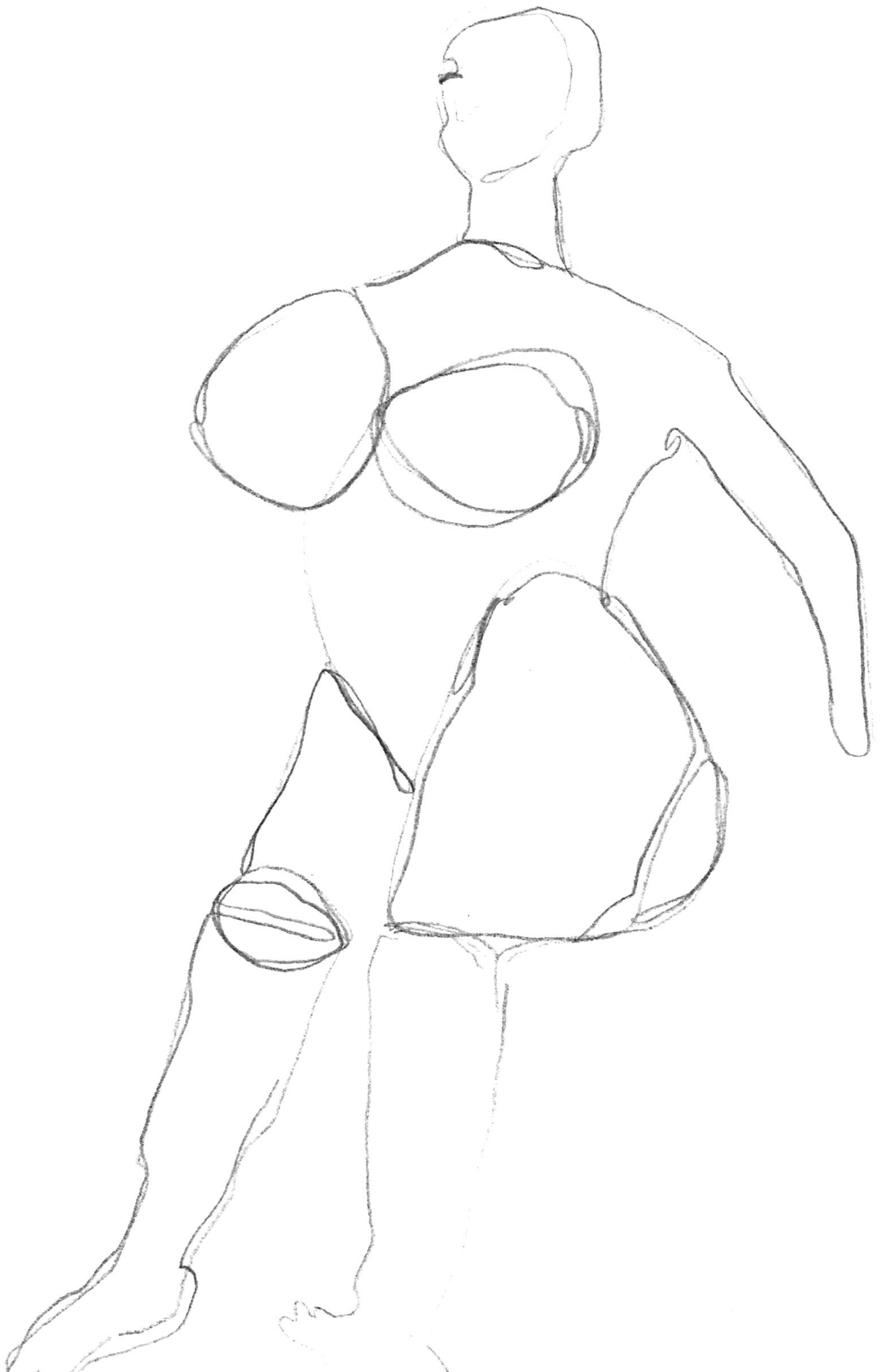

CHAPTER VIII

Childhood Drawings

Do you remember when you made this drawing?
What's the story behind it?
What's your strongest childhood clothing memory?
Is there a garment that you will always cherish?

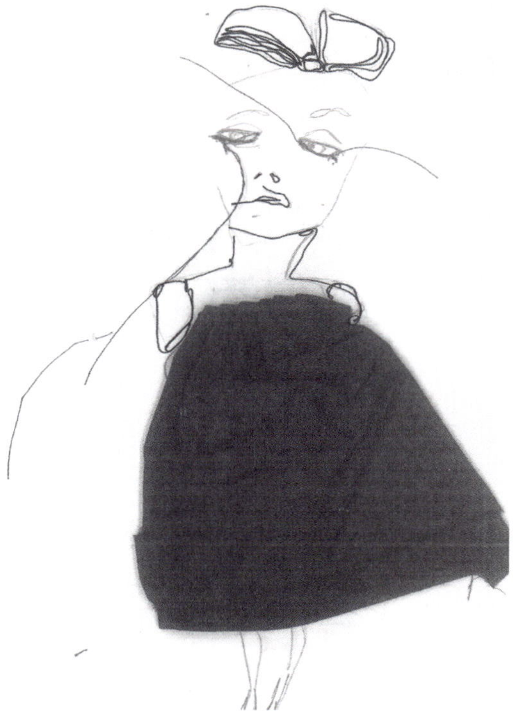

SIMONE ROCHA, DESIGNER

I made these drawings just coming out of secondary school. You can see how I loved highlighting the physicality of the body and the volume in the dress. Growing up in Ireland, my strongest childhood memory of clothing is my brown school uniform with a white shirt, white knee socks, a red tie and brown shoes. The garments that I will always cherish are no longer my own, but the clothing of my daughters.

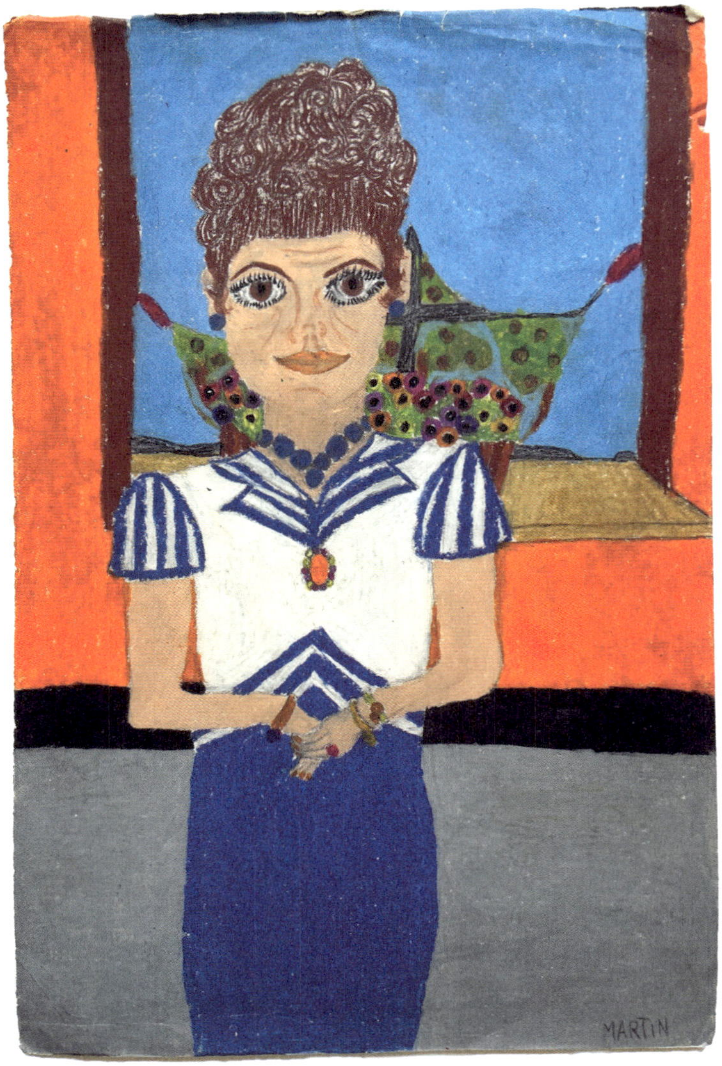

MARTIN MARGIELA, DESIGNER

A Portrait of My Grandmother (1967)

This is the woman who supported my passion for fashion all her life. My grandmother was a seamstress and taught me everything about clothes. I adored and respected her but had a different point of view when it came to fashion. In 1988, at the end of my first show in Paris, she came backstage and said, smiling: 'What a success by doing everything I told you not to do'.

My strongest childhood clothing memory is seeing André Courrèges on the evening news showing his collection for 1964. I remember asking my mother in shock what it was about and got the answer: 'He is a couturier in Paris'. At that moment I knew what I wanted to become in the future without knowing what couturier meant and also not knowing where Paris was situated.

JEAN PAUL GAULTIER, DESIGNER

I made this drawing in 1966 when I was fourteen. At that age, I made imaginary fashion shows with my creations and even interviewed myself about them. The drawing on the right is from 1968. I sent it to Pierre Cardin. A few years later, on the 24th of April of 1970, I started working for him. It was the day of my eighteenth birthday.

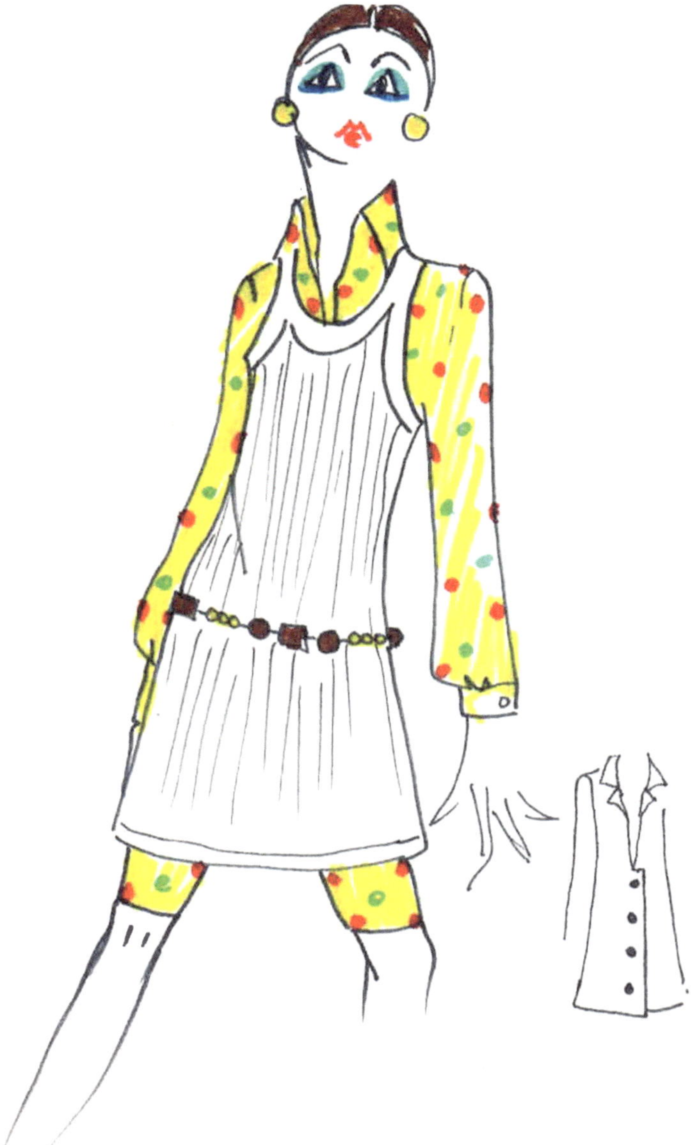

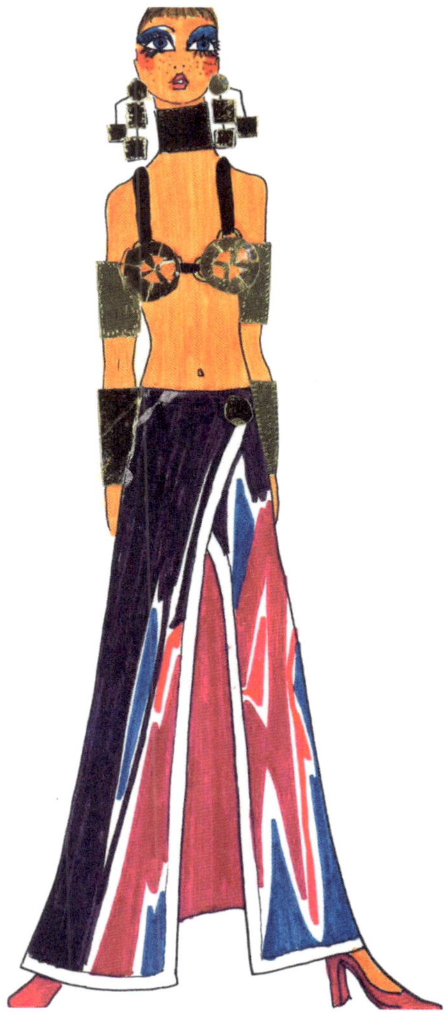

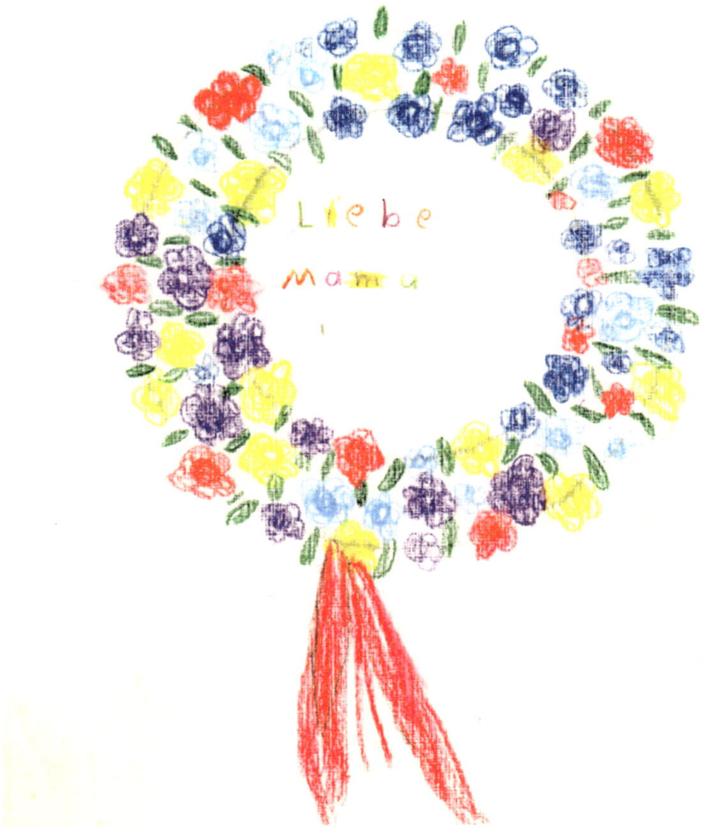

BERNHARD WILLHELM, DESIGNER

I never drew much as a child. I was mostly into origami and string figures, and into growing flowers. I keep some of my childhood drawings in Paris, but this one is special because it was saved by my mum at home. I made the card for her and there is a kind of love dedication on the inside. The circle of flowers is a *Meekranz* and this circle shape reappears in many of my later collections and lookbooks, such as Spring-Summer 2019 and Spring-Summer 2022. I was always more interested in nature than in clothing and have no sentimental memories connected to clothing from my childhood, but my collection of cacti is alive and well.

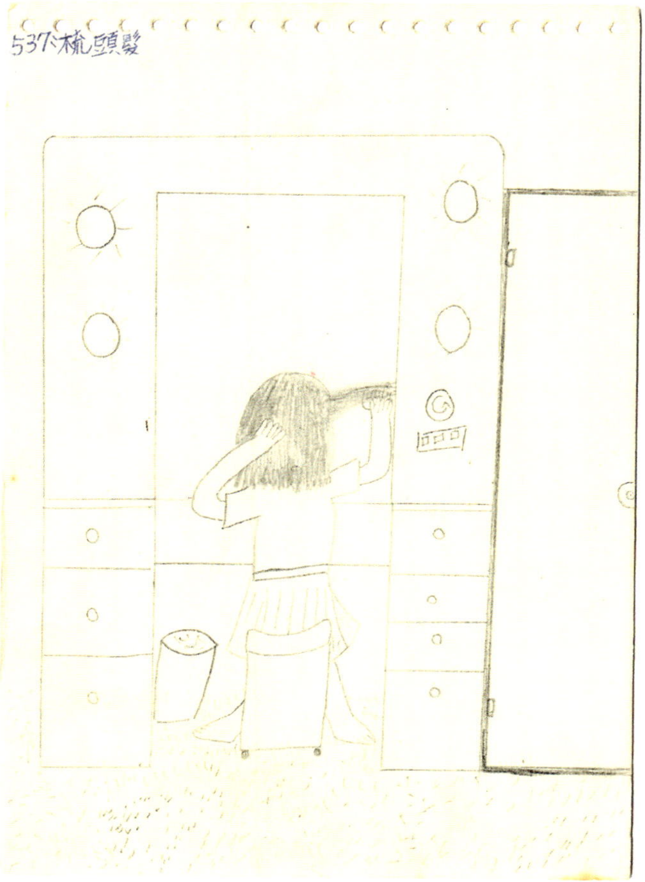

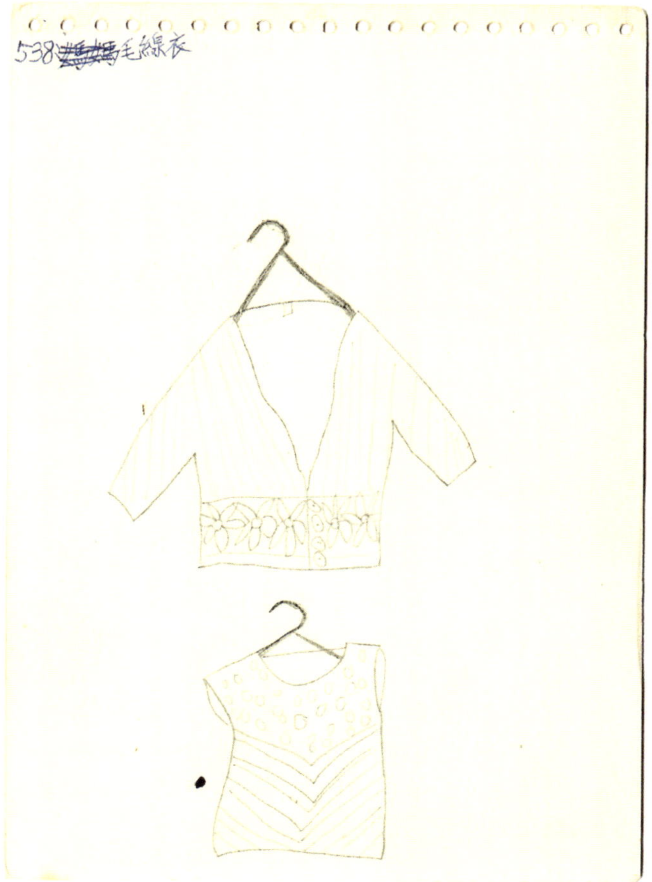

JEN-FANG SHUEH —— JENNY FAX, DESIGNER

You can see me from the back in my school uniform combing my hair sitting at my mum's dressing table. When I was ten, my art teacher told us he would hand out an award to the student who drew the most after school. The prize was a painter's kit containing 24 colours of water paint, crayons and lovely coloured pens. The dream! I started drawing like crazy and made more than 1,000 drawings in a few months. I mainly found my subjects in my ordinary life. The day our teacher decided to hand me the award, he forgot his wallet and could not buy me the kit. This strange bittersweet emotion of feeling both proud and disappointed, of feeling happy and sad, inspires me to this today.

As a kid I loved making my own accessories, and my strongest memory is always wishing for a white lace princess dress. I hoped to get one every year. Garments from my childhood and dreamy princess dresses are recurring themes in my work.

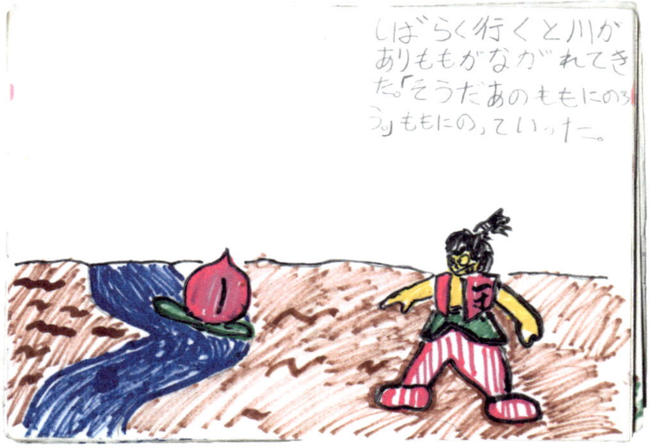
しばらく行くと川が
ありももがながれてき
た。「そうだあのももにのろ
う」ももにの」ていった。

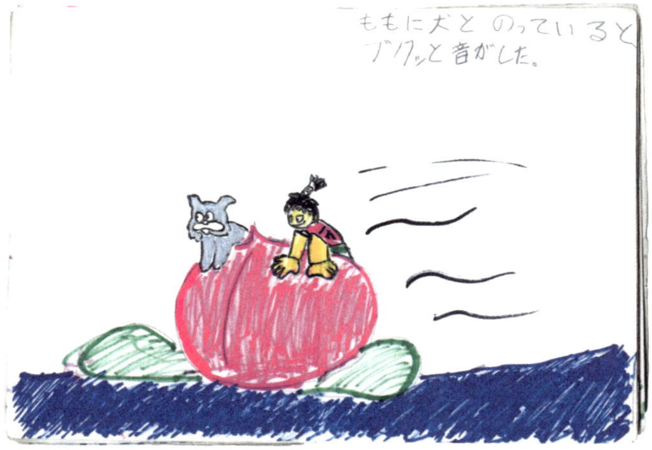
ももに犬と のっていると
ブクッと音がした。

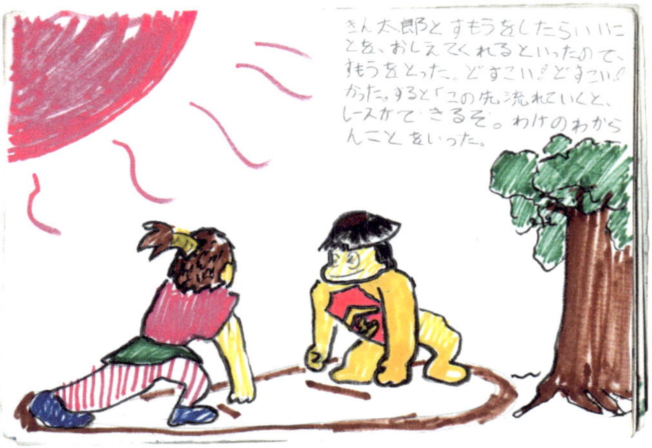
きん太郎とすもうをしたらいいに
とを、おしえてくれるといったので、
すもうをとった。どすこい!どすこい!
かった。すると「この先流れていくと、
レースができるぞ。わけのわから
んことをいった。

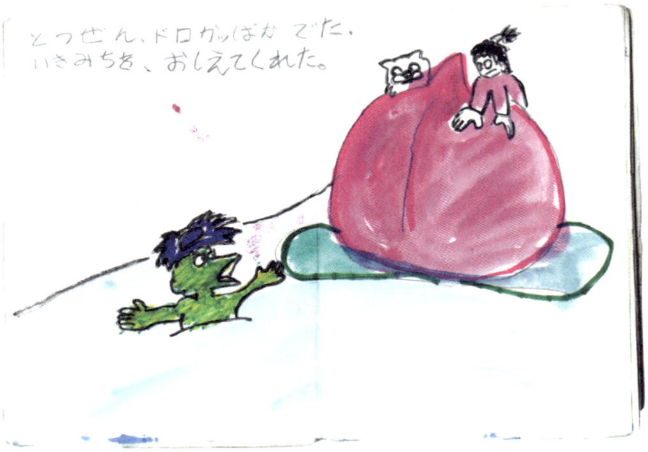
とつぜん、ドロガッぱが でた.
いきみちを、おしえてくれた。

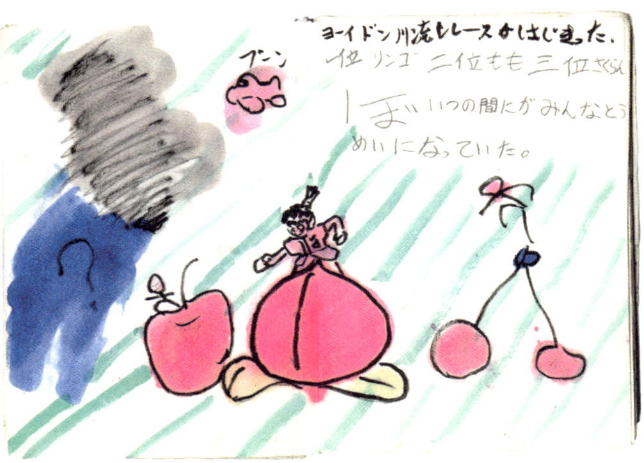
ブーン
ヨーイドン川流しレースがはじまった.
一位リンゴ 二位もも 三位さくらん
ぼ いつの間にかみんなとう
めいになっていた。

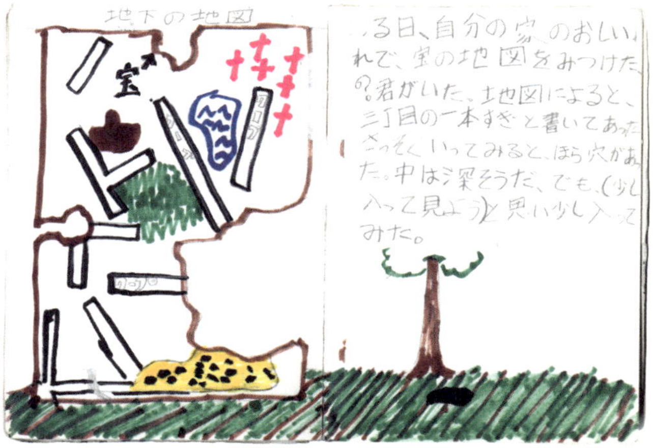

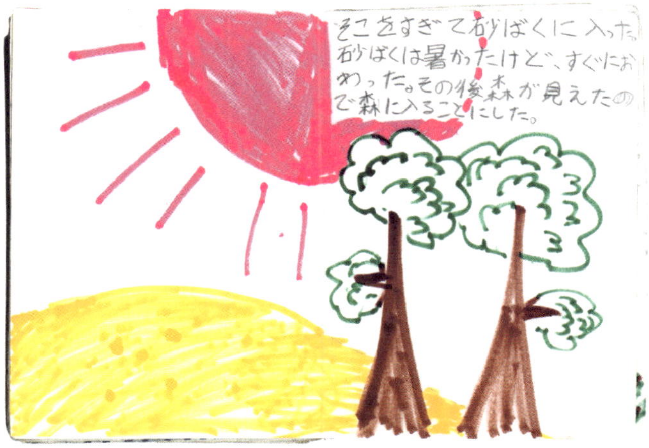

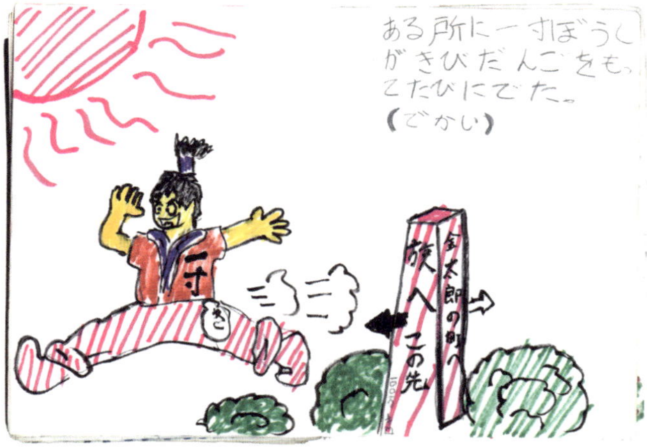

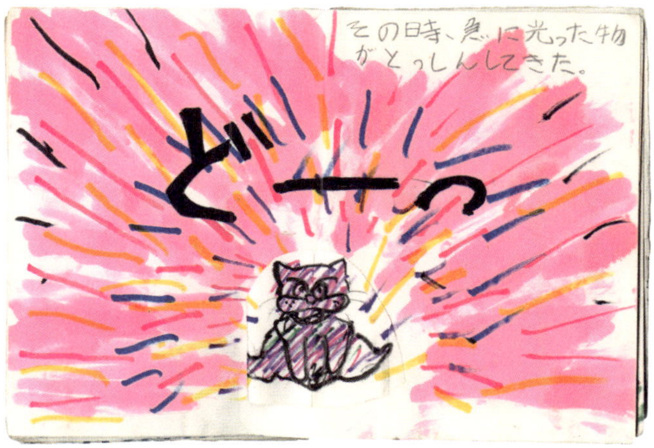

MIKIO SAKABE, DESIGNER

As a child, I made this small book filled with colourful 3D pop-outs, in which I mixed Japanese anime with *Dragon Quest* game characters. I do not remember the exact story I wanted to tell, but it shows how much I preferred fantasy over reality. My strongest childhood clothing memory is my blue Ralph Lauren polo shirt. These shirts were a real trend in Japan for a while, and I remember wearing it with pride. I have always been attracted to strong colours, and as I child I wore red and blue shirts under a mustard-coloured coat. I loved to combine the strangest colours, which still inspires me today.

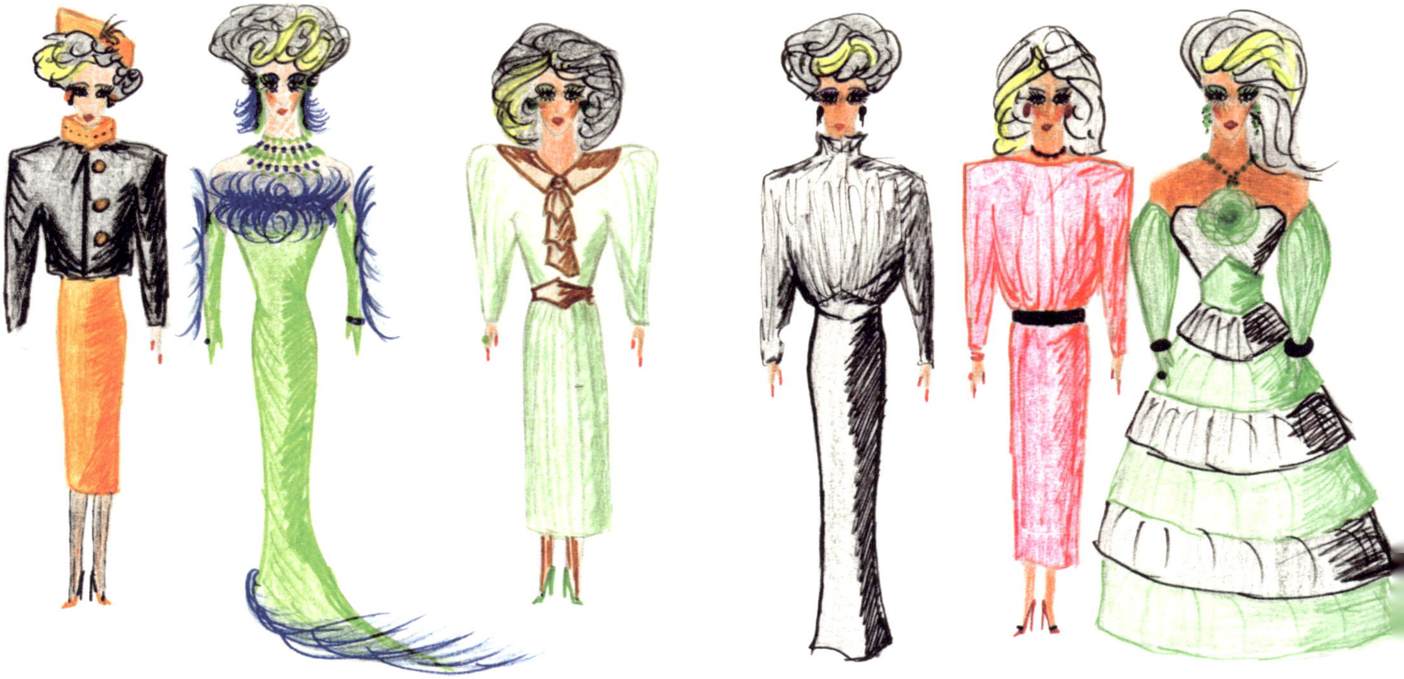

JURGI PERSOONS, DESIGNER

I made these drawings in the early 1980s. I was eleven at the time, and you can see I was obsessed with glamour, colour and extravagance. I drew dream worlds where I had all the freedom to create all kinds of events and occasions. These drawings were like comic strips that gave me a chance to indulge my fantasies. It was my way of escaping reality.

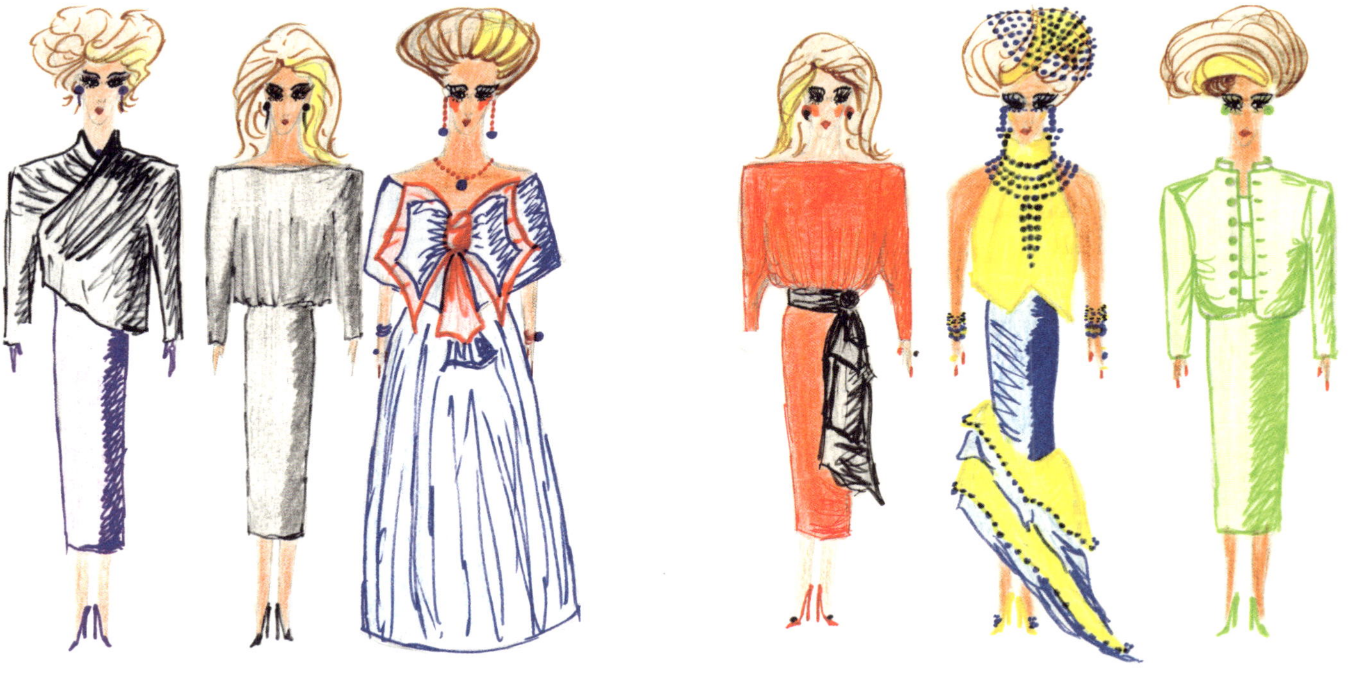

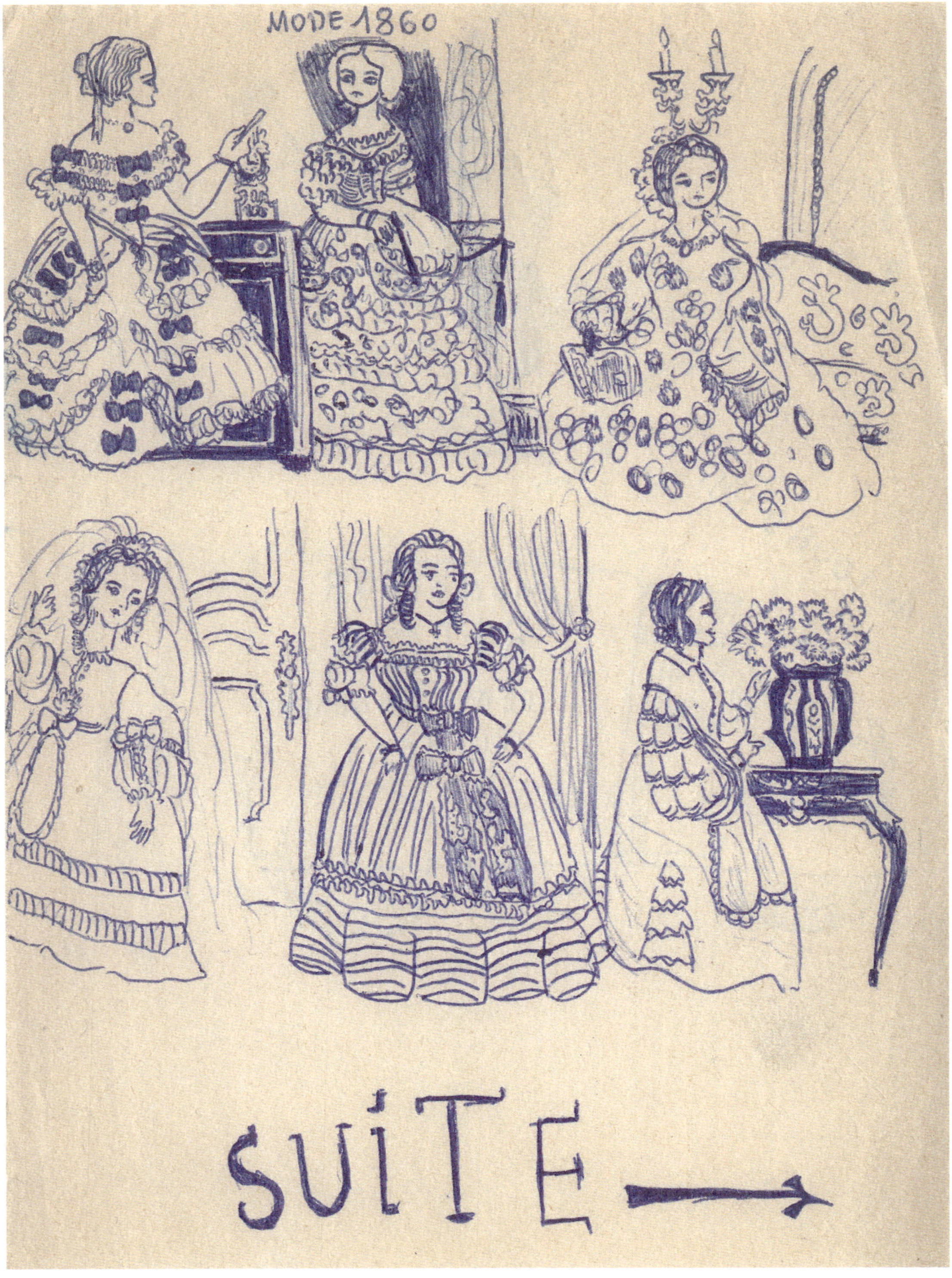
MODE 1860
SUITE

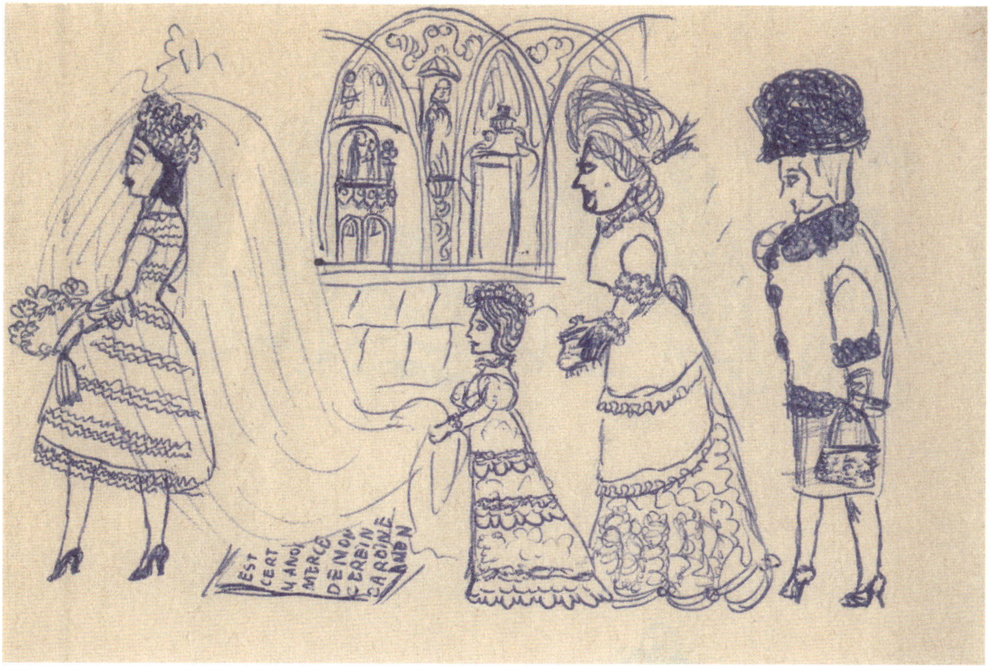

CHRISTIAN LACROIX, DESIGNER

I was born in 1951 when the *New Look* by Dior was still fashionable. When I was two or three, I loved going underneath these tulle voluminous petticoats. I remember my mother's clothes and her act of dressing when she was going out: the thin satin and lace slips under her dresses, the tartan taffeta linings of her coats, the way she positioned her berets.

I vividly remember making my first drawings on 'bloc notes' my father had brought home from his office. It was quite rough paper used for stenography. I remember sitting next to the kitchen window and drawing for hours. My oldest toddler scribbles were thrown away when my parents and grandparents were moving. I was very productive as a kid, but my parents were not too conservative with archiving them, so not many survived.

Even as a child, I was fascinated by the past, especially by the Louis XIV period, the late eighteenth-century fashions and the Belle Époque. I was also intrigued by my mother's contemporary magazines and the ones that I read at her dressmaker's. I keep a box of my old fashion sketches. These drawings were made in 1960. What is astounding to me is that even in my first attempts, I was already mixing and matching anachronistic elements. I never stopped chasing pictures and documents of historical costumes in a passionate, hectic and almost pathological way. Even to the present day, 65 years later, I have never stopped using elements, emotions and stories from past centuries in my work.

In these drawings, you can see my obsession with the bride. It has always been the bride for me. In Charles Dickens's *Great Expectations* (1861), there is a mad old lady, Miss Havisham, who wears the same silk wedding dress that she wore as a young woman. She is forever waiting for a groom who will never come. That is why every haute couture collection I made included a long gown bearing the imprint of the past.

OLIVIER THEYSKENS, DESIGNER

I made this drawing when I was about nine or maybe ten. For years I had been drawing characters wearing stylish dresses or historical costumes, but these had not been set within a fashion context. At the time of this drawing, I had started to sketch my first 'fashion' silhouettes, and I liked to sketch them fast, mimicking the 1980s energy one would see in fashion illustration then. Fashion shows were suddenly becoming more popular and were reported during the news on television, which is one of the reasons I started aspiring to create fashion myself. I remember the feeling of inventing something new —— or so I believed —— with these 'butterfly' puffy sleeves, also very 1980s. I also liked silhouettes with a 1920s look: lean and tubular with boas and accessories. I admired the photographs of Serge Lutens. You can see a derivation of his view on beauty in the way I sketched the faces.

I remember playing with clothes as a child, and I loved fancy dress-ups. There was a trunk at home filled with discarded stuff. I would play with it for days and create my costumes. It all took place in a room we called *l'atelier*; it was a room my mother used for sewing. I will forever associate the presence of the sewing machine, the clutter of small needle boxes, fabric coupons and thread bobbins with that kind of playtime. I still clearly remember everything the trunk contained.

I have clear memories of closing the cuff buttons of my shirt for the first time, which took me lots of time and focus... My strongest childhood clothing memory is wearing a floor-length deep red cape my mother made me out of old curtains. It was pure joy to run around wearing it in and outside the house. I thought I was a marquis!

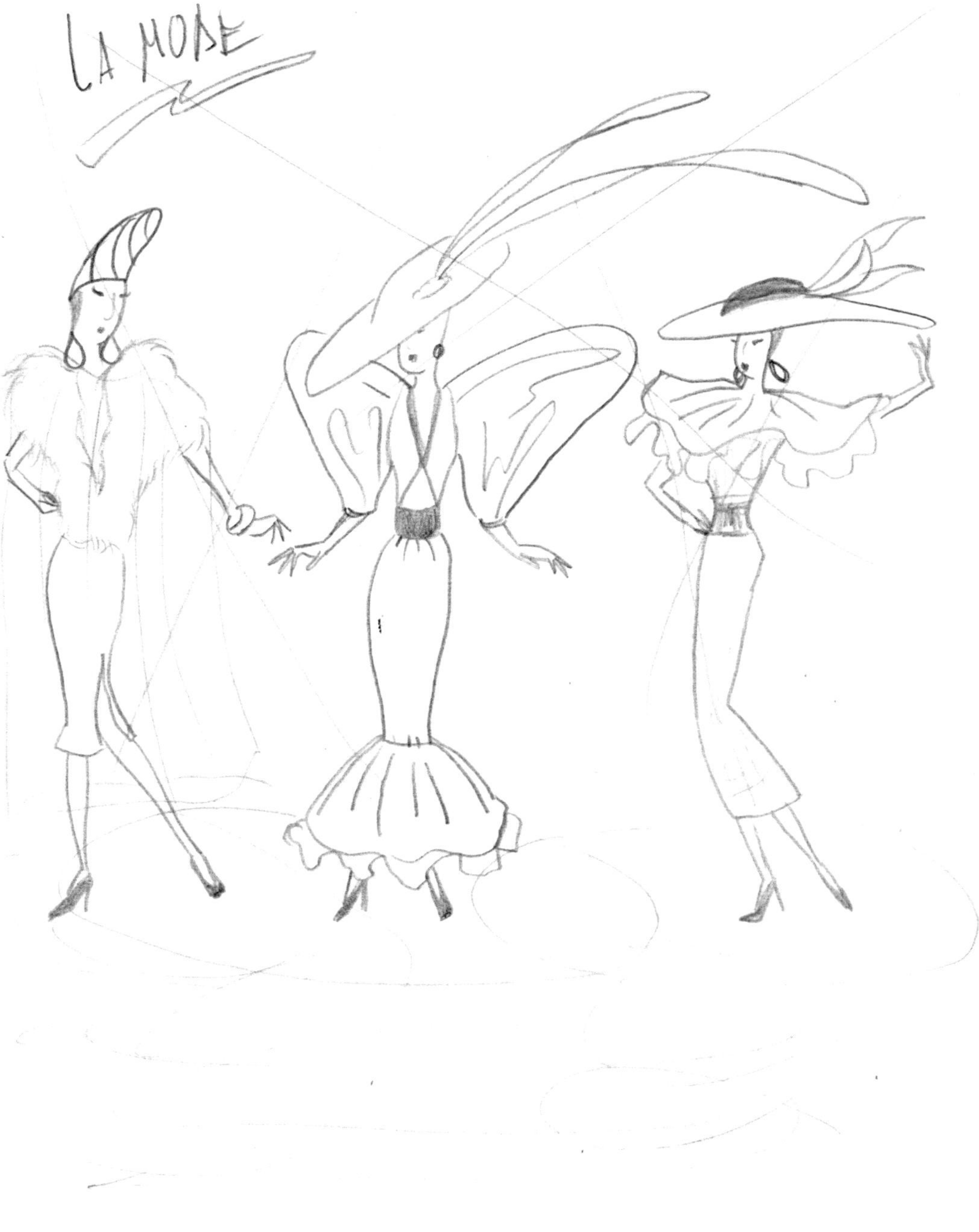
LA MODE

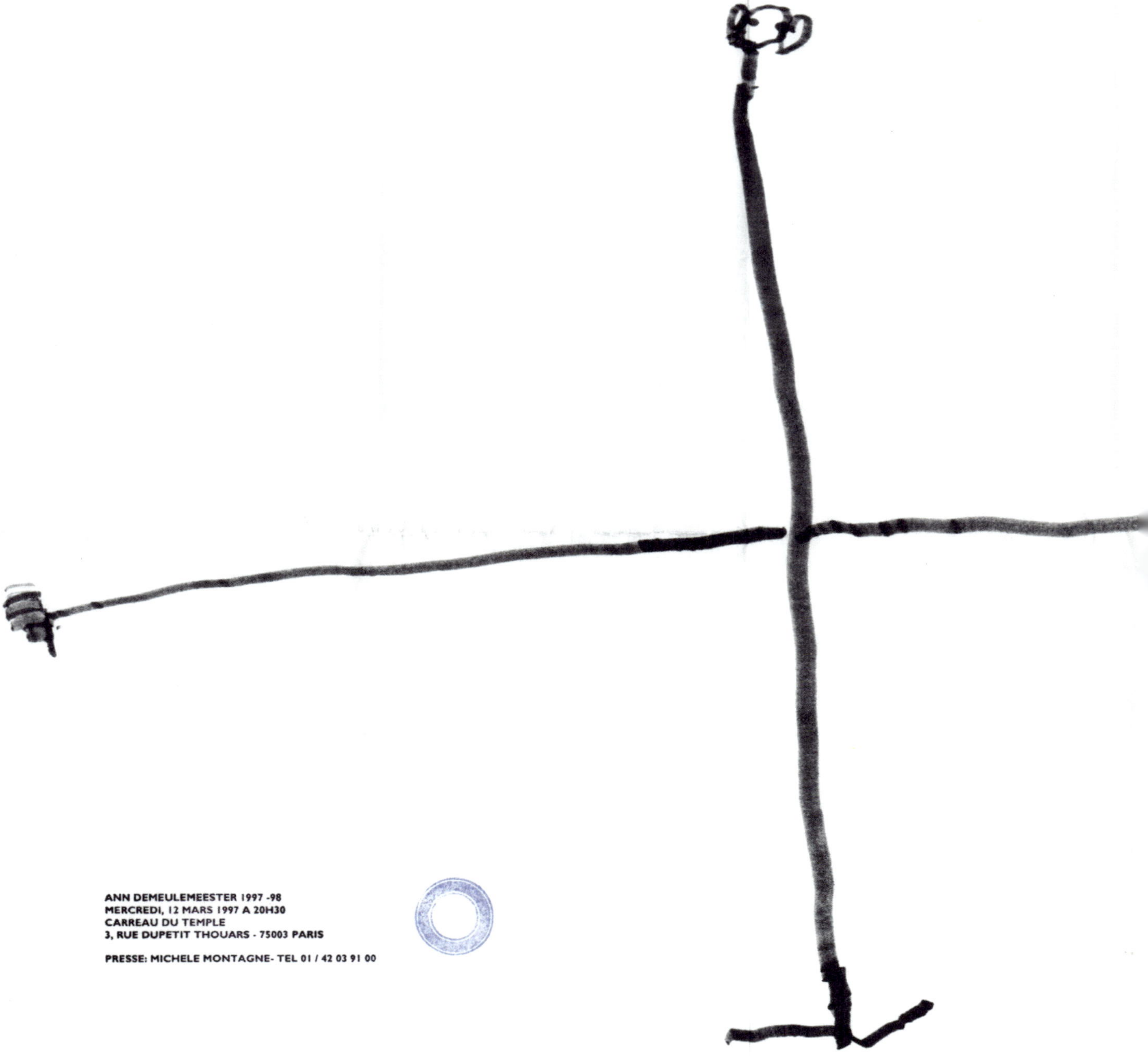
ANN DEMEULEMEESTER 1997 -98
MERCREDI, 12 MARS 1997 A 20H30
CARREAU DU TEMPLE
3, RUE DUPETIT THOUARS - 75003 PARIS
PRESSE: MICHELE MONTAGNE- TEL 01 / 42 03 91 00

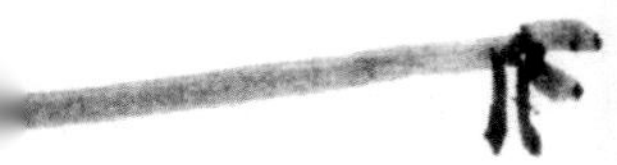

ANN DEMEULEMEESTER, DESIGNER

I do not have any of the drawings I made as a child, but as a girl, I loved to draw and drew a lot. I had a big wall in my room painted with blackboard paint, and every day for years, I made chalk drawings on it. Each day was a fresh start. I had always dreamt of having such a huge blackboard and kept nagging until I finally got one. This is my son Victor's first drawing. I used it as the show invitation of my Autumn-Winter 1997-98 collection.

PAUL BOUDENS, GRAPHIC DESIGNER

I made this drawing sometime in the early 1970s, so I must have been six. I think these are supposed to be three princesses, as the third one is wearing a cape, though none of them is wearing a crown. To be honest, I really wanted to be a princess myself. I find the little dog endearing, but I frown at the marks I was giving myself as a child. I am clearly as self-critical today as I was then. [*laughs*]

There are a couple of garments that are burnt into my memory. In 1968 I wore an adorable twin set in grey tweed with a white collar and puff pants with white socks and shoes —— I am still wearing white sneakers today. I also remember swimming trunks in a red, blue and white Hawaii print, a white Fina polo with fine blue and red borders, and my first communion look was Marine striped. I am still a sucker for stripes!

In the early 1990s I was the proud owner of a Comme des Garçons jacket with tweed print and hoodie. It was love at first sight. It cost me a small fortune as a student, but I wore it until it fell apart. It is still hanging in my wardrobe as a memory of my carefree thirties.

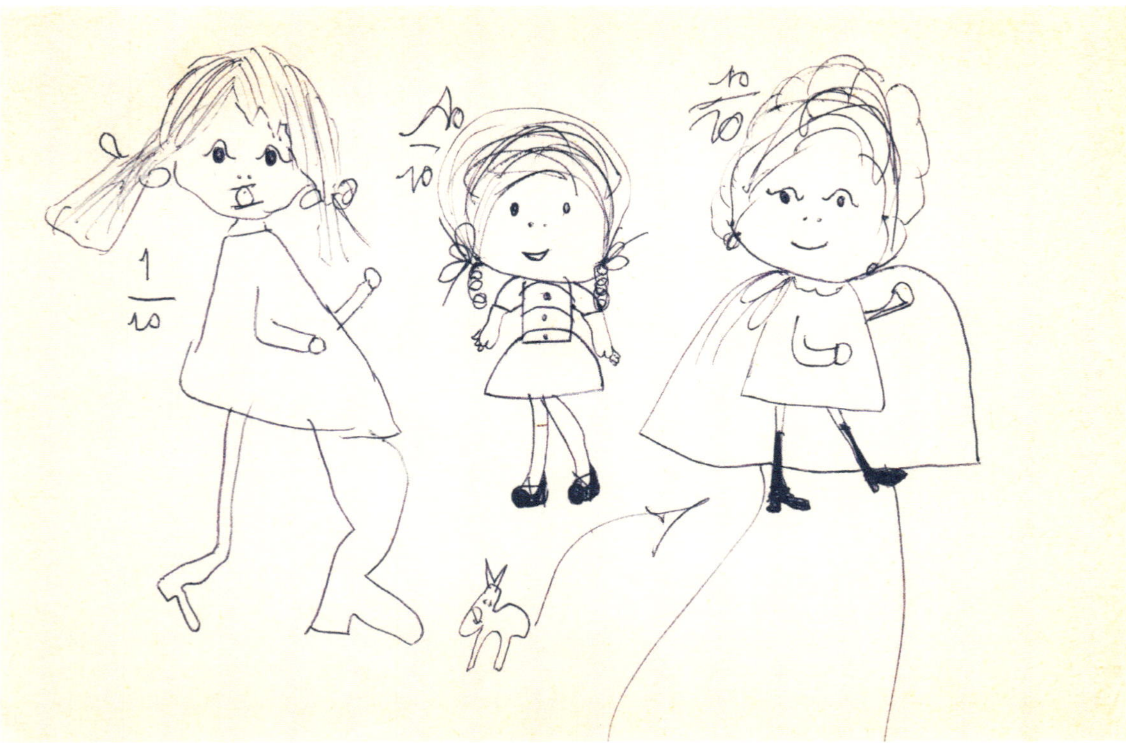

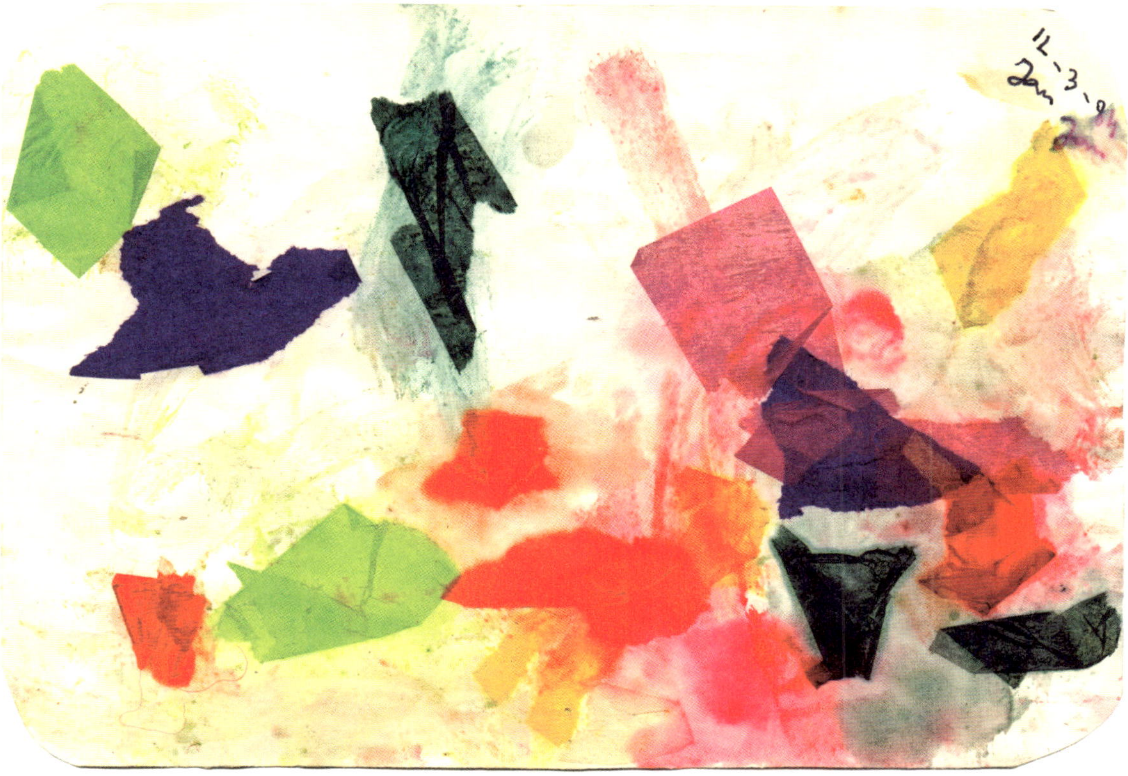

JAN-JAN VAN ESSCHE, DESIGNER

I have kept quite a lot of drawings from my time at school, but none of them prominently feature clothing. This drawing was the oldest one I have; it is an abstract expression of colour.

I clearly remember some of my favourite childhood garments, in particular a denim perfecto jacket with some sort of camouflage motif in blues and purples. I can fully visualise this jacket down to the minutest details, even though I was probably only about six years old. I felt so cool and empowered wearing it. It was the first time I remember experiencing how a garment can really affect your mood and become a way to express yourself.

I will always cherish the tuxedo my grandfather made for his own marriage. The idea that he made his own wedding clothes is so valuable to me. He was a tailor, but I never saw him in action; he retired before I was born. But by wearing the piece I got to appreciate his craftsmanship and dedication.

JANINA PEDAN, SET DESIGNER

I think I drew this shortly after we arrived in Sweden from Ukraine when I was six years old. We lived in a couple of different refugee facilities while waiting for our asylum case to be processed. It was the first time I encountered Western popular culture and was mesmerised and terrified after seeing Michael Jackson's 'Thriller' video. The zombie is a direct reference to the video, with its burnt-red jacket. I think the scene represents a birthday party or a wedding of a royal couple and their baby. Something bad is about to happen, clouds gather, and a zombie tries to kidnap the child, but an angel saves the day. My grandmother, to whom I was very close and who we left behind in Ukraine, used to cut the edges of family photos with a special type of scissors that made a shaped decorative edge. I tried to mimic the effect on the drawing using regular scissors.

My mother is a brilliant seamstress. With five children to take care of, she did not have much time to sew, but she would make us spectacular dresses for the end of school celebrations. When we were small, these dresses made us look like Victorian dolls. I think my sisters felt awkward in them, like dressed-up cats, but I loved mine. She still makes dresses for my daughters.

When my first child was born, the hospital provided a little hat with a pom-pom to cover its head. I thought it was extremely sweet, as it was clearly homemade. Later, I read it was part of a project where volunteers knitted thousands of hats for the hospital with green, orange or red pom-poms. It was a simple signalling system for the staff to observe babies who might be at risk from complications. My child's white hat with a red pom-pom took on a different meaning: still sweet, but embodying the difficulty and intertwining of death and life at childbirth.

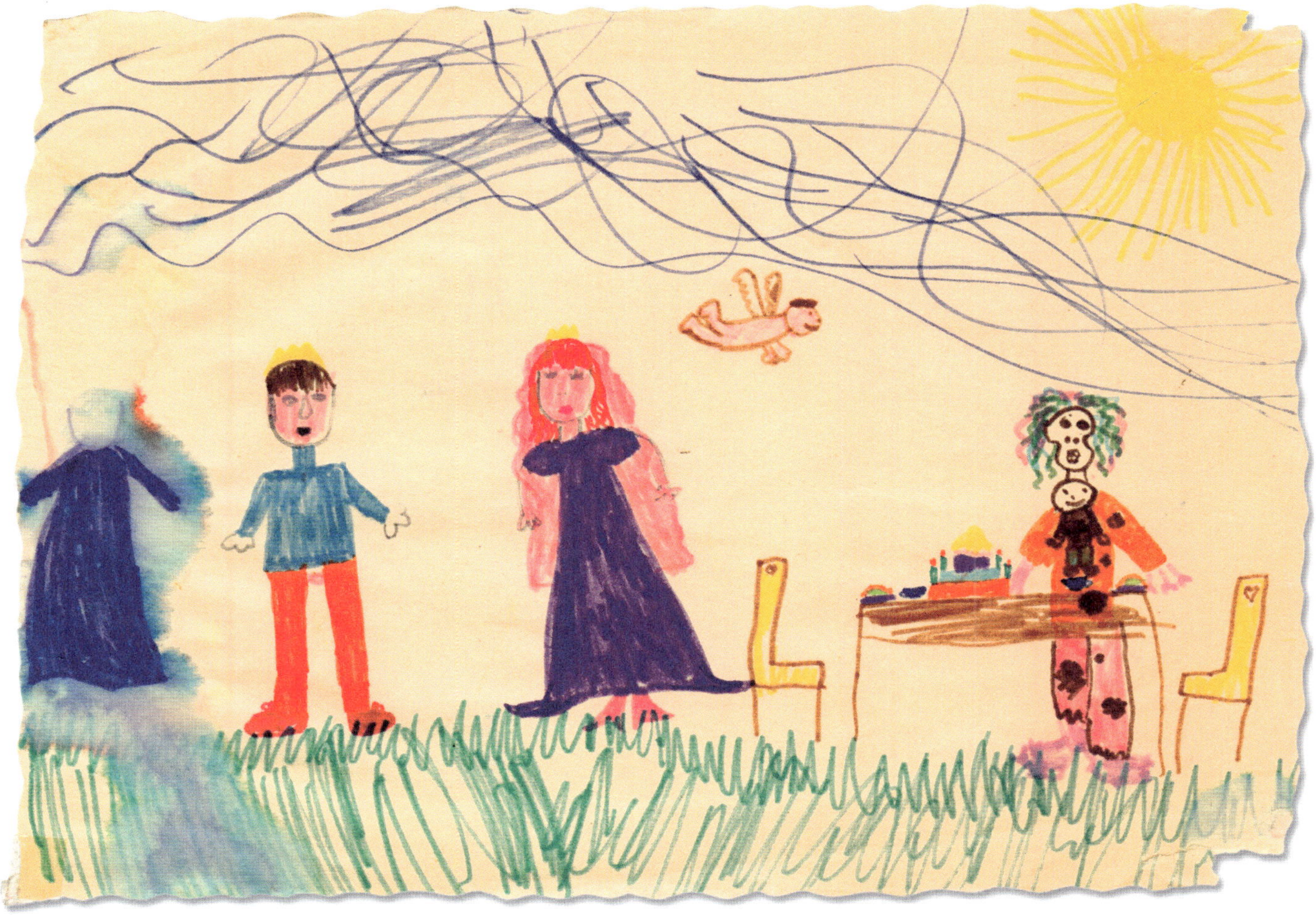

P4 Emil Larsson
P6 Courtesy Simone Rocha
P8 Photo Christopher Burke,
© The Easton Foundation/SABAM Belgium 2023
P11 Herman Sorgeloos
P12 Collection Whitney Museum of American Art, New York. Photo Peter Bellamy,
© The Easton Foundation/SABAM Belgium 2023
P15 Harley Weir
P16 Photo Christopher Burke,
© The Easton Foundation/SABAM Belgium 2023
P17 Harley Weir
P19 Thierry De Mey
P20 Petra Collins
P21 Photo Christopher Burke,
© The Easton Foundation/SABAM Belgium 2023
P23 Colin Dodgson/Art Partner
P24 Private Collection, New York, Courtesy Xavier Hufkens, Brussels, photo Christopher Burke,
© The Easton Foundation/SABAM Belgium 2023
P25 Photo Christopher Burke,
© The Easton Foundation/SABAM Belgium 2023
P26 Collection The Easton Foundation, New York. Photo Christopher Burke,
© The Easton Foundation/SABAM Belgium 2023
P29 Private Collection, New York, Courtesy Xavier Hufkens, Brussels, photo Christopher Burke,
© The Easton Foundation/SABAM Belgium 2023
PP30-31 Photo Christopher Burke,
© The Easton Foundation/SABAM Belgium 2023
P32 Photo Jacob Lillis
P33 Courtesy Simone Rocha
P34 Photo Christopher Burke,
© The Easton Foundation/SABAM Belgium 2023
P38 Photo Pascal Gambarte, styling Tamara Rothstein, hair Teiji Utsumi, makeup Jessica Taylor
P40-41 Courtesy of the Artist and Xavier Hufkens, Brussels
P42 Courtesy the Artist and Lehmann Maupin, New York, Hong Kong, Seoul, and London.
P43 Lafayette Anticipations —— Fonds de dotation Famille Moulin. Exhibition view 'L'Intruse', 2014. Courtesy Marcelle Alix, Paris, photo Aurélien Mole
P44-45 Harley Weir
P46 Courtesy of the Artist and Xavier Hufkens, Brussels, photo HV-StudioF
P47 Ruben Diaz
P48 Laila Gohar
P49 Collection City of Antwerp inv. nr. T23/1378/1-10, photo Pierre Antoine
PP50-51 Courtesy of the Artist and Dvir Gallery, Brussels, exhibition views from CIAP/CMINE © Michiel De Cleene
P52 © Alex Van Gelder / Art: © The Easton Foundation/ SABAM Belgium 2023
PP56-57 © The Easton Foundation/SABAM Belgium 2023
PP59-60 © Alex Van Gelder
P62 William Waterworth
P65 Eoin McLoughlin (*top*);
Colin Dodgson/Art Partner (*below*)
PP66-67 Alice Neale/Artistry Global
PP70-71 Courtesy Simone Rocha
P74-75-76-77 Jacob Lillis
PP81-82 Jacob Lillis
P83 Rosie Marks
P84 Casper Sejersen/Artistry Global
P87 Herman Sorgeloos
PP88-89 Jean-Luc Tanghe
P90 Herman Sorgeloos
PP92-93, 94 Herman Sorgeloos
P95 Anne Van Aerschot
P96 Herman Sorgeloos
P98 Anne Van Aerschot
P99 Herman Sorgeloos
P101 Anne Van Aerschot
PP102-103 Herman Sorgeloos
P104 Anne Van Aerschot
PP106-107 Anne Van Aerschot
P109 Casper Sejersen/Artistry Global
P122 Private Collection, New York, Photo Christopher Burke,
© The Easton Foundation/SABAM Belgium 2023
P125 Photo Christopher Burke,
© The Easton Foundation/SABAM Belgium 2023

P37, P73, PP126-149

TEXT CONTRIBUTIONS
Elisa De Wyngaert
Wim Mertens
Kim Verkens
Birgit Ansoms

PHOTOGRAPHY
Frederik Vercruysse

ASSISTANT PHOTOGRAPHER
Julien Hayard

SET DESIGN
Janina Pedan

PRODUCTION
Elisa De Wyngaert
Juliette de Waal

COLLECTION AND OBJECT CARE
Kim Verkens
Frédéric Boutié
Birgit Ansoms
Eva Van den Ende
Danicia van Glanen-Weijgel
Ellen Machiels
Pieter Pauwels
Bas Verwaetermeulen
Robbe Vanderhaeghe

PHOTOGRAPHY AGENT
I.N.I.T.I.A.L.S. L.A.

PP110-121

PHOTOGRAPHY
Frederik Vercruysse

ASSISTANT PHOTOGRAPHER
Julien Hayard

SET DESIGN
Janina Pedan

OBJECT CARE
Frédéric Boutié

PRODUCTION
Elisa De Wyngaert
Juliette de Waal

PHOTOGRAPHY AGENT
I.N.I.T.I.A.L.S. L.A.

IN COLLABORATION WITH
Rosas

This book is published in conjunction with the exhibition *ECHO. Wrapped in Memory* on view at MoMu —— Fashion Museum Antwerp, from 14 October 2023 to 25 February 2024

CURATOR
Elisa De Wyngaert

EXHIBITION DESIGN
Janina Pedan

GRAPHIC DESIGN
Paul Boudens

A special gratitude goes to The Easton Foundation New York and Xavier Hufkens.

The work of Louise Bourgeois would not have played such a key role in this publication and exhibition without their trust and advice.

This publication and exhibition would equally not have been possible without the time, help and thoughtful generosity of Simone Rocha and Anne Teresa De Keersmaeker and their teams.

MOMU —— FASHION MUSEUM ANTWERP

DIRECTOR
Kaat Debo

BUSINESS MANAGEMENT
Sara Joukes

CURATORS
Romy Cockx
Elisa De Wyngaert

ASSISTANT CURATOR
Juliette de Waal

PRODUCTION MANAGEMENT
Marie Vandecasteele

COLLECTION MANAGEMENT
Wim Mertens
Esther Bellefroid
Frédéric Boutié
Ellen Machiels
Pieter Pauwels
Belgiz Polat
Kim Verkens
Bas Verwaetermeulen
Ykje Wildenborg

LIBRARY AND DRIES VAN NOTEN STUDY CENTRE
Birgit Ansoms
Ester Claes
Bram Fierens
Eva Van den Ende
Dieter Suls
Tobias Hendrickx
Michelle Suykerbuyk
Hadewych Bal

PRESS AND COMMUNICATIONS
David Flamée
Wouter Pauwels
Lies Verboven

EDUCATION AND EVENTS
Leen Borgmans
Klaartje Patteet
Noëlle Opdebeek
Iris Adriaenssens

ADMINISTRATION
Simon Goyvaerts
Diane Van Osta

MERCHANDISING MANAGER
Annik Pirotte

HOSPITALITY MANAGER
An Teyssen

WELCOME DESK
Maaike Delsaerdt
Veronique De Man
Raphaël Lauwers
Kristel Van den Wyngaert

FACILITY MANAGEMENT
Justin Vanneste

SECURITY
Interne bewakingsdienst van de
AG Culturele Instellingen Antwerpen

MAINTENANCE
Isabel Suengue
Maria Sebastiao Viegas

LENDERS
Clémance and Didier Krzentowski
Lafayette Anticipations
The Easton Foundation
Dvir Gallery
Harley Weir Studio
Jean Paul Gaultier
Laila Gohar
Lehmann Maupin
Maya Barrera
Rosas
Simone Rocha
Xavier Hufkens

AND ALL PRIVATE LENDERS

WITH SPECIAL THANKS TO
Aminata Samba

COLOPHON

AUTHORS
Elisa De Wyngaert
Charlie Porter
Ellen Sampson
Lou Stoppard

GRAPHIC DESIGN
Paul Boudens

IMAGE RESEARCH AND COPYRIGHT
Birgit Ansoms
Elisa De Wyngaert

PROJECT MANAGEMENT
Astrid Devlaminck

TRANSLATIONS
Dutch——English: Lisa Holden
English——Dutch: Robrecht Vandemeulebroecke

EDITING
English: Amy Haagsma
Dutch: Nathalie Houfflijn

PROOFREADING
English: Amy Haagsma
Dutch: Nathalie Houfflijn

PHOTO ENGRAVING
Steurs

PRINTING AND BINDING
Wilco

COVER IMAGES
Louise Bourgeois, *Dawn* (detail), 2006
Photo: Christopher Burke
© The Easton Foundation/SABAM Belgium 2023

Simone Rocha, Autumn-Winter 2019-20
© Harley Weir

Dries Van Noten, Autumn-Winter 2021-22,
collection film choreographed by
Anne Teresa De Keersmaeker
© Casper Sejersen/Artistry Global

PUBLISHED BY LANNOO PUBLISHERS

WWW.LANNOO.COM

Sign up for our newsletter with news about new and forthcoming publications on art, interior design, food & travel, photography and fashion, as well as exclusive offers and events. If you have any questions or comments about any of the material in this book, please do not hesitate to contact our editorial team: art@lannoo.com.

D/2023/45/329 —— NUR452/644
ISBN 978 94 014 96667